God's Warriors

God's Warriors

Religious Violence and the Global Crisis of Secularism

NILAY SAIYA

OXFORD
UNIVERSITY PRESS

Oxford University Press is a department of the University of Oxford.
It furthers the University's objective of excellence in research, scholarship,
and education by publishing worldwide. Oxford is a registered trade mark of
Oxford University Press in the UK and in certain other countries.

Published in the United States of America by Oxford University Press
198 Madison Avenue, New York, NY 10016, United States of America.

© Oxford University Press 2025

All rights reserved. No part of this publication may be reproduced, stored in a retrieval system, transmitted, used for text and data mining, or used for training artificial intelligence, in any form or by any means, without the prior permission in writing of Oxford University Press, or as expressly permitted by law, by license or under terms agreed with the appropriate reprographics rights organization. Inquiries concerning reproduction outside the scope of the above should be sent to the Rights Department, Oxford University Press, at the address above.

You must not circulate this work in any other form
and you must impose this same condition on any acquirer.

Library of Congress Cataloging-in-Publication Data
Names: Saiya, Nilay, author.
Title: God's warriors : religious violence and the global crisis of
secularism / Nilay Saiya.
Description: New York, NY : Oxford University Press, [2025] |
Includes bibliographical references.
Identifiers: LCCN 2025007920 (print) | LCCN 2025007921 (ebook) |
ISBN 9780197813546 (hardback) | ISBN 9780197813553 (paperback) |
ISBN 9780197813560 (epub) | ISBN 9780197813584
Subjects: LCSH: Violence—Religious aspects. |
Secularism—Poltical aspects. | Religion and politics.
Classification: LCC BL65.V55 S25 2025 (print) | LCC BL65.V55 (ebook) |
DDC 201/.72—dc23/eng/20250518
LC record available at https://lccn.loc.gov/2025007920
LC ebook record available at https://lccn.loc.gov/2025007921

DOI: 10.1093/9780197813584.001.0001

Paperback Printed by Integrated Books International, United States of America
Hardback Printed by Bridgeport National Bindery, Inc., United States of America

The manufacturer's authorized representative in the EU for product safety is Oxford
University Press España S.A., Parque Empresarial San Fernando de Henares,
Avenida de Castilla, 2 - 28830 Madrid (www.oup.es/en).

For Neha, Jacob, Isaac, Winnie, and Maisy

Contents

Introduction	1
Why Religious Violence (Still) Matters	3
Explanations for Religious Violence	7
Argument of the Book	14
Outline of the Book	24

PART I

1. Religious Violence and the Global Crisis of Secularism	31
What Is Secularism?	32
Why Secularism Is in Crisis	44
How the Crisis of Secularism Begets Religious Violence	49
Summary	59

PART II

2. Christianity	63
American Christian Nationalism and Violence	64
European Christian Civilizationalism and Violence	81
Christian Nationalism and Violence in the Developing World	90
Summary	95
3. Islam	96
How Political Secularism Is Undermined in the Muslim World	98
Muslim Privilege and Islamist Violence	104
The Problem of Blasphemy Codes	117
Can Muslim-Majority Countries Accept Political Secularism?	122
Summary	131
4. Hinduism	134
Political Secularism in India	136
Hindu Nationalism and Violence	143
The Problem of Anticonversion Laws	152
Summary	158
5. Buddhism	162
Sri Lanka	164

Myanmar	172
Thailand	181
Summary	186
6. Judaism	**189**
Political Secularism in Israel	191
Jewish Nationalism and Violence	196
Summary	205

PART III

7. Finding Unity in Diversity	**209**
Covenantal Pluralism: An Antidote to the Crisis of Secularism?	210
Covenantal Pluralism in Practice	214
Christianity: The Case of Botswana	215
Islam: The Case of Senegal	216
Hinduism: The Case of India	219
Buddhism: The Case of Singapore	222
Judaism: The Case of Israel	224
Concluding Thoughts	226
Appendix	228
Statistical Analysis	228
Case Studies	232
Index	235

Introduction

On January 6, 2021, supporters of American president Donald Trump stormed the U.S. Capitol, wherein they desecrated the home of Congress to an extent not seen since the War of 1812. The rioters, moved by the president's claim that the 2020 presidential election had been rigged and stolen from him, sought to overturn the election outcome by violently disrupting a joint session of Congress assembled to formally certify Joe Biden's electoral victory. Five people perished in the attack or in its immediate aftermath; 140 police officers were assaulted. One of the most shocking aspects of the Capitol siege was its religious character. The rioters proudly brandished Bibles, wooden crosses, Christian flags, signs declaring "Jesus Saves," and pictures of Jesus decked out in gear declaring "Make America Great Again." They sang praise and worship songs and knelt in prayer as they cried out to God to overturn the election results and save the country. The insurrectionists were quite literally attempting to take back the country for God. Breaching the Senate chamber, Jacob Angeli Chansley, the horn-wearing, bare-chested self-proclaimed "Q-Anon Shaman"—the most recognizable figure involved in the insurrection—led the rioters in a prayer in which he thanked God for "allowing the United States of America to be reborn" and for "allowing us to get rid of the communists, the globalists, and the traitors within our government." He saw the uprising as an opportunity to send a clear message to the enemies of God: "this is our country, not theirs."[1]

***

The Capitol insurgency failed to achieve its goal of keeping Trump in power; three weeks later Biden assumed the presidency. One of Biden's most important foreign policy decisions during his first year in office involved withdrawing American troops from Afghanistan, officially ending America's longest war. The troop withdrawal gave way to an escalating wave of violence by jihadist groups, especially the regional chapter of the Islamic State terror outfit, Islamic State of Iraq and Syria–Khorasan Province (ISIS-K). The extremist Islamist group exploited the void left by the United States

---

[1] *New Yorker*, "A Reporter's Footage from Inside the Capitol Siege," YouTube, January 18, 2001, https://www.youtube.com/watch?v=270F8s5TEKY.

to challenge the authority of the Taliban regime in Kabul, which had reassumed power following its takeover of the country. The leaders of the Islamic State in Afghanistan denounced the Taliban's takeover, criticizing their version of Islamic rule as insufficiently hardline and pious.[2] After Washington quit Afghanistan, ISIS-K waged a terrorist campaign in and around Kabul and against Taliban forces in outlying provinces such as Nangarhar. On August 26, 2021, the group carried out a strike outside Kabul's Hamid Karzai International Airport, killing 169 civilians and 13 American service members. Both ISIS-K and the Taliban harness violence in an attempt to mold Afghanistan in line with their respective visions of a proper Islamic theocracy and, in the case of ISIS-K, beyond.

***

On February 1, 2021, the Burmese military (Tatmadaw) wrested power from the civilian government of Myanmar in a coup d'état, declaring a one-year state of emergency. Seven months later, it took the extraordinary step of releasing from prison Ashin Wirathu, a firebrand Buddhist nationalist monk whose sermons had helped inspire the violent persecution of Rohingya Muslims over the previous decade—a persecution so serious that Zeid Ra'ad al-Hussein, the United Nations High Commissioner for Human Rights, cited it as a "textbook example of ethnic cleansing."[3] The violence has resulted in the deaths of tens of thousands of Rohingya Muslims and the forced exodus of over 1 million to surrounding countries, creating one of the world's worst humanitarian crises. Myanmar's Buddhist nationalists like Wirathu believe that the country is under siege from the Rohingya minority, despite the fact that many Rohingya families have lived in Myanmar for generations and Rohingya Muslims collectively comprise only 4 percent of the total population.

***

On April 1, 2017, a gang of Hindu vigilantes dragged a Muslim man, Pehlu Khan, and his two sons out of their truck in the city of Alwar, Rajasthan, and began beating them. Soon dozens more men streamed in and joined the attack. Khan was beaten unconscious and later succumbed to his injuries.[4]

---

[2] Asfandyar Mir, "The ISIS-K Resurgence," Wilson Center, October 8, 2021, https://www.wilsoncenter.org/article/isis-k-resurgence.

[3] United Nations, "UN Human Rights Chief Points to 'Textbook Example of Ethnic Cleansing' in Myanmar," *UN News*, September 11, 2017, https://news.un.org/en/story/2017/09/564622-un-human-rights-chief-points-textbook-example-ethnic-cleansing-myanmar.

[4] Eliza Griswold, "The Violent Toll of Hindu Nationalism in India," *New Yorker*, March 5, 2019, https://www.newyorker.com/news/on-religion/the-violent-toll-of-hindu-nationalism-in-india.

What offense had the Khans committed that led to the savage attack? They were dairy farmers transporting cows in the back of their truck.[5] The attack on the Khans is an example of a growing phenomenon in India known as "cow vigilantism." Cow vigilantes, known locally as *gau rakshaks*, take it upon themselves to protect cows, which many Hindus consider sacred. These groups of vigilantes often use violence against those they suspect to be involved in cow slaughter or beef consumption. In many such cases, the vigilantes have been emboldened by the police and members of the ruling political party. At the root of cow vigilantism and other forms of Hindu violence in India lies Hindutva, a national-cultural project rooted in an exclusionary political doctrine that envisions India as a nation for the majority Hindu population alone to the exclusion of those belonging to other religious traditions.

***

In early 2021, violence erupted in Jerusalem. The proximate cause of the hostility involved the imminent expulsion of a number of Palestinian families from Sheikh Jarrah, a predominantly Palestinian neighborhood in East Jerusalem. During the Islamic holy month of Ramadan, right-wing Jewish youth marched through the streets of Sheikh Jarrah chanting "Death to Arabs" as they accosted Palestinian residents. The demonstration was organized by Lehava, a violent Jewish extremist organization.[6] Communal violence between Arab and Jewish Israelis quickly broke out on the streets of cities across Israel at a level unseen in years, including attacks on Palestinian homes and businesses as well as assaults on individual Palestinians. The violence in Jerusalem ultimately led to an eleven-day war between Israel and Hamas, resulting in the deaths of hundreds of Palestinians, including scores of children.

Why Religious Violence (Still) Matters

These five cases are examples of contemporary violence in the world's major religious traditions: Christianity, Islam, Hinduism, Buddhism, and Judaism. "Religious violence" refers to acts of physical hostility, aggression, or conflict

---

[5] Hamza Kahn, "Pehlu Khan Lynching Case: All Held in the Case Are Out on Bail," *Indian Express*, September 29, 2017, https://indianexpress.com/article/india/pehlu-khan-lynching-case-all-held-in-the-case-are-out-on-bail-4866368/.

[6] Jill Jacobs, "American Jews, Stop Funding Jewish Terrorism," *Haaretz*, May 2, 2021, https://www.haaretz.com/us-news/.premium.HIGHLIGHT-american-jews-stop-funding-jewish-terrorism-1.9765063.

that are motivated or justified by religious beliefs, ideologies, or identities. It involves individuals or groups using violence as a means to promote, defend, or enforce their religious views or to target individuals or communities based on their religious affiliation.[7] It can be interreligious or intrareligious, carried out by majorities or minorities. Religious violence is not representative of the beliefs or teachings of the broader religious communities from which violent religious actors hail. Rather, it is often perpetrated by extremist individuals or groups who distort the teachings of their faith, manipulating them for political or ideological reasons. Religion can inform various forms of violence, such as civil wars and terrorism, mob or sectarian violence, destruction of property, and physical displacement. Many studies find that religious belief fashions a uniquely deadly form of violence, attributing this relative lethality to the transcendent, utopian goals that are part and parcel of religious belief.[8]

This book is concerned with a specific category of religious violence known as "violent religious hostilities," which I define as the use of force, aggression, or physical harm committed by private individuals, organizations, or informal groups in society who claim to be acting on their faith-based commitments. Those who carry out these acts are clearly motivated by their faith beliefs or religious identities, while the targets are chosen for theirs. Violent religious hostilities can assume various forms: religion-related riots, terrorist attacks, honor killings, attacks on holy sites, hate crimes, communal violence, and genocide. Specific examples include the destruction of Ahmadiyya mosques in Indonesia, sectarian conflict between Muslims and Christians in Nigeria, conversion-related violence against religious minorities in India, mob violence against evangelicals in Vietnam, the ethnic cleansing of Rohingya Muslims in Myanmar, hate crimes against Jews and Muslims throughout the United States and Europe, and religion-related vigilante violence in Syria. Violent religious hostilities can be interreligious, occurring between individuals or groups of altogether different religions, or intrareligious, occurring between members

---

[7] Monica Duffy Toft, "Getting Religion? The Puzzling Case of Islam and Civil War," *International Security* 31, no. 4 (2007): 97–131; Matthew Isaacs, "Sacred Violence or Strategic Faith? Disentangling the Relationship between Religion and Violence in Armed Conflict," *Journal of Peace Research* 53, no. 2 (2016): 211–225; Monica Duffy Toft, "Getting Religion Right in Civil Wars," *Journal of Conflict Resolution* 65, no. 9 (2021): 1607–1634.

[8] Bruce Hoffman, *Inside Terrorism* (New York: Columbia University Press, 1998); Mark Juergensmeyer, *Global Rebellion: Religious Challenges to the Secular State, from Christian Militias to al Qaeda* (Berkeley: University of California Press, 2008); Michael C. Horowitz, "Long Time Going: Religion and the Duration of Crusading," *International Security* 34, no. 2 (2009): 162–193.

of the same religion. Of course, violence against religious groups and individuals can also be orchestrated by the governments of states.[9] Nevertheless, although violent government persecution of religious groups is indeed an important and understudied subject, I do not consider it to be "religious violence," and therefore it remains outside the scope of this book.

That religion carries the potential to inspire violence has long been recognized by scholars, pundits, and policymakers. But why does violence rooted in religion persist in a world characterized by scientific advancement, economic development, and the free flow of ideas? Indeed, scholarship has found that religious violence has been *increasing* since the end of the Cold War. Political scientist Monica Toft reports that 71 percent of ongoing civil wars feature religion as a central or peripheral issue.[10] Likewise, political scientists Isaak Svensson and Desirée Nilsson find that conflicts rooted in religion have seen a steady upward trend since 1975.[11] At the time of this writing, possible genocides against people of faith are being carried out in Myanmar and China, and wars tinged with religion are raging in Ukraine and Gaza.

The global surge in religious conflict has been a surprising development that few social scientists would have predicted when the Iron Curtain fell. In fact, for the better half of the twentieth century, social scientists broadly agreed that religion—and by extension religious conflict—was on the decline. The founding fathers of modern social science—Marx, Weber, Comte, and Durkheim—expected that people would lead progressively secular lives and that religion's influence in society would eventually disappear altogether. This massive shift away from religion would be motored by scientific advancement, rationalism, and education. The emergence of secular, rational worldviews made possible by the spread of scientific knowledge would render superstitious religious explanations of the world obsolete, in time resulting in lowered levels of religiosity across society, the displacement of religion from the center of everyday life, and the weakening of religious institutions. In 1968, sociologist Peter Berger famously predicted that in "the twenty-first century, religious believers are likely to be found

---

[9] Daniel Philpott and Timothy Samuel Shah, eds., *Under Caesar's Sword: How Christians Respond to Persecution* (New York: Cambridge University Press, 2018).
[10] Toft, "Getting Religion Right in Civil Wars."
[11] Isak Svensson and Desirée Nilsson, "Disputes over the Divine: Introducing the Religion and Armed Conflict (RELAC) Data, 1975 to 2015," *Journal of Conflict Resolution* 62, no. 5 (2017): 1127–1148.

only in small sects, huddled together to resist a world-wide secular culture. ... The predicament of the believer is increasingly like that of a Tibetan astrologer on a prolonged visit to an American university."[12] Many believers in the "secularization thesis" also celebrated religion's demise in a normative sense; the triumph of secularism would necessarily mean less religious hostility and conflict in the world.[13]

Not only did predictions of secularization fail to materialize, but the exact opposite occurred. Even as secularization theorists prematurely heralded the end of religion, the world began experiencing a religious resurgence.[14] Owing to processes like modernization, globalization, and democratization—the very developments that the secularization thesis predicted would kill off religion—coupled with the evident failures of secular projects and ideologies in developing countries, the major world religions have experienced a newfound relevance in the modern world.[15] Even today, some 85 percent of the global population subscribes to some form of religious belief.[16] Consequently, political struggles became redefined in religious terms across the world. Indeed, the growth in religious extremism can be understood as an effort to combat the secularism that had become the basis for global politics during the first half of the twentieth century. By 1999, Berger had come full circle, humbly recanting his belief that the world was

---

[12] *New York Times*, "A Bleak Outlook Is Seen for Religion," February 25, 1968, https://www.nytimes.com/1968/02/25/archives/a-bleak-outlook-is-seen-for-religion.html.

[13] Thomas Woolson, *Works of Thomas Woolston* (London: J. Roberts, 1733); Anthony F. C. Wallace, *Religion: An Anthropological View* (New York: Random House, 1966); Steve Bruce, *God Is Dead: Secularization in the West* (Oxford: Blackwell, 2002); Steve Bruce, *Secularization: In Defence of an Unfashionable Theory* (New York: Oxford University Press, 2014).

[14] José Casanova, *Public Religions in the Modern World* (Chicago: University of Chicago Press, 1994); Peter Berger, *The Desecularization of the World: Resurgent Religion and World Politics* (Grand Rapids, MI: Eerdmans, 1999); Scott M. Thomas, "Taking Religious and Cultural Pluralism Seriously: The Global Resurgence of Religion and the Transformation of International Society," *Millennium* 29, no. 3 (2000): 815–841; Jonathan Fox, "Religion as an Overlooked Element of International Relations," *International Studies Review* 3, no. 3 (2001): 53–72; Fabio Petito and Pavlos Hatzopoulos, *Religion in International Relations: The Return from Exile* (New York: Palgrave, 2003); Jonathan Fox and Shmu'el Sandler, *Bringing Religion into International Relations* (New York: Palgrave Macmillan, 2004); Jürgen Habermas, "Religion in the Public Sphere," *European Journal of Philosophy* 14, no. 1 (2006): 1–25; Monica Duffy Toft and Timothy Samuel Shah, "Why God Is Winning," *Foreign Policy* 155 (2006): 38–43; Daniel Philpott, "Has the Study of Global Politics Found Religion?," *Annual Review of Political Science* 12 (2009): 183–202; Rodney Stark, *The Triumph of Faith: Why the World Is More Religious Than Ever* (Wilmington, DE: ISI Books, 2015); Gregorio Bettiza, *Finding Faith in Foreign Policy: Religion and American Diplomacy in a Postsecular World* (New York: Oxford University Press, 2019); Jeffrey Haynes, *Religion, Conflict and Post-secular Politics* (London: Routledge, 2020).

[15] Monica Duffy Toft, Daniel Philpott, and Timothy Samuel Shah, *God's Century: Resurgent Religion and Global Politics* (New York: W. W. Norton, 2011).

[16] Pew Research Center, "The Global Religious Landscape," December 18, 2012, http://www.pewforum.org/2012/12/18/global-religious-landscape-exec/.

becoming more secular. He now conceded that the world was "as furiously religious as it ever was, and in some places more so than ever."[17] Arguably, religion is today a more salient feature of international politics than at any point in the past three hundred years.

In summary, religion has defied the confident predictions of the secularization paradigm. Whereas different versions of the secularization thesis anticipated that religion would become less relevant in a world marked by access to education, scientific advancement, and the generation of wealth, religion remains significant, influential, and prevalent in most parts of the world. Because religion has not gone away, neither has religious conflict. On the contrary, violent religious hostilities have been increasing dramatically around the world since the end of the Cold War. The following section examines some of the most important proposed causes of religious violence in the modern world.

Explanations for Religious Violence

Having covered what religious violence is and why it remains an urgent problem, I now turn attention to what existing explanations claim lies behind acts of religious violence of the sort described at the beginning of this chapter. Policymakers and academics have long struggled to understand how religions which proclaim a message of peace and love can become weaponized in the murder of innocent civilians.[18] What explains this unique form of violence?

Explanations for religious violence come in four general varieties: *essentialist* explanations that blame religion itself for violence in the modern world; *instrumentalist* explanations that hold that religion masks secular, rational motivations for violence; *denialist* explanations that reject that religious and nonreligious violence can be effectively differentiated; and *ideological extremist* explanations that aver that particular religious ideologies lie at the root of faith-based violence.

The first explanation for religious violence—essentialism—blames religion itself. Especially influential here are the arguments of the "new atheist" movement and especially its "four horsemen": Christopher Hitchens, Daniel

---

[17] Berger, *The Desecularization of the World*, 2.
[18] Charles Kimball, *When Religion Becomes Evil: Five Warning Signs* (San Francisco: Harper, 2008).

Dennett, Richard Dawkins, and Sam Harris.[19] In books with titles such as *The End of Faith, Breaking the Spell, The God Delusion,* and *God Is Not Great,* they argue that religion necessarily leads to absolutism, division, irrationality, extremism, and violence.[20] The subtitle of Hitchen's book *The God Delusion* succinctly encapsulates this standpoint: *Religion Poisons Everything.* As Dawkins put it in an op-ed written for *The Guardian* four days after the attacks of September 11, 2001, "To fill a world with religion, or religions of the Abrahamic kind, is like littering the streets with loaded guns. Do not be surprised if they are used."[21] Religious studies scholar Charles Kimball makes a similar, albeit more qualified argument to that of the neo-atheists, but one with which the neo-atheists would certainly agree: "History clearly shows that religion has often been linked directly to the worst examples of human behavior. It is somewhat trite, but nevertheless sadly true, to say that more wars have been waged, more people killed and these days more evil perpetuated in the name of religion than by any other institutional force in human history."[22]

Another essentialist take on the conflict-prone nature of religion, especially in contexts of pluralism, is the influential and controversial "clash of civilizations" thesis championed by the late Harvard scholar Samuel Huntington.[23] In contrast to those who believed that liberal democracy and free-market capitalism would flourish with the end of the Cold War, Huntington predicted the return of primordial conflicts, arguing that the "the principal conflicts of global politics will occur between nations and groups of different civilizations" rather than between peoples within civilizations.[24] In Huntington's framework, these civilizations are based primarily on predominant religious traditions, such as Western and Eastern Orthodox Christianity, Islam, Buddhism, and Hinduism. Because the clash thesis sees conflict in the modern world arising from clashing cultures enabled largely by increasing religious diversity, it necessarily recommends that civilizations

---

[19] Christopher Hitchens, Richard Dawkins, Sam Harris, and Daniel Dennett, *The Four Horsemen: The Conversation That Sparked an Atheist Revolution* (New York: Random House, 2019).

[20] Sam Harris, *The End of Faith: Religion, Terror, and the Future of Reason* (New York: W. W. Norton, 2005); Daniel C. Dennett, *Breaking the Spell: Religion as a Natural Phenomenon* (New York: Viking, 2006); Richard Dawkins, *The God Delusion* (Boston: Houghton Mifflin, 2006); Christopher Hitchens, *God Is Not Great: How Religion Poisons Everything* (New York: Twelve, 2008).

[21] Richard Dawkins, "Religion's Misguided Missiles," *The Guardian,* September 15, 2001, https://www.theguardian.com/world/2001/sep/15/september11.politicsphilosophyandsociety1.

[22] Kimball, *When Religion Becomes Evil,* 190.

[23] Samuel P. Huntington, *The Clash of Civilizations and the Remaking of World Order* (New York: Simon & Schuster, 2006).

[24] Samuel P. Huntington, "The Clash of Civilizations?," *Foreign Affairs* 72, no. 3 (1993): 22.

should maintain their unity by promoting intracivilizational cooperation and limiting multiculturalism and immigration.[25] After 9/11, the clash of civilizations theory gained newfound respect among certain policymakers who used Huntington's logic to understand the roots of religious violence.

Both the neo-atheists and Huntington take particular aim at Islam. The neo-atheists highlight various violent passages in the Qur'an as proof that Islam is inherently prone to violence. In their view, Islam's foundational doctrines and sacred texts mandate violence against non-Muslims. Accordingly, individuals such as Osama bin Laden, Ayman al-Zawahiri, and Abu Bakr al-Baghdadi are not necessarily marginal figures in the Muslim world as much as they are representatives of innate Muslim hostility to the West. The clash of civilizations thesis traces the roots of Muslim rage to residual animosity from the Crusades, the downfall of the Ottoman Empire, and Islam's inability to separate religion and politics in the way that Christianity did following the Peace of Westphalia.[26] "In Islam . . . God is Caesar," Huntington explained. He further warned, "The underlying problem for the West is not Islamic fundamentalism. It is Islam."[27]

Both of these essentialist explanations for religious violence in the modern world are deficient. Of course, the neo-atheists are correct in their assessment that religion *can* lead to violence. The same, though, can be said of virtually any nonreligious ideology. Indeed, the greatest mass murderers of the twentieth century were moved not by religious belief but by nonreligious ideologies—fascism, communism, and secular nationalism. Furthermore, there is no evidence that religious belief systems lead to greater levels of bloodshed than secular systems of thought. Yes, some of the world's most notoriously violent groups are clearly driven by religion, but so too are some of history's greatest human rights activists and peacemakers. Research has consistently shown that religiosity is a poor predictor of support for or participation in violent activities.[28] Thus, it is much more worthwhile to focus

---

[25] Samuel P. Huntington, *Who Are We: The Challenges to America's National Identity* (New York: Simon & Schuster, 2004).

[26] Bernard Lewis, "The Roots of Muslim Rage," *The Atlantic*, September 1990, https://www.theatlantic.com/magazine/archive/1990/09/the-roots-of-muslim-rage/304643/.

[27] Huntington, *Clash of Civilizations*, 70.

[28] C. Christine Fair and Bryan Shepherd, "Who Supports Terrorism? Evidence from 14 Muslim Countries," *Studies in Conflict & Terrorism* 29, no. 1 (2006): 51–74; C. Christine Fair, Neil Malhotra, and Jacob N. Shapiro, "Faith or Doctrine? Religion and Support for Political Violence in Pakistan," *Public Opinion Quarterly* 76, no. 4 (2012): 688–720; Richard A. Nielsen, *Deadly Clerics: Blocked Ambition and the Paths to Jihad* (Cambridge: Cambridge University Press, 2017).

on the *conditions* that empower the "darker side of religion."[29] Likewise, the clash of civilizations thesis is beset with problems. While Huntington correctly predicted the heightened role religion would play in the politics of a post–Cold War world—a stunningly prescient forecast that his critics often fail to recognize—the clash of civilizations thesis itself has not stood the test of time. While some religiously plural countries do experience violent religious conflict, many others do not. What is more, the religious violence that occurs in these countries is not generally attributable to the causes theorized by Huntington. While a few studies have found that religious diversity (a proxy for clashing civilizations) correlates with increased levels of conflict along religious lines,[30] the vast majority of empirical tests of the clash thesis fail to corroborate the proposition that global conflict can be attributed to clashing civilizations.[31] Indeed, there appear to be more violent conflicts *within* civilizations than *between* them.[32] Finally, despite numerous scholarly works debunking the thesis that Islam is more prone to violence than other faith traditions,[33] this myth continues to remain influential in analyses

---

[29] Isak Svensson, "Civil War and Religion: An Overview," in *The Oxford Encyclopedia of Politics and Religion*, ed. Paul A. Djupe, Mark J. Rozell, and Ted G. Jelen (Oxford: Oxford University Press, 2019), 3.

[30] Rudolph J. Rummel, "Is Collective Violence Correlated with Social Pluralism?," *Journal of Peace Research* 34, no. 2 (1997): 163–175; Philip G. Roeder, "Clash of Civilizations and Escalation of Domestic Ethnopolitical Conflicts," *Comparative Political Studies* 36, no. 5 (2003): 509–540.

[31] Errol A. Henderson and Richard Tucker, "Clear and Present Strangers: The Clash of Civilizations and International Conflict," *International Studies Quarterly* 45, no. 2 (2001): 317–338; Jonathan Fox, "Clash of Civilizations or Clash of Religions: Which Is a More Important Determinant of Ethnic Conflict?," *Ethnicities* 1, no. 3 (2001): 295–320; Jonathan Fox, "Ethnic Minorities and the Clash of Civilizations: A Quantitative Analysis of Huntington's Thesis," *British Journal of Political Science* 32, no. 3 (2002): 415–434; Giacomo Chiozza, "Is There a Clash of Civilizations? Evidence from Patterns of International Conflict Involvement, 1946–97," *Journal of Peace Research* 39, no. 6 (2002): 711–734; Pippa Norris and Ronald Inglehart, "Islamic Culture and Democracy: Testing the 'Clash of Civilizations' Thesis," in *Human Values and Social Change*, ed. Ronald Inglehart (London: Brill, 2003), 5–33; Errol A. Henderson, "Mistaken Identity: Testing the Clash of Civilizations Thesis in Light of Democratic Peace Claims," *British Journal of Political Science* 34, no. 3 (2004): 539–554; Jonathan Fox, "Paradigm Lost: Huntington's Unfulfilled Clash of Civilizations Prediction into the 21st Century," *International Politics* 42, no. 4 (2005): 428–457; Jonathan Fox, "Civilizational Clash or Balderdash? The Causes of Religious Discrimination in Western and European Christian-Majority Democracies," *Review of Faith & International Affairs* 17, no. 1 (2019): 34–48.

[32] Indra De Soysa and Ragnhild Nordås, "Islam's Bloody Innards? Religion and Political Terror, 1980–2000," *International Studies Quarterly* 51, no. 4 (2007): 927–943.

[33] Jonathan Fox, "Is Islam More Conflict Prone Than Other Religions? A Cross-Sectional Study of Ethnoreligious Conflict," *Nationalism and Ethnic Politics* 6, no. 2 (2000): 1–24; Jonathan Fox, "Do Muslims Engage in More Domestic Conflict Than Other Religious Groups?," *Civil Wars* 6, no. 1 (2003): 27–46; Süveyda Karakaya, "Religion and Conflict: Explaining the Puzzling Case of 'Islamic Violence,'" *International Interactions* 41, no. 3 (2015): 509–538; M. Steven Fish, Francesca R. Jensenius, and Katherine E. Michel, "Islam and Large-Scale Political Violence: Is There a Connection?," *Comparative Political Studies* 43, no. 11 (2010): 1327–1362; Mora Deitch, "Is Religion a Barrier to Peace? Religious Influence on Violent Intrastate Conflict Termination," *Terrorism and Political Violence* 34, no. 7 (2020): 1454–1470.

of religious violence and in popular discourse. Accordingly, political scientist Jonathan Fox finds "identity-based theories" of religious conflict to be "the most problematic in the literature on religion and politics."[34]

A second approach—instrumentalism—cautions against blaming religion for "religious violence." This view holds that religion functions as a smokescreen for violence undertaken to achieve some quintessentially nonreligious objective. In contrast to the first school of thought, which holds that religion itself is the cause of much of the violence in the contemporary world, these scholars argue that religion is only a secondary consideration in violence, masking the "real" underlying causes of violent conflict: endemic poverty, foreign military occupation, political marginalization, humiliation, alienation, or the innate desire for "brotherhood."[35] These studies do not dismiss religion's role in violence altogether, but instead claim that religious leaders sometimes exploit faith in order to make the use of violence acceptable to a wider constituency in service to achieving some nonreligious objective; theological beliefs are not, however, the main source of contemporary violence.[36] As such, religious violence does not constitute a unique category of bloodshed.

It is certainly the case that religious militants do pursue temporal goals. However, whereas this rationalist explanation for religious violence sees religion only as a mobilizing force used to gain leverage in sectarian conflicts, religion shapes these temporal goals in fundamental ways. Consider the example of the relationship between foreign military occupation and religious violence, often thought to be a straightforward demonstration of the rationalist character of contemporary religious conflict. In point of fact, religion can shape one's devotion to a particular piece of territory as a "holy

---

[34] Jonathan Fox, *An Introduction to Religion and Politics: Theory and Practice*, 2nd ed. (New York: Routledge, 2018), 32.

[35] Karen Rasler, "Concessions, Repression, and Political Protest in the Iranian Revolution," *American Sociological Review* 61 (1996): 132–152; Ibrahim Elbadawi and Nicholas Sambanis, "How Much War Will We See? Explaining the Prevalence of Civil War," *Journal of Conflict Resolution* 46, no. 3 (2002): 307–334; James D. Fearon and David D. Laitin, "Ethnicity, Insurgency, and Civil War," *American Political Science Review* 97, no. 1 (2002): 75–90; Robert A. Pape, "The Strategic Logic of Suicide Terrorism," *American Political Science Review* 97, no. 3 (2003): 343–361; Paul Collier and Anke Hoeffler, "Greed and Grievance in Civil War," *Oxford Economic Papers* 56, no. 4 (2004): 563–595; Håvard Hegre and Nicholas Sambanis, "Sensitivity Analysis of Empirical Results on Civil War Onset," *Journal of Conflict Resolution* 50, no. 4 (2006): 508–535; David L. Richards and Ronald D. Gelleny, "Banking Crises, Collective Protest and Rebellion," *Canadian Journal of Political Science/Revue Canadienne de Science Politique* 39, no. 4 (2006): 777–801; Robert A. Pape and James K. Feldman, *Cutting the Fuse: The Explosion of Global Suicide Terrorism and How to Stop It* (Chicago: University of Chicago Press, 2010).

[36] Andra Filote, Niklas Potrafke, and Heinrich Ursprung, "Suicide Attacks and Religious Cleavages," *Public Choice* 166, no. 1 (2016): 3–28.

land" by conceiving of it as a sacred space that offers the faithful the possibility of communing with the divine and achieving deeper insight into issues of transcendence.[37] Competing claims over sacred land are an enduring feature of many contemporary religious conflicts, which, to an outsider, may appear as mere squabbles over territorial demarcation. Perhaps nowhere is the link between religion and nationalism more evident than in Israel. It is impossible to understand the violent conflicts that have surrounded the city of Jerusalem—the holiest city in Judaism and Christianity and the third holiest in Islam—for millennia without taking religious factors into account.

A third explanation for contemporary religious violence—ideological extremism—makes a more nuanced argument, asserting that particular religious beliefs rather than religion itself motivates bloodshed in the name of God.[38] These theologies of violence offer a metanarrative that justifies bloodshed against religious outsiders and are usually built upon a selective reading and interpretation of sacred texts. For the religious militant, violence is a holy act undertaken with the sanction of a higher power. According to sociologist Mark Juergensmeyer, it is violence for which religion supplies "the motivation, the justification, the organization, and the worldview."[39] In this view, religious militants carry out violent acts because they are motivated by religious rewards, usually in an afterlife. Accordingly, religious violence is especially destructive. Scholars in this camp have pointed to three general theologies that appear to be especially important in motivating the violence of religious militants in the modern world: fundamentalism, apocalypticism, and religious nationalism.[40]

Theologies of violence surely matter in explaining contemporary religious violence. However, theological explanations often elide the question of why violent theologies—and corresponding religious violence—are more prevalent in some contexts than in others. While these studies are tremendously helpful in elucidating the psychological reasoning of the individual religious militant, they do not attempt to put forth generalizable and testable

---

[37] Ron E. Hassner, *War on Sacred Grounds* (Ithaca, NY: Cornell University Press, 2009).
[38] Magnus Ranstorp, "Terrorism in the Name of Religion," *Journal of International Affairs* 50 (Summer 1996): 41–60; Mark Juergensmeyer, *Terror in the Mind of God: The Global Rise of Religious Violence* (Berkeley: University of California Press, 2003); Jessica Stern, *Terror in the Name of God: Why Religious Militants Kill* (New York: Harper Collins, 2003).
[39] Juergensmeyer, *Terror in the Mind of God*, 7.
[40] Heather Selma Gregg. "Three Theories of Religious Activism and Violence: Social Movements, Fundamentalists, and Apocalyptic Warriors," *Terrorism and Political Violence* 28, no. 2 (2016): 338–360.

propositions for why some countries are rife with violent religious conflict but others are free from it. Starting from the assumption that political theologies of violence can plausibly take root anywhere, this book aims to ascertain why these theologies are more pervasive and destructive in some countries than in others. Are there certain contexts or special situations that serve to spread bellicose beliefs throughout society? To answer this question, we need to complement a theological approach with a structural one, an element largely missing from ideological explanations for religious violence.

A fourth view—denialism—argues that because religion is an inherently nebulous concept with imprecise boundaries, the distinction between "religious" and "secular" violence is artificial and unjustifiable on both conceptual and empirical grounds, and that the religious/secular dichotomy is best avoided altogether.[41] For example, theologian William Cavanaugh believes that "the very distinction between secular and religious violence is unhelpful, misleading, and mystifying."[42] He argues that religious violence is a "myth," born of the idea that "religion is a transhistorical and transcultural feature of human life, essentially distinct from 'secular' features such as politics and economics, which has a peculiarly dangerous inclination to promote violence."[43]

The denialist view of religious violence, however, ignores empirical research on the fundamental differences between religious and nonreligious violence. This body of work has shown that the two *can* be effectively differentiated and that religious violence is unique in its lethality and resilience. Because religious militants look to their faith as a source of inspiration, legitimation, and worldview, a totally different incentive structure emerges than exists for their secular counterparts.[44] As explained by Juergensmeyer, religious violence is "particularly savage and relentless" because "its perpetrators have placed such religious images of divine struggle—cosmic war—in the service of worldly political battles."[45] Several studies have shown that

---

[41] Talal Asad, *Genealogies of Religion: Discipline and Reasons of Power in Christianity and Islam* (Baltimore: Johns Hopkins University Press, 1993); Terry Nardin. "Review: *Terror in the Mind of God: The Global Rise of Religious Violence*," *Journal of Politics* 63, no. 2 (2001): 683–684; William T. Cavanaugh, *The Myth of Religious Violence: Secular Ideology and the Roots of Modern Conflict* (New York: Oxford University Press, 2009); Jeroen Gunning and Richard Jackson. "What's So 'Religious' about 'Religious Terrorism'?," *Critical Studies on Terrorism* 4, no. 3 (2011): 369–388.
[42] Cavanaugh, *The Myth of Religious Violence*, 7.
[43] Cavanaugh, *The Myth of Religious Violence*, 3.
[44] Juergensmeyer, *Terror in the Mind of God*, 125–126.
[45] Juergensmeyer, *Terror in the Mind of God*, 146.

the sacred basis of religious violence renders it a uniquely deadly form of violence in the modern world, which results in greater levels of bloodshed and overall devastation than nonreligious forms of violence.[46] The relative lethality of religious violence can be attributed to the exceptionally high stakes involved. That religious militants seek to impose their version of a religiously pure society on everyone makes conflicts rooted in divergent value systems extraordinarily difficult to resolve.

In summary, existing explanations for religious violence can be grouped into four categories. The first involves essentialist accounts that pin the blame for religious violence on the very nature of religion. The second offers instrumentalist interpretations that have little to do with religion itself. The third looks instead at particular religious beliefs that generate violence. Finally, the fourth contends that religious and nonreligious violence cannot be effectively differentiated. As argued, each of these explanations has important limitations.

Argument of the Book

In contrast to these explanations for religious violence, this book emphasizes a concept known as the "ambivalence of the sacred."[47] To say that religion is politically ambivalent means that it is fundamentally malleable and can be used to support any number of political positions—even contradictory ones like violence and peace. Religion is ambivalent because spiritual beliefs and practices cannot be reduced to a reified ontological category from which political worldviews are determined a priori. Religions are instead dynamic and complex systems; while peace and love represent one face of religion, every one of the world's major faith traditions also carries the potential for violence. The world's religions are multivocal, containing within them numerous doctrinal currents and interpretations—some peaceful, others violent. Religion spawns the terrorist and the insurrectionist, just as it

---

[46] Jonathan Fox, "Ethnoreligious Conflict in the Third World: The Role of Religion as a Cause of Conflict," *Nationalism and Ethnic Politics* 9, no. 1 (2003): 101–125; Isak Svensson, "Fighting with Faith," *Journal of Conflict Resolution* 51, no. 6 (2007): 930–949; Toft, "Getting Religion?"; Isak Svensson and Emily Harding, "How Holy Wars End: Exploring the Termination Patterns of Conflicts with Religious Dimensions in Asia," *Terrorism and Political Violence* 23, no. 2 (2011): 133–149; Peter S. Henne, "The Ancient Fire: Religion and Suicide Terrorism," *Terrorism and Political Violence* 24, no. 1 (2012): 38–60; Desirée Nilsson and Isak Svensson, "Resisting Resolution: Islamist Claims and Negotiations in Intrastate Armed Conflicts," *International Negotiation* 25, no. 3 (2020): 389–412.

[47] R. Scott Appleby, *The Ambivalence of the Sacred: Religion, Violence, and Reconciliation* (Lanham, MD: Rowman & Littlefield, 1999).

does the peacemaker and the human rights activist. While religion's inherent ambivalence and malleability have long been recognized by scholars of religion and politics, less understood is *why* religion is sometimes violent and at other times peaceful.

What kinds of environments encourage or discourage religious violence? Of particular importance here is the interaction between religious and political institutions. In a pioneering work, political scientist Daniel Philpott argued that the "political theologies" of religious groups interact with governmental treatment of religion to produce religious violence in the forms of communal conflict and terrorism. He found that religious actors who remain independent from the state and hold a political theology conducive to tolerance and liberalism were likely to support democracy, peace, and reconciliation. On the other hand, religious actors in a close relationship with the state and holding theologies conducive to violence were likely to support authoritarianism and engage in faith-based conflict.[48]

Following the trail blazed by Philpott, several other scholars applied the idea of religion-state arrangements to the study of religious violence, including civil wars, terrorism, and mob violence, arguing that states and societies which do not attempt to impose a religious monopoly or selectively subsidize religious groups in a partial manner allow for a wide range of religious practices and doctrinal interpretations to flourish. This work consistently finds that contexts marked by an amicable separation of religion and state, and especially religious freedom, tend to experience fewer problems with religious violence.[49] Separation and freedom have the effect of weakening the narrative of religious extremists that their faith is under attack by the state, thus making violence less likely. In these settings, radicals have their views challenged and critiqued in the marketplace of ideas and have to defend them, thus dampening the impetus toward violence. For this reason, religious actors who do not find themselves sidelined by laws or violent suppression are much less likely to pursue their aims through violence than groups which do not have the capacity to carry out activities central to

---

[48] Daniel Philpott, "Explaining the Political Ambivalence of Religion," *American Political Science Review* 101, no. 3 (2007): 505–525.

[49] Thomas F. Farr, *World of Faith and Freedom: Why International Religious Liberty Is Vital to American National Security* (New York: Oxford University Press, 2008); Nil S. Satana, Molly Inman, and Jóhanna Kristín Birnir, "Religion, Government Coalitions, and Terrorism," *Terrorism and Political Violence* 25, no. 1 (2013): 29–52; Nilay Saiya, *Weapon of Peace: How Religious Liberty Combats Terrorism* (New York: Cambridge University Press, 2018).

their faith and bring those ideas to bear in the public realm. Otherwise militant-minded individuals and groups have the ability to exact change through legitimate institutional mechanisms through which they can influence the character of the state and its religious identity by means other than violence. The political engagement of faith groups—voting, running for office, grassroots activism, and other forms of civic engagement—helps induce moderation and the formation of cross-cutting cleavages, as politically active religious groups have to vie with each other for votes and must appeal to the political center in order to capture the widest proportion of the electorate.[50]

As important as this body of work is, one of its deficiencies is that it fails to distinguish who actually is responsible for the violence in conflict-ridden societies, arguing instead that the lack of differentiation between religion and state produces general "violent religious hostilities" or "religious terrorism." The overwhelming majority of quantitative, cross-country analyses on the correlates of religious violence aggregate attacks by groups in society, making it impossible to assess if, in fact, the violence is being principally carried out by marginalized and aggrieved faith communities. To the extent that previous studies assess the source of religious violence, they tend to see it arising from embattled religious minorities,[51] though a couple of studies find otherwise.[52]

The logic linking minority discrimination to violence has a long pedigree in the contentious politics literature, dating back to Ted Gurr's seminal work *Why Men Rebel*.[53] Since then, a number of studies have indeed demonstrated a link between minority discrimination and various forms of large-scale

---

[50] Jillian Schwedler, *Faith in Moderation: Islamist Parties in Jordan and Yemen* (New York: Cambridge University Press, 2007); Johanna Kristin Birnir and Nil S. Satana, "Religion and Coalition Politics," *Comparative Political Studies* 46, no. 1 (2013): 3–30.

[51] Jonathan Fox, "The Influence of Religious Legitimacy on Grievance Formation by Ethno-religious Minorities," *Journal of Peace Research* 36, no. 3 (1999): 289–307; Jonathan Fox, "The Effects of Religious Discrimination on Ethno-religious Protest and Rebellion," *Journal of Conflict Studies* 20, no. 2 (2000): 16–43; Yasemin Akbaba and Zeynep Taydas, "Does Religious Discrimination Promote Dissent? A Quantitative Analysis," *Ethnopolitics*, 10, nos. 3–4 (2011): 271–295.

[52] Matthias Basedau, Jonathan Fox, Jan H. Pierskalla, Georg Strüver, and Johannes Vüllers, "Does Discrimination Breed Grievances—and Do Grievances Breed Violence? New Evidence from an Analysis of Religious Minorities in Developing Countries," *Conflict Management and Peace Science* 34, no. 3 (2017): 217–239; Nilay Saiya, Stuti Manchanda, and Rahmat Wadidi, "Faith-Based Discrimination and Violent Religious Hostilities," *Journal of Conflict Resolution*, doi:https://doi.org/10.1177/0022002731188901.

[53] Ted Robert Gurr, *Why Men Rebel* (Princeton, NJ: Princeton University Press, 1970); Ted Robert Gurr, "Why Minorities Rebel," *International Political Science Review* 14, no. 2 (1993): 161–201; Ted Robert Gurr, *Minorities at Risk* (Washington, DC: U.S. Institute of Peace, 1993).

political violence, including civil wars and rebellions.[54] The logic linking minority discrimination to communal conflict is as follows. Selective discrimination against minorities produces a ubiquitous sense of "relative deprivation" among targeted groups when they compare their inferior status to that of similar groups in society. When they see that other groups are objectively better off economically, politically, or socially, they feel relatively deprived. Relative deprivation erodes tolerance, engenders grievances, fuels social polarization, and reinforces a sense of in-group solidarity among marginalized communities. If these communities are able to overcome their collective action problems, they will attempt to mobilize, sometimes violently, resulting in various forms of conflict behavior, including rebellion, revolution, and war. This dynamic is exacerbated in contexts where states not only discriminate against minorities but also have policies in place that favor political or ethnic majorities, including special legal privileges or the ability to regulate public life at the expense of others.

This "minority backlash" explanation for conflict is especially prevalent in the field of terrorism studies.[55] Many of the seminal works on the causes of terrorism claim that governments which discriminate against minorities generate sympathy for extremist groups, provoke people to turn to these groups for protection, and increase the costs of remaining peaceful for

---

[54] Mark Irving Lichbach, "Deterrence or Escalation? The Puzzle of Aggregate Studies of Repression and Dissent," *Journal of Conflict Resolution* 31, no. 2 (1987): 266–297; Will H. Moore, "Repression and Dissent: Substitution, Context, and Timing," *American Journal of Political Science* 42, no. 3 (1988): 851–873; Ted Robert Gurr and Will H. Moore, "Ethnopolitical Rebellion: A Cross-sectional Analysis of the 1980s with Risk Assessments for the 1990s," *American Journal of Political Science* 41, no. 4 (1997): 1079–1103; Ted Robert Gurr, *Peoples versus States: Minorities at Risk in the New Century* (Washington, DC: U.S. Institute of Peace Press, 2000); Ted Robert Gurr, "Nonviolence in Ethnopolitics: Strategies for the Attainment of Group Rights and Autonomy," *PS: Political Science and Politics* 33, no. 2 (2000): 155–160; Matthew R. Cleary, "Democracy and Indigenous Rebellion in Latin America," *Comparative Political Studies* 33, no. 9 (2000): 1123–1153; Patrick M. Regan and Daniel Norton, "Greed, Grievance, and Mobilization in Civil Wars," *Journal of Conflict Resolution* 49, no. 3 (2005): 319–336; Victor Asal and Brian J. Phillips, "What Explains Ethnic Organizational Violence? Evidence from Eastern Europe and Russia," *Conflict Management and Peace Science* 35, no. 2 (2018): 111–131.

[55] James A. Piazza, "Poverty, Minority Economic Discrimination, and Domestic Terrorism," *Journal of Peace Research* 48, no. 3 (2011): 339–53; James A. Piazza, "Types of Minority Discrimination and Terrorism," *Conflict Management and Peace Science* 29, no. 5 (2012): 521–546; Seung-Whan Choi and James A. Piazza, "Ethnic Groups, Political Exclusion and Domestic Terrorism," *Defence and Peace Economics* 27, no. 1 (2016): 37–63; Sambuddha Ghatak, "Challenging the State: Effect of Minority Discrimination, Economic Globalization, and Political Openness on Domestic Terrorism," *International Interactions* 42, no. 1 (2016): 56–80; Kristian Skrede Gleditsch and Sara M. T. Polo, "Ethnic Inclusion, Democracy, and Terrorism," *Public Choice* 169, no. 3 (2016): 207–229; Holley E. Hansen, Stephen C. Nemeth, and Jacob A. Mauslein, "Ethnic Political Exclusion and Terrorism: Analyzing the Local Conditions for Violence," *Conflict Management and Peace Science* 37, no. 3 (2020): 280–300.

ordinary citizens.[56] This framework suggests that those who are most suppressed in society—particularly ethnic, political, or religious minorities—should be the most likely to employ terrorism. Therefore a key solution to terrorism would involve the accommodation of minority demands.

While most studies of relative deprivation, grievance formation, and violence focus on the political, economic, and cultural grievances of ethnic minorities,[57] the straightforward logic linking repression and resistance can also be applied to repressed *religious* communities. When states limit the practice of religion by minority groups, they implicitly favor adherents of dominant religious traditions, either purposely or unintentionally, thereby creating an unbalanced religious playing field. Discrimination often leads oppressed minority communities to seek redress from the state. A government unresponsive to the just claims of minorities intensifies grievances, produces a common narrative of disenfranchisement, and exacerbates existing sectarian tensions, sometimes leading to civil unrest and minority violence against those perceived to be responsible for their marginalization and suppression.[58] Political scientists Yasemin Akbaba and Zeynep Taydas straightforwardly argue that "religious discrimination leads to the generation of grievances, which in turn encourages ethnoreligious minorities to engage in peaceful and violent opposition against the state." They further contend that "severe inequalities in access to political, economic and social resources between culturally defined groups serve as the basis for inter-group hostility." Violence ensues when "[r]ebels who feel subordinate stop perceiving the state as a neutral entity but rather identify the state as

---

[56] Martha Crenshaw, "The Causes of Terrorism," *Comparative Politics* 13, no. 4 (1981): 379–399; Jeffrey Ian Ross, "Structural Causes of Oppositional Political Terrorism: Towards a Causal Model," *Journal of Peace Research* 30, no. 3 (1993): 317–329; Walter Laqueur, *The New Terrorism* (Oxford: Oxford University Press, 1999); Gordon H. McCormick, "Terrorist Decision Making," *Annual Review of Political Science* 6, no. 1 (2003): 473–507.

[57] Gudrun Østby, "Polarization, Horizontal Inequalities and Violent Civil Conflict," *Journal of Peace Research* 45, no. 2 (2008): 143–162; Andreas Wimmer, Lars-Erik Cederman, and Brian Min, "Ethnic Politics and Armed Conflict: A Configurational Analysis of a New Global Data Set," *American Sociological Review* 74, no. 2 (2009): 316–337; Lars-Erik Cederman, Andreas Wimmer, and Brian Min, "Why Do Ethnic Groups Rebel? New Data and Analysis," *World Politics* 62, no. 1 (2010): 87–119; Lars-Erik Cederman, Nils B. Weidmann, and Kristian Skrede Gleditsch, "Horizontal Inequalities and Ethnonationalist Civil War: A Global Comparison," *American Political Science Review* 105, no. 3 (2011): 478–495; Lars-Erik Cederman, Kristian Skrede Gleditsch, and Halvard Buhaug, *Inequality, Grievances, and Civil War* (New York: Cambridge University Press, 2013); Lars-Erik Cederman, Kristian Skrede Gleditsch, and Julian Wucherpfennig, "Predicting the Decline of Ethnic Civil War: Was Gurr Right and for the Right Reasons?," *Journal of Peace Research* 54, no. 2 (2017): 262–274.

[58] Philpott, "Explaining the Political Ambivalence of Religion," 518–521; Farr, *World of Faith and Freedom*, 243–272.

an agent responsible for promoting the identity of the dominant group."[59] Their empirical analysis finds that discrimination against minorities does indeed increase the likelihood of armed conflict. Similarly, political scientists Monica Toft, Daniel Philpott, and Timothy Shah argue that "repression of religion" leaves "religious actors feeling oppressed and resentful."[60] Targets of violence may include state officials, members or holy sites of other religious groups, or the population at large. Numerous studies, both quantitative and qualitative, have demonstrated a connection between religious repression, grievance formation, and political violence.[61]

My own previous work has used a "minority backlash" lens to understand violent religious conflict.[62] I have argued that when religious minorities

---

[59] Akbaba and Taydas, "Does Religious Discrimination Promote Dissent?," 271, 273, 277.

[60] Toft, Philpott, and Shah, *God's Century*, 132.

[61] Denis O'Hearn, "Catholic Grievances, Catholic Nationalism: A Comment," *British Journal of Sociology* 34, no. 3 (1983): 438–445; David C. Rapoport, "Some General Observations on Religion and Violence," *Terrorism and Political Violence* 3, no. 3 (1991): 118–140; Lisa Anderson, "Fulfilling Prophecies: State Policy and Islamist Radicalism," in *Political Islam: Revolution, Radicalism, or Reform?*, ed. John L. Esposito (London: Lynne Rienner, 1997), 17–31; Mohammed M. Hafez, *Why Muslims Rebel: Repression and Resistance in the Islamic World* (Boulder, CO: Lynne Rienner, 2003); Mohammed M. Hafez, "From Marginalization to Massacres: A Political Process Explanation of GIA Violence in Algeria," in *Islamic Activism: A Social Movement Theory Approach*, ed. Quintan Wiktorowicz (Bloomington: Indiana University Press, 2003), 37–60; Brian J. Grim and Roger Finke, *The Price of Freedom Denied: Religious Persecution and Conflict in the 21st Century* (New York: Cambridge University Press, 2011); Roger Finke, "Origins and Consequences of Religious Freedoms: A Global Overview," *Sociology of Religion* 74, no. 3 (2013): 297–313; David Muchlinski, "Grievances and Opportunities: Religious Violence across Political Regimes," *Politics and Religion* 7, no. 4 (2014): 684–705; Melanie Kolbe and Peter S. Henne, "The Effect of Religious Restrictions on Forced Migration," *Politics & Religion* 7, no. 4 (2014): 665–683; Pazit Ben-Nun Bloom, "State-Level Restriction of Religious Freedom and Women's Rights: A Global Analysis," *Political Studies* 64, no. 4 (2016): 832–853; Matthias Basedau, Birte Pfeiffer, and Johannes Vüllers, "Bad Religion? Religion, Collective Action, and the Onset of Armed Conflict in Developing Countries," *Journal of Conflict Resolution* 60, no. 2 (2016): 226–255; Peter S. Henne, "Government Interference in Religious Institutions and Terrorism," *Religion, State and Society* 47, no. 1 (2019): 67–87.

[62] Nilay Saiya, "Explaining Religious Violence across Countries: An Institutional Perspective," in *Mediating Religion and Government: Political Institutions and the Policy Process*, ed. Kevin R. den Dulk and Elizabeth Oldmixon (New York: Palgrave, 2014), 209–240; Nilay Saiya, "The Religious Freedom Peace," *International Journal of Human Rights* 19, no. 3 (2015): 369–382; Nilay Saiya and Anthony Scime, "Explaining Religious Terrorism: A Data-Mined Analysis," *Conflict Management and Peace Science* 32, no. 5 (2015): 487–512; Nilay Saiya, "Religion, Democracy and Terrorism," *Perspectives on Terrorism* 9, no. 6 (December 2015): 51–59; Nilay Saiya, "Religious Freedom, the Arab Spring and U.S. Middle East Policy," *International Politics* 54, no. 1 (February 2017): 43–53; Nilay Saiya and Joshua Fidler, "Taking God Seriously: The Struggle against Extremism," *Middle East Policy* 25, no. 1 (Spring 2018): 80–95; Nilay Saiya, "Religion, State and Terrorism: A Global Analysis," *Terrorism and Political Violence* 31, no. 2 (April 2019): 204–223; Nilay Saiya and Anthony Scime, "Comparing Classification Trees to Discern Patterns of Terrorism," *Social Science Quarterly* 100, no. 4 (June 2019): 1420–1444; Nilay Saiya, "Pluralism and Peace in South Asia," *Review of Faith & International Affairs* 17, no. 4 (2019): 12–22; Nilay Saiya, "Confronting Apocalyptic Terrorism: Lessons from France and Japan," *Studies in Conflict & Terrorism* 43, no. 9 (2020): 375–395; Nilay Saiya and Stuti Manchanda, "Do Burqa Bans Make Us Safer? Veil Restrictions and Terrorism in Europe," *Journal of European Public Policy* 27, no. 12 (2020): 1781–1800; Nilay Saiya, "Who Attacks America? Islamist Attacks on the American Homeland," *Perspectives on Terrorism* 15, no. 5 (2021): 187–201;

suffer from an institutional bias in the form of legal discrimination—laws or official policies that restrict the building and maintenance of minority houses of worship, the wearing of certain types of religious garments in public, proselytizing and conversion, and blasphemy and apostasy—extremists from these communities are more likely to turn to the gun over their second-class status. They are also more likely to garner support from embattled minority constituencies. I thus offered the following explanation for religious violence in an earlier work: "Often embattled religious communities, perceiving their faith to be under attack, subscribe to a ubiquitous narrative of communal disillusionment, sometimes leading to violence against those perceived to be responsible for their marginalized and suppressed status.... When religious groups find themselves ostracized through laws or violent suppression, they are much more likely to pursue their aims through violence as well."[63] In short, straightforward repression by the state generates minority grievances and motivates various forms of mobilization—sometimes peaceful, at other times violent.

Several cases anecdotally demonstrate the connection between minority religious discrimination and violence. In Northern Ireland, systematic discrimination against Catholics directly fueled the activities of the Irish Republican Army throughout the 1980s and 1990s. In India, the militant wing of the Sikh resistance movement arose in response to centuries of brutal repression by successive national governments stemming back to the Mughal Empire. In Sri Lanka, discrimination against Hindu Tamils led to the rise of the Tamil Tigers and paved the way for a sanguinary civil war between the country's Hindu and Buddhist communities. In Sudan, embattled minority groups fought a war against the regime in Khartoum, which had allied with Islamists to impose a draconian form of Islamic law throughout the entire country.[64] Eventually, the conflict led to the division of the country altogether. In Europe, widespread religious profiling of nonviolent Muslims has been seized on by ISIS to gain sympathy for its cause.

Nilay Saiya, Stuti Manchanda, and Rahmat Wadidi, "Faith-Based Discrimination and Violent Religious Hostilities: A Global Analysis," *Journal of Conflict Resolution* 68, no. 6 (2024): 1109–1138; Xun Cao, Haiyan Duan, Chuyu Liu, and Yingjie Wei, "Local Religious Institutions and the Impact of Interethnic Inequality on Conflict," *International Studies Quarterly*, 62, no. 4 (2018): 765–781; Saiya, *Weapon of Peace*, 34–37.
[63] Saiya and Scime, "Explaining Religious Terrorism," 492–493.
[64] Francis M. Deng, "Sudan—Civil War and Genocide: Disappearing Christians of the Middle East," *Middle East Quarterly* 8, no. 1 (2001): 13–21.

In short, the repression-resistance thesis has a great deal of face validity and finds support in the historical record. To be sure, the argument that religious minorities turn to the gun in response to objective conditions of marginalization, discrimination, oppression, and inequality is correct. When any community experiences a gap between what Gurr called "value expectations" (that which people believe they are rightly entitled to) and "value capabilities" (that which they are actually capable of attaining) they are more likely to seek redress for their grievances by turning to the gun.[65] Such a logic would also certainly apply to religious as much as nonreligious groups.

However, a singular focus on violence by minority groups misses the paradoxical reality that *the vast preponderance of contemporary religious violence is carried out principally by religious majorities and not religious minorities*—a reality that has received relatively little attention from scholars and policymakers.[66] This paradox can be seen in the examples that opened this book. The violence of the 2021 U.S. Capitol insurrection occurred largely at the hands of those identifying with America's largest religion, namely Christianity. In Afghanistan, both the Taliban and ISIS-K claim to represent the country's majority-Muslim population. The violence that began the 2021 war between Israel and Hamas was carried out by Jews in the world's only Jewish-majority state. In India, a Hindu-majority country, extremist Hindus have been responsible for a preponderance of violence, sometimes inviting retaliation from the country's other religious traditions. Finally, the ethnic cleansing of Myanmar's Rohingya population has been supported by Buddhist nationalists in a Buddhist-majority country. Elsewhere, countless individuals belonging to minority faith traditions or none at all have been threatened, beaten, harassed, vilified, jailed, tortured, or even killed for their rejection of the faith practiced by the majority of the country. Examples abound: Jehovah's Witnesses in Russia, Jews in Europe, Baha'is in Iran, and atheists around the world. In each of these cases, empowered religious majorities and not beleaguered religious minorities have been principally responsible for the religious violence engulfing their countries. The main instigators of violence did not hail from disaffected or marginalized communities but rather from dominant and empowered communities that enjoyed special prerogatives from the state.

---

[65] Gurr, *Why Men Rebel*, 13.
[66] James A. Piazza, "Intolerance of Non-Muslim Political Rights and Engagement in Political Violence: A Study of Public Opinion in 11 Arab Countries," unpublished manuscript.

My analysis of global religious violence from 1998 to 2018 shows that about 90 percent of all identifiable cases of religious violence around the world can be attributed to religious majorities—those religious communities comprising the largest faith traditions within a country. This figure may strike readers as counterintuitive. It is easy to see how states practicing religious favoritism create a fertile ground for backlash violence from marginalized, suppressed, and weaker minority religious communities. But why would majority groups that enjoy special prerogatives from the state turn to violence? Would not a state favoring a religious tradition important to the majority of its citizens decrease grievances among members of that majority and promote stability? Paradoxically, as this book argues, state favoritism of religion also has serious drawbacks.[67]

Although the discriminatory treatment of minority groups may well provoke targeted minorities to seek revenge, it is far more likely to encourage vigilante violence by *dominant and favored* religious majorities who use their privileged stations as a justification to attack out-groups. Whereas religious violence is commonly believed to be a "weapon of the weak," carried out by aggrieved religious minorities, in reality it is more often a "weapon of the strong," wielded by politically empowered religious communities, often against those of minority faith traditions.[68] Majoritarian militants coalesce around a common religious identity when they perceive a threat to that identity stemming from forces external to the faith, especially the presence of religious outsiders.[69] When religious identity becomes politicized in this way, religious theologies can easily become weaponized in service to violence, which is justified on the premise that the targeted group threatens the established social and moral order. The argument that contemporary religious violence occurs at the hands of empowered religious majorities and is dispensed against religious minorities upends the conventional wisdom on religious violence held by many in the West, a view strongly shaped by images of Muslim extremists such as the 9/11 hijackers or the *Charlie Hebdo* attackers waging war against Western societies.

---

[67] Ani Sarkissian, *The Varieties of Religious Repression: Why Governments Restrict Religion* (New York: Oxford University Press, 2015), 27; Grim and Finke, *The Price of Freedom Denied*, 209.

[68] Peter S. Henne, Nilay Saiya, and Ashlyn W. Hand, "Weapon of the Strong: Government Support for Religion and Majoritarian Terrorism," *Journal of Conflict Resolution* 64, no. 10 (2020): 1943–1967; Virginia Page Fortna, "Is Terrorism Really a Weapon of the Weak? Debunking the Conventional Wisdom," *Journal of Conflict Resolution* 67, no. 4 (2023): 642–671.

[69] Assaf Moghadam, *The Globalization of Martyrdom: Al Qaeda, Salafi Jihad, and the Diffusion of Suicide Attacks* (Baltimore: Johns Hopkins University Press, 2009), 46.

It is also worth noting that majoritarian violence is theoretically much deadlier than violence by minorities for two reasons. First, by definition, religious majorities are greater in number than minorities. This simple fact means that majorities have more people in society who can become radicalized and that there is potentially more support within society at large for majoritarian violence. Some studies have found that when a majority comprises a greater percentage of the overall population, conflict becomes more likely.[70] Second, majorities expectedly seek more grandiose goals than do minorities, such as overthrowing and replacing a government with one that is more religiously pure. Minorities, by contrast, are much less likely to desire such ambitious objectives and are more likely to seek more limited goals such as equal rights. Taken together, these observations suggest that previous work has perhaps placed too much emphasis on the conflict behavior of minorities and not enough on that of majorities.

In summary, this book argues that politics and not religion lies at the root of contemporary religious violence. Two points here require clarification. First, this is not to suggest that theology and religious identity do not matter in the production of faith-based violence; clearly they do. I take the view, however, that because religion is fundamentally malleable, it can be marshaled in service to violence or peace. Second, to say that religious violence is political does not mean that religion merely serves as a smokescreen for self-serving political goals. Rather, it suggests that the key consideration in the production of contemporary violent religious hostilities involves an inescapably political dimension, namely the relationship that exists between religious and state institutions. I argue that contemporary religious violence stems centrally from environments of political privilege, where historically and culturally dominant religious communities enjoy the favor of the state. In countries marked by privilege, the government actively favors adherents of the majority religion over followers of different faiths in its laws and policies. States that favor certain religions and discriminate against others encourage militancy not only by those bearing the brunt of their inequitable laws and policies but also by extremists from the very religious communities favored by the state. We might think of this counterintuitive claim as a

---

[70] Tanja Ellingsen, "Colorful Community or Ethnic Witches' Brew? Multiethnicity and Domestic Conflict during and after the Cold War," *Journal of Conflict Resolution* 44, no. 2 (2000): 228–249; Matthias Basedau, Georg Strüver, Johannes Vüllers, and Tim Wegenast, "Do Religious Factors Impact Armed Conflict? Empirical Evidence from Sub-Saharan Africa," *Terrorism and Political Violence* 23, no. 5 (2011): 752–779.

"paradox of privilege."[71] As I will argue, because the paradox of privilege is so widespread, it has contributed to a global crisis of secularism.

Outline of the Book

This book is divided into three parts. The first part (chapter 1) explains how a global crisis of political secularism has created a rising tide of religious violence. The second part (chapters 2 through 6) considers contemporary religious violence across the world's major faith traditions. Each chapter examines the relationship between privilege and violence in one of the world's major religious traditions: Christianity, Islam, Hinduism, Buddhism, and Judaism. The third part (chapter 7) argues that an approach to religion called "covenantal pluralism"—an inclusive social framework wherein different religious groups coexist and interact while retaining their distinct identities—offers a promising antidote to the crisis of secularism and the attendant violence afflicting the world. The following contains a more detailed summary of each of the chapters.

The first chapter argues that global religious violence results from a dearth of political secularism. From the late 1970s onward, governments and assertive religious actors around the world have deeply entwined religious and state institutions, undermining political secularism and heightening the political salience of religious identities. This chapter covers three issues: what secularism is, why it is in crisis, and how it begets religious violence.

The next five chapters examine the paradox of privilege in the world's major religions: Christianity, Islam, Hinduism, Buddhism, and Judaism. Together these religions comprise about 80 percent of the global population and about 90 percent of the global religious population. Of course, there are other important faith traditions, such as Sikhism, Zoroastrianism, the Baha'i faith, and various folk religions. The reason this book does not deal with these other faith traditions pertains to the main argument that religious violence results from the state's privileging of a majoritarian religious tradition. Because religions outside of the "big five" do not comprise the dominant religion in any country—and therefore are not the beneficiaries of religious privilege—they remain beyond the scope of this book.

---

[71] Nilay Saiya, *The Global Politics of Jesus: A Christian-Case for Church-State Separation* (New York: Oxford University Press, 2022).

The second chapter examines the roots of contemporary religious violence in the world's largest religion, Christianity. In his most famous teaching, the Sermon on the Mount, Jesus commanded his followers to practice the way of peace by turning the other cheek, going the extra mile, and blessing their persecutors.[72] "Blessed are the peacemakers, for they will be called children of God," he taught.[73] Yet, despite the clarity of these teachings, Christianity has a long and troubling history of violence, seen in the various European wars over religion, the inquisitions, and wars of colonial expansion. Violence in the Christian tradition is not an artifact of the past, however. Today Christian violence tends to arise from an ideology known as "Christian nationalism," a political theology and cultural framework that advocates for the fusion of Christianity and a country's civic and political life and for a privileged place for Christianity in the public square. This chapter argues that where the state privileges Christianity in its laws or policies relative to other religions, *Christian* violence increases. It examines the dramatic increase of Christian violence in both the West and the developing world, showing that structures of privilege have emboldened violent Christian extremists.

The third chapter turns to Islam, the world's second largest religion. For many, the subject of religious violence likely brings to mind images of Muslim extremists. There are understandable reasons for this association. The vast majority of religious violence that occurs around the world is indeed perpetrated by Islamist extremists. The scenes of 9/11, 11/9, and 10/7 have been permanently emblazoned in the memories of those who witnessed those events. This chapter explores the relationship between Islam and violence by looking at specific ways that political secularism is violated in Muslim-majority states and how this deficiency produces religion-related violence. Importantly, this chapter shows that political secularism is undermined in the Muslim world in two different ways. The first is through the ideology of Islamism, a political theology that seeks to infuse public life with Islamic principles, including the political, economic, legal, and social realms. Islamists believe that Islam should be the law of the land and that their states should grant Islam special privileges not accorded other faith traditions. Because Islamism views the state as a vehicle for promoting the Islamization of society—including family life, entertainment, education, and religious

---

[72] Matthew 5:38–40.
[73] Matthew 5:9.

practice—it necessarily restricts the rights of those belonging to a minority faith, no faith, or a nonconformist version of Islam. A second way Muslim-majority countries undermine political secularism is through an ideology I call "pseudo-secularism." Based on imported versions of Western secular models of religion and state, particularly the French model of laïcité, pseudo-secularism seeks to manage and control the expression of religion so as to make space for the development of secular forms of nationalism, economic development, and Enlightenment-based notions of modernity. Though an antireligious ideology, pseudo-secularism accomplishes this goal by extending religious privileges to the predominant form of Islam in exchange for its support, while restricting other religions. Both Islamism and pseudo-secularism have worked to produce the Muslim world's unusually high levels of religious violence.

Chapter 4 examines the case of Hinduism, the world's oldest and third-largest religious tradition. Whereas both Christianity and Islam comprise the majority religions in dozens of countries, Hinduism is the majority religion in only three—India, Mauritius, and Nepal—with around 95 percent of the global Hindu population living in India alone. Thus this chapter examines Hindu-state relations in India, revealing how a country that embraced political secularism upon its independence has today become a country based in Hindu privilege and the marginalization of religious minorities. The increasing integration of Hinduism and the state has also encouraged majority-on-minority violence in the form of Hindu vigilantism. In attempt to maintain the Hindu purity of the country, Hindu extremists have taken part in antiminority pogroms, riots, terrorism, and hate crimes. This form of political Hinduism has taken an especially dangerous turn with the ascendance of the Hindu nationalist Bharatiya Janata Party and its charismatic, ultranationalist firebrand leader Narendra Modi.

The fifth chapter turns attention to the fourth-largest of the five major world religions: Buddhism. Like Hinduism, Buddhism is an Eastern tradition that arose in India. From there it expanded into Southeast and East Asia. Today Buddhism makes up the majority religion in Bhutan, Cambodia, Laos, Mongolia, Myanmar, Sri Lanka, and Thailand. It is also the dominant religion in several other Asian countries. Whereas Islam is stereotypically associated with violence, Buddhism is conversely believed to be a pacifist religion. However, just as the stereotype surrounding Islam is empirically false, so is the belief that Buddhism is always a religion of peace. In countries where Buddhism has been the recipient of special favor from the state, it too has assumed violent forms. This chapter takes a look at three Asian countries that have been especially ravaged by Buddhist violence: Sri Lanka, Myanmar, and Thailand.

Chapter 6 explores the relationship between a lack of secularism and religious violence in the smallest of the world's major religious traditions, Judaism. The global Jewish population (about 15 million) is tiny compared to the number of followers commanded by the world's other major religious traditions. Although sizable Jewish communities can be found in some countries, such as the United States, France, Canada, and Russia, Judaism comprises the majority religion in only one state: Israel. Among advanced industrial countries, Israel has a highly unique relationship governing religion and state. Although a democratic state with a legal framework supportive of freedom for all of its citizens, Israel is also the only democratic state founded as a homeland for a specific religious group. Israel is the least secular democracy in the world and, as such, has given rise to violence emanating not only from marginalized minority communities but also from *Jewish* groups who enjoy special privileges not afforded to non-Jews.

While the aforementioned five chapters examine how deficits in political secularism encourage violence across faith traditions, the final chapter turns attention to the positive relationship between political secularism and societal harmony. Returning again to the world's major religious traditions, this chapter takes a brief look at "exemplar" countries, each dominated by one of the religions explored in previous chapters, which have gotten the relationship between religion and state right. Owing to the robust presence of political secularism, each of these countries experiences little by way of societal religious hostilities. The cases again highlight the political ambivalence of religion, showing that the world's different religious traditions, though containing violent extremists, also are capable of living in peace with their neighbors. This chapter argues that "covenantal pluralism"—an approach to interreligious relations marked by respect for diversity, shared values, inclusive citizenship, mutual recognition, and solidarity—has the potential to counteract the pernicious effects the global crisis of secularism has helped to produce.

PART I

Chapter 1
Religious Violence and the Global Crisis of Secularism

In 1978, protests broke out in dozens of Iranian cities against the oppressive, corrupt, and brutal regime of Mohammed Shah Reza Pahlavi, an authoritarian leader backed by Western powers. By August the protests had ballooned to include hundreds of thousands of demonstrators, some of them turning violent. A deadly massacre of regime opponents at the hands of security forces occurred on September 8, resulting in the deaths of sixty-four protestors. Eventually, though, the protests succeeded in toppling the shah, who formally stepped down from power in December. Although the majority of demonstrators who took to the streets were not motivated by a fundamentalist vision of Islam, toward the end of the year the protests had assumed a religious character. The Iranian Revolution replaced the Imperial State of Iran and the Pahlavi dynasty with the Islamic Republic of Iran, led by a religious cleric, Ayatollah Ruhollah Khomeini. Iran thus became the first modern religious nation-state.

Not only did the Iranian Revolution formally mark the end of Iran's historical, secular monarchy and the beginning of a theocratic government based on the concept of *velâyat-e faqih* (guardianship of the Islamic jurist) that remains in place to this day; it also sparked a new form of confrontational religious politics elsewhere. Although the Iranian Revolution caught many in the West by surprise, it quickly inspired religious movements, sometimes violent ones, across the world of Islam. In time, religious nationalism would also emerge in the world's other religious traditions. This new wave of fundamentalism aimed to combat the secularism that formed the basis of global politics during the first half of the twentieth century. Religious believers decried the destruction of faith-based values in public life and sought to replace corrupt and self-serving secular political orders with a politics having spiritual underpinnings that conformed to religious texts and principles. The different visions that these new religious societies would take became acrimonious points of contention that often culminated in bloodshed.

God's Warriors. Nilay Saiya, Oxford University Press. © Oxford University Press (2025).
DOI: 10.1093/9780197813584.003.0002

The previous chapter argued that contemporary religious violence tends to be carried out by majoritarian religious communities with far more frequency than minority religious communities. It also contended that this phenomenon is linked to the political empowerment of majoritarian communities. The present chapter explains why this is the case. It argues that nonsecular states empower vigilantes from majoritarian religious communities to attack religious and nonreligious out-groups. Politically secular states, by contrast, do not encourage violent forms of religious expression precisely because they do not enter into alliances with dominant faith traditions.

This chapter proceeds in three parts. The first poses the question "What is secularism?" Though secularism is commonly equated with atheism, secular humanism, secularity, or hostility toward religion, this is a misunderstanding. Secularism is instead a *political* arrangement governing relations between religious and state institutions. The more that states embrace religious (or antireligious) dogma, the less secular they are. Secular states remain equidistant from the different religions found in society, while nonsecular states seek out alliances with dominant religious communities. The second section demonstrates that there is a global crisis in secularism. Since the end of the Cold War, many countries have been steadily moving away from secularism, including several long-standing secular democracies. The chapter attributes the crisis of secularism to both religious and nonreligious ideologies. The third part shows that the global crisis of secularism has corresponded to increasing faith-based violence around the world. It also offers an explanation for why this is the case.

What Is Secularism?

"Secularism" is among the most misunderstood and, among people of faith, the most maligned terms in the modern political lexicon.[1] Commonly associated with atheism, Marxism, secularization, and general religious hostility, many assume that secularism is incompatible with religion.[2] Critics of secularism point to political ideologies such as communist totalitarianism, fascism, and secular Arab nationalism—all of which in different

---

[1] Jacques Berlinerblau, *Secularism: The Basics* (London: Routledge, 2021).
[2] Charles Taylor, *A Secular Age* (Cambridge, MA: Harvard University Press, 2007).

ways sought to sharply control religious expression—as evidence that confirms their verdict. The idea of secularism as religious subjugation also emerges in the writings of the new atheists discussed in the previous chapter.

Such a view, however, conflates *philosophical* secularism and *political* secularism. Philosophical secularism interprets human life on the basis of material concerns rather than supernatural beliefs. Political secularism, by contrast, is a mode of governance that prescribes a certain relationship between religious and state institutions.[3] It does not presuppose atheism or hostility toward religion, nor does it seek to banish or privatize religion. Sociologist José Casanova argues that political secularism does not espouse "negative assumptions about religion" nor assume "any progressive historical development that will make religion increasingly irrelevant." Instead, he contends that secularism is "compatible with a positive view of religion as a moral good, or as an ethical communitarian reservoir of human solidarity and republican virtue."[4] In fact, many of the political systems grounded in philosophical secularism actually violate one or more of political secularism's core principles. Accordingly, political secularism is a virtue that can be supported by people of faith and those of none.

Properly understood, secularism is not hostile to religion but necessary for its flourishing. Scholar of religion Jacques Berlinerblau correctly defines political secularism as "a political philosophy which, at its core, is preoccupied with, and often deeply suspicious of, any and all relations between government and religion."[5] As used here, secularism refers to the idea that religious and political life should be differentiated and that the state should reign supreme in public matters.[6] Government has a distinct raison d'être and should not be controlled or manipulated by religion, which has a raison

---

[3] Rajeev Bhargava, "What Is Secularism For?," in *Secularism and Its Critics*, ed. Rajeev Bhargava (New Delhi: Oxford University Press, 1998), 486–542; Rajeev Bhargava, "Political Secularism," in *The Oxford Handbook of Political Theory*, ed. John S. Dryzek, Bonnie Honig, and Anne Phillips (Oxford: Oxford University Press, 2006), 636–655; Jonathan Fox, *Political Secularism, Religion, and the State: A Time Series Analysis of Worldwide Data* (New York: Cambridge University Press, 2015); Jacques Berlinerblau, "Political Secularism," in *The Oxford Handbook of Secularism*, ed. Phil Zuckerman and John R. Shook (Oxford: Oxford University Press, 2017), 85–102; Jonathan Fox, "Political Secularism and Democracy in Theory and Practice," in Zuckerman and Shook, *The Oxford Handbook of Secularism*, 103–123.

[4] José Casanova, "The Secular and Secularisms," *Social Research: An International Quarterly* 76, no. 4 (2009): 1057.

[5] Jacques Berlinerblau, *How to Be Secular: A Call to Arms for Religious Freedom* (New York: First Mariner Books), xv.

[6] Elizabeth Shakman Hurd, *The Politics of Secularism in International Relations* (Princeton, NJ: Princeton University Press, 2008).

d'être of its own. Essentially, secular states do not privilege religion generally or any specific religion, nor do they punish the lack of religious belief.[7]

Political secularism is ordinarily believed to originate from foundational events such as the Peace of Westphalia and the Enlightenment, which transferred temporal ruling prerogatives from religious institutions and ideas (i.e., the Catholic Church and the "divine right of kings") to secular sources of political legitimacy, resulting in a diminution of religious influence in the political realm and also of the ability of religious rulers to coerce adherence to a particular dogma.[8] In actuality, secularism has much deeper and *religious* roots. The basis for secularism can be found in the Christian tradition and traced to the very teachings of Jesus Christ, who commanded his followers to "render unto Caesar the things that are Caesar's and to God the things that are God's" and taught them that his kingdom was not "of this world."[9] These teachings of Christ would be taken up and developed in the writings of numerous Christian intellectuals, all of whom saw the separating of the "things of Caesar" and the "things of God" as integral to the Christian faith. These thinkers included Augustine of Hippo in Late Antiquity; Pope Gelasius, William of Ockham, and Marsilius of Padua in the Middle Ages; and the reformers Martin Luther and John Calvin in the Early Modern Period. The most important Christian progenitor of modern political secularism, however, was John Locke, who argued in his *Letter concerning Toleration* that the conflation of ecclesial power and civil authority "jumbles heaven and earth together, the things most remote and opposite ... which are ... infinitely different from each other." Accordingly he concluded, "There is absolutely no such thing under the gospel as a Christian commonwealth."[10] Locke, unlike most of his Christian predecessors, believed that the character of the state should be nonsectarian, nonaligned with any particular religious confession. Locke's ideas would strongly influence the American founders, who undertook the world's first experiment in secular democracy. For all these individuals, the state was seen as a distinct body politic with a raison d'être entirely separate from spiritual matters.

Some argue that because political secularism was formed in the crucible of the Western experience—in religiously homogeneous societies and through

---

[7] John Rawls, *Political Liberalism* (New York: Columbia University Press, 1993), 151.

[8] Daniel Philpott, *Revolutions in Sovereignty: How Ideas Shaped Modern International Relations* (Princeton, NJ: Princeton University Press, 2001), 73–150.

[9] Matthew 22:21; Mark 12:17; John 18:36.

[10] John Locke, *A Letter concerning Toleration* (1689), ed. James H. Tully (Indianapolis, IN: Hackett, 1983), 33, 44.

historically unique events such as the European wars of religion and the French Revolution—it has limited applicability in the non-Western world.[11] Although political secularism, especially the notion of church-state separation, has Christian roots and was developed by Western intellectuals— Niccolò Machiavelli, Thomas Hobbes, Jean-Jacques Rousseau, Adam Smith, Immanuel Kant, and Locke—this does not mean that it is the sole province of the West and holds no resonance in non-Western countries. In the contemporary world, India, Japan, Kazakhstan, Singapore, South Korea, Türkiye, and many African countries have developed their own versions of political secularism, though they take different forms from the secularism found in the West.[12] Political secularism, wherever it emerges, is strongly conditioned by the particular history and culture of a country. Furthermore, several Western countries have waxed and waned in their commitment to secularism; many of the Western countries widely believed to be bastions of political secularism have retreated from their secular commitments in recent years. Thus the belief in a natural connection between political secularism and the West is likely overstated.

Political secularism contains four core components: *separation, neutrality, equality,* and *freedom*. Separation refers to the idea that religion and state constitute different realms of authority. In contexts marked by separation between religious and political institutions, both religious actors and political authorities maintain their own spheres of influence, and each renounces interference in the other's realm; they regard each other as legitimate and independent. Political scientist Alfred Stepan famously referred to this mutual acceptance of the independence of political and religious institutions as the "twin tolerations."[13] The state does not interfere in the ability of religious groups to appoint their leaders, determine their offices, or practice their worship; similarly, religious actors do not hold standing offices in the political realm or constitutional prerogatives that allow

---

[11] Asad, *Genealogies of Religion*; Huntington, *The Clash of Civilizations*, 70; Talal Asad, *Formations of the Secular: Christianity, Islam, Modernity* (Stanford, CA: Stanford University Press, 2003); Elizabeth Shakman Hurd, *Beyond Religious Freedom: The New Global Politics of Religion* (Princeton, NJ: Princeton University Press, 2015); Saba Mahmood, *Religious Difference in a Secular Age: A Minority Report* (Princeton, NJ: Princeton University Press, 2015); Winnifred Fallers Sullivan, Elizabeth Shakman Hurd, Saba Mahmood, and Peter G. Danchin, eds., *Politics of Religious Freedom* (Chicago: University of Chicago Press, 2015).

[12] Alfred C. Stepan, "The Multiple Secularisms of Modern Democratic and Non-Democratic Regimes," in *Rethinking Secularism*, ed. Craig Calhoun, Mark Juergensmeyer, and Jonathan VanAntwerpen (New York: Oxford University Press, 2011), 114–144.

[13] Alfred C. Stepan, "Religion, Democracy, and the 'Twin Tolerations,'" *Journal of Democracy* 11, no. 4 (2000): 37–57.

them to mandate public policy or impose their beliefs on the rest of society.[14] Separation entails the disestablishment of religion, the prohibition on public funds being used for religious purposes, the disentangling of a country's legal and educational systems from religion, and the banning of religious tests for public office. Separation does not mean that religion cannot have a public voice—as excluding religion from civic life would itself be a violation of political secularism—only that religious actors cannot be supported by the state in exercising it.[15] The opposite of religion-state separation is religious establishment, an arrangement that confers official privileges on favored religious groups in the areas of law, politics, economics, or education—privileges which are not granted to nonprivileged faiths or those who practice a different form of the established faith. Any state that has the power to establish religion may also attempt to foist that particular religion's dogma on nonconformists.

Secularism is not reducible to religion-state separation, however, and the absence of an established religion does not necessarily indicate that a state is politically secular. The former Soviet Union and present-day North Korea provide two extreme examples of officially separated states that cannot in any way be considered secular, owing to their attempts to establish a religion of the state grounded in atheism while eradicating the rest.[16] In these two cases, the attempt to replace transcendent reality with the deification of the state contributed to brutal forms of totalitarianism. Accordingly, such states would be better characterized as "antireligious" rather than "secular."[17] Proponents of political secularism are just as committed to condemning these sorts of governments as they are to castigating theocratic regimes, both of which are functionally similar. While separating religion and state is necessary to ensure an inclusive society and polity, it is also insufficient on its own. Political secularism must therefore also include three other arguably more important elements.

Secular neutrality, the second essential component of political secularism, requires that the state remain equidistant from all religious traditions,

---

[14] Stepan, "Religion, Democracy, and the 'Twin Tolerations,'" 39–40; Toft, Philpot, and Shah, *God's Century*, 34–37.

[15] Veit Bader, "Religious Pluralism: Secularism or Priority for Democracy?," *Political Theory* 27, no. 5 (1999): 597–633.

[16] Daniel Peris, *Storming the Heavens: The Soviet League of the Militant Godless* (Ithaca, NY: Cornell University Press, 1998); Dae Young Ryu, "Kim Il-Sung and Christianity in North Korea," *Journal of Church and State* 61, no. 3 (2019): 403–430.

[17] Ahmet T. Kuru, "Passive and Assertive Secularism: Historical Conditions, Ideological Struggles, and State Policies toward Religion," *World Politics* 59, no. 4 (2007): 570.

in this way ensuring impartiality.[18] According to political scientist John Madeley, state neutrality in religious affairs means that government actions neither benefit nor impair any way of life more than any other, resulting in neutral government action vis-à-vis religious bodies.[19] Just as a referee remains independent of the sports teams actually playing the match and fairly and neutrally enforces the rules of the game in a way that neither benefits nor disadvantages either side, the task of the state is to remain independent of religion, ensuring that no faith tradition enjoys advantages that others do not. As philosopher Roger Trigg explains, "The state's neutrality means that it should not use the force of law to impose its own favored viewpoint on recalcitrant citizens."[20] Neutral states do not recognize an official religion, grant monopoly or primacy to a specific faith, have laws in place that benefit one religion more than others, or otherwise identify themselves with one particular religion or worldview. Neutrality also means that states eschew "civil religion"—a country's nonsectarian, quasi-religious faith that combines a vague spirituality and a country's history and perceived destiny—insofar as civil religion often incorporates the dominant faith tradition's religious references into its public rituals, symbols, national holidays, and historical monuments, thus implicitly privileging members of that religious tradition and disadvantaging those holding nonreligious or heterodox beliefs. A religiously neutral state is separated from not just a single religion but all religious traditions. In neutral countries, no religious group can claim that the state belongs singularly to it, nor can all communities of faith, banding together, say that the state is collectively theirs alone. Conversely, neutrality also means that the state cannot be friendlier to the nonreligious than those who affirm a transcendent faith.

Closely related to neutrality is the third core ingredient of political secularism: equality. Secular equality means that state laws and policies do not discriminate on the basis of religious belief or lack thereof by privileging communities based on their religious identity. It treats all faiths equally and gives them equal opportunities, in this way creating a level religious

---

[18] John T. S. Madeley and Zsolt Enyedi, eds., *Church and State in Contemporary Europe: The Chimera of Neutrality* (London: Routledge, 2004).

[19] John T. S. Madeley, "European Liberal Democracy and the Principle of State Religious Neutrality," *West European Politics* 26, no. 1 (2003): 1–22.

[20] Roger Trigg, "Religious Freedom in a Secular Society," in Zuckerman and Shook, *The Oxford Handbook of Secularism*, 310.

playing field.[21] Equality protects minorities—both religious and nonreligious—from what John Stuart Mill famously referred to as the "tyranny of the majority."[22] John Locke believed that such protections must be in place for those who find themselves in positions where they may be forced to violate their conscience. Minorities must be free to practice their faith and not forced to observe the traditions of the majority religion. Precisely for this reason, religious minorities and dissidents have often been the greatest champions of secularism historically, seeing it as integral to the preservation of the rights of all citizens.[23] Jews in Muslim-majority countries are natural secularists, as are Muslims in Christian-majority states. Importantly, that all religious groups in society must be treated equally does not entail moral relativism or imply that the ideas held by these groups are equal and that society cannot adjudicate between them. Rather, equality necessitates that all groups in society must be free to advance their views—no matter how unpopular, unfashionable, illiberal, or repugnant—peacefully in the marketplace of ideas. Secularism even provides space for those holding antisecular, including theocratic, views. These views, however, are also open to challenges from those who do not agree with them, and the state, while accommodating the right of illiberal groups to exercise their voice, does not align itself with their goals. "People are equal, but beliefs are not," writes Trigg.[24] A crucial but often overlooked aspect of secular equality concerns the status of nonreligious individuals and groups, who frequently find themselves in a minority position in a highly religious world.

Finally, freedom refers to the idea that secular states nonpreferentially protect the religious rights of individuals and groups to follow their convictions of conscience, to practice their faith privately as they choose, and to engage in public religious acts like celebrating festivals, establishing corporate houses

---

[21] Roger Finke, "Religious Deregulation: Origins and Consequences," *Journal of Church and State* 32, no. 3 (1990): 609–626; Rodney Stark and Roger Finke, *Acts of Faith: Explaining the Human Side of Religion* (Berkeley: University of California Press, 2000); Brian Grim and Roger Finke, "International Religion Indexes: Government Regulation, Government Favoritism, and Social Regulation of Religion," *Interdisciplinary Journal of Research on Religion* 2 (2006); Amartya Sen, "Secularism and Its Discontents," in *Secularism and Its Critics*, ed. Rajeev Bhargava (New Delhi: Oxford University Press, 1998), 454–485; Roger Finke, "Origins and Consequences of Religious Restrictions: A Global Overview," *Sociology of Religion* 74, no. 3 (2013): 297–313.

[22] John Stuart Mill, *On Liberty* (1859), in *On Liberty, Utilitarianism, and Other Essays*, ed. Mark Philip and Frederick Rosen (London: Oxford University Press, 2015).

[23] Stathis N. Kalyvas, *The Rise of Christian Democracy in Europe* (Ithaca, NY: Cornell University Press, 1996), 3.

[24] Trigg, "Religious Freedom in a Secular Society, 311.

of worship, publishing literature, fundraising, and even participating in politics.[25] Freedom of religion also protects the rights of individuals to challenge, reject, or leave the dominant religion and to adopt another or remain religiously uncommitted. Religiously free countries refrain from coercing individuals in matters of faith and discriminating against religious communities in their faith-based expression. The freedom aspect of political secularism belies a conventional understanding that views it as an attempt to remove religion from the public square and replace it with values based in atheism—a condition once referred to by Pope Benedict XVI as "negative secularism."[26] Properly understood, political secularism protects and does not impede religious freedom. The point was made well by Jawaharlal Nehru, the leader of the Indian nationalist movement and India's first prime minister: "Some people think [political secularism] means something opposed to religion. That obviously is not correct. What it means is that it is a state which honors all faiths equally and gives them equal opportunities."[27] For Pope Benedict and Nehru, negative secularism was not genuine secularism.

Of course, freedom of religion, like any freedom, presupposes justifiable limits, most notably when the right to act on one's religious beliefs infringes on the rights of others, undermines the common good, endangers the rule of law, or threatens the secular foundations of the state. These caveats acknowledged, a secular state guarantees freedom to religious groups and individuals to the fullest extent possible, in this way circumscribing its own power and ambit by acknowledging what many people consider to be most important in their lives. This same freedom of conscience also extends to atheists for whom the rejection of the supernatural forms a central part of their existence. The rejection and criticism of religious beliefs, too, are part and parcel of religious freedom. Properly understood, a robust understanding of freedom encompasses both freedom *of* religion and freedom *from* it, including the right to openly criticize or challenge a country's religious status quo.

In short, secular states treat religion as neither a courtier nor a captive, but instead allow religious bodies to govern themselves free from governmental

---

[25] Paul A. Marshall, *Religious Freedom in the World* (Lanham, MD: Rowman & Littlefield, 2008).
[26] Alfonso Aguilar, "Secularization, Good and Bad," *National Catholic Register*, December 8, 2008, https://www.ncregister.com/commentaries/secularization-good-and-bad.
[27] Sarvepalli Gopal, ed., *Jawaharlal Nehru: An Anthology* (New Delhi: Oxford University Press, 1980), 330.

interference. In properly secular states, no faith tradition has the power to order a country's political structures according to its religious vision either through coercion of citizens or political representatives or any other extra-institutional means. The state possesses a monopoly on the legitimate use of force, and the order imposed by the state allows people of faith or those of none to pursue transcendent truth in accordance with the dictates of their conscience or to reject this spiritual quest altogether. At the same time, the state renounces the ability to regulate or suppress the right of individuals to exercise their religious beliefs freely, so long as religious (or irreligious) beliefs do not infringe on the rights of others or undermine the common good.

Secularism should not be understood in a binary manner that sees states as being either secular or not secular but rather as a continuum on which states are more or less secular, ranging from full-fledged theocracy with no institutional separation between religion and state to institutionally separated secular states that remain generally neutral in religious affairs, ensure equality, and provide for religious freedom.[28] In between these two extremes lies a large middle ground of sundry arrangements: liberal states that, despite having officially established religious bodies, extend religious liberty to the rest of society (e.g., Argentina, Armenia, El Salvador, Georgia, Great Britain), states that officially recognize more than one religious tradition (e.g., Indonesia), nontheocratic states that nonetheless single out particular religions for special treatment and discriminate against others (e.g., Myanmar and Sri Lanka), states that have a civil religion (e.g., United States), and states that ban religion (e.g., North Korea). These categories represent only some of the myriad possibilities that religion-state relationships can take.

From this understanding of secularism, it is clear that there are various forms of secularism but also that secularism itself is an ideal that is never realized fully. In other words, states widely considered to be secular may in reality not be as secular as commonly believed. Some attempt to control religion; others interfere in religious affairs; still others offer support for religious institutions, including educational and nonprofit organizations, and activities such as festivals and pilgrimages. Jonathan Fox's research reveals

---

[28] Ahmet Kuru, *Secularism and State Policies toward Religion: The United States, France, and Türkiye* (Cambridge: Cambridge University Press, 2009); Michael Warner, Jonathan VanAntwerpen, and Craig J. Calhoun, eds., *Varieties of Secularism in a Secular Age* (Cambridge, MA: Harvard University Press, 2013).

that no democracies in the world display a complete institutional separation of religion and state. In Western Europe, for example, every country engages some form of antisecular behavior. Interestingly, he also finds that government involvement in religious affairs has been steadily increasing in many long-standing democracies.[29]

The opposite of secularism is religious privilege—a form of corporatism that has existed across time, space, and religious traditions. Privilege does not simply concern security for a particular religious community or a seat at the political table; instead, it accommodates a religious group's desire for supremacy over other faith communities. Privilege demarcates the boundaries of national belonging by dividing the citizenry into insiders and outsiders. The state, for example, may grant a particular religion constitutional recognition as the official religion of the land, impose penalties for sacrilege and apostasy, enforce conformity with respect to dress and speech, or grant religious elites political powers. In religious states, the government gains legitimacy by propagating a particular religious ideology in various aspects of social and political life and coercing religious conformity via laws governing religious conduct. Such states also suppress religious minorities and heterodox believers in the majority faith who depart from the official religious doctrine. The constitutional and legal partiality shown to a privileged religion in these countries results in situations where either the state promotes the objectives of the favored religion through legislation and judicial powers or, as in the case of Iran, certain religious groups hold special prerogatives in the government. In short, in nonsecular countries, the authority of the dominant religion and the authority of the state are profoundly intertwined, often to the detriment of religious minorities. Thus states marked by a religion-state arrangement of privilege treat one religious group (usually the dominant faith tradition) better than others, even as they restrict, sometimes harshly, the practice of nonfavored faith traditions. As discussed later, if privileged religions enjoy powers that impinge on the personal beliefs and practices of members of other faiths, or if these religions possess veto or authorizing power over legislative outcomes, violent religious conflict becomes much more likely.

---

[29] Jonathan Fox, "World Separation of Religion and State into the 21st Century," *Comparative Political Studies* 39, no. 5 (2006): 537–569; Jonathan Fox, "Do Democracies Have Separation of Religion and State?," *Canadian Journal of Political Science/Revue Canadienne de Science Politique* 40, no. 1 (2007): 1–25; Jonathan Fox, *A World Survey of Religion and the State* (New York: Cambridge University Press, 2008); Jonathan Fox, "Separation of Religion and State in Stable Christian Democracies: Fact or Myth?," *Journal of Law, Religion and State* 1, no. 1 (2012): 60–94.

At its most extreme, religious privilege takes the form of theocracy, in which the governing apparatus of the state is amalgamated with a particular religious order. Theocracies are ruled according to divine laws mediated by a priestly order that claims to rule on the basis of supernatural revelation. Historical examples include ancient Israel from the time of Moses to the inauguration of King Saul, medieval Christendom, John Calvin's Geneva, and the Ottoman Empire ruled by a sultan-caliph. Islamist regimes in Afghanistan, Iran, and Saudi Arabia come closest to modern-day theocracies. In theocracies, religious minorities enjoy few rights and are often ruthlessly suppressed.

Not every state that grants special privileges to a favored religious community is a theocracy, however. Roughly one-quarter of countries in the world today feature an official establishment of religion, most of which are not theocracies.[30] Nontheocratic countries with religious establishments exhibit formal or symbolic alliances between a single faith tradition and the state, while still retaining at least some differentiation between the political and spiritual spheres. Religious and political institutions are separate enough to have distinct identities and roles. Still, establishment is a contravention of political secularism. Most common in the Islamic world today, states that feature a religious establishment afford religious actors the capability of regulating political life to varying extents.[31] In these settings, the state extends special legal privileges or other forms of patronage to a particular religious community, which, in turn, legitimates the authority of the government, further obfuscating the boundaries between religion and state.[32] (It is sometimes the case that religious minorities are the ones that enjoy the privilege of the state, as seen in prewar Cote d'Ivoire, Iraq, and Syria, but it is far more often true that the privileged faith traditions also happen to be the dominant ones in society.)

It is important to distinguish religious privilege from the general category of religious repression or persecution. Repression and persecution *can*

---

[30] Jonathan Fox and Jori Breslawski, "State Support for Religion and Government Legitimacy in Christian-Majority Countries," *American Political Science Review* 117, no. 4 (2023): 1395–1409.

[31] Olivier Roy, *The Failure of Political Islam*, trans. Carol Volk (London: I. B. Tauris, 1994); Dale F. Eickelman and James Piscatori, *Muslim Politics* (Princeton, NJ: Princeton, 1996); L. Carl Brown, *Religion and State: The Muslim Approach to Politics* (New York: Columbia University Press, 2000); Nazih Ayubi, *Political Islam: Religion and Politics in the Arab World* (New York: Routledge, 2003); Timur Kuran, *The Long Divergence: How Islamic Law Held Back the Middle East* (Princeton, NJ: Princeton University Press, 2012).

[32] Peter L. Berger, *The Sacred Canopy: Elements of a Sociological Theory of Religion* (New York: Doubleday, 1967); David Martin, *A General Theory of Secularization* (New York: Harper & Row, 1978).

involve a dynamic of privilege. But repression and persecution can also refer to many other forms of religious restriction, including varieties that restrict the practice of the majority faith tradition along with that of minorities.[33] Countries regulating religion in this manner seek to put religion under state control due to political leaders' fear or suspicion of religion.[34] North Korea, for example, is likely the most religiously repressive country in the world, but it is also a state where there is little discernible privilege among religious groups. Although minorities in these cases may sometimes fare worse than majorities, because repression targets all religions the *differential* treatment of minorities and majorities is less pronounced. Religious privilege, by contrast, involves the differential treatment of a country's faith communities, often denying minorities the rights and privileges accorded to the majority religious tradition. In this way, environments of privilege artificially distort the religious playing field, tilting it in favor of some religions and against others. This dynamic is seen most clearly in religious states such as Iran and Saudi Arabia, where regimes derive legitimacy from their willingness to support a particular religious tradition through laws and policies. Privilege does not necessarily mean that the majority is free from any sort of religious restriction, but it does suggest that the majority faith tradition is in a much better position vis-à-vis other religions.

In summary, political secularism, properly understood, strives to create a political and social space in which no single religious community or institution enjoys privileges not granted to all people, regardless of their religious (or irreligious) beliefs. Secularism in this context conforms to international human rights standards on matters pertaining to religion, such as Article 18 of the Universal Declaration of Human Rights and the International Covenant on Civil and Political Rights. It consists of four key components—separation, neutrality, equality, and freedom—the absence of any of which degrades the quality of secularism. The opposite of political secularism is religious privilege, the idea that the government should prefer one religion over others, that religion should be privileged over nonreligion, that nonreligion should be privileged over religion, or that one's religious affiliation determines one's standing in the civic community. Finally, secularism is an

---

[33] Jonathan Fox, "Equal Opportunity Oppression: Religious Persecution Is a Global Problem," *Foreign Affairs*, August 31, 2015, www.foreignaffairs.com/articles/2015-08-31/equal-opportunityoppression.

[34] Karrie J. Koesel, *Region and Authoritarianism: Cooperation, Conflict, and the Consequences* (New York: Cambridge University Press, 2014).

ideal that is never perfectly realized, and many states commonly believed to be secular violate its core principles.

Why Secularism Is in Crisis

Importantly, political secularism is not a static label that can be permanently affixed to countries; states can become more or less secular over time. In some cases, countries have moved in a decidedly antisecular direction.[35] Since the turn of the century, political secularism has generally been in retreat in many parts of the world, including Europe, North and South America, Asia, and Africa.[36] Compiling and analyzing prodigious data on religion-state arrangements worldwide, Fox has consistently revealed a steady increase in governmental involvement in religion since the end of the Cold War or, to use the language of this book, a decline in political secularism. He also shows that privileges for majority religions (and related discrimination against minorities) are ubiquitous around the world and across religious traditions.[37] Consider the following examples from each of these regions.

The United States is the world's oldest experiment in political secularism, but the country's secular orientation has always been challenged by those who believe that the country was founded as a "Christian nation." American Christian nationalists have grown increasingly bolder in recent years and now hold several seats in Congress. These politicians openly decry the separation of church and state and advocate for Christian privilege. For example, congressional representative Lauren Boebert of Colorado has been an outspoken proponent of Christian nationalism, once declaring to an enthused audience, "The church is supposed to direct the government.... I'm tired of this separation of church and state junk that's not in the Constitution."[38] Boebert's comments are typical of American Christian nationalists. From 2019

---

[35] Sumantra Bose, *Secular States, Religious Politics: India, Türkiye, and the Future of Secularism* (New York: Cambridge University Press, 2018).

[36] Daniel Nilsson DeHanas and Marat Shterin, "Religion and the Rise of Populism," *Religion, State, and Society* 46, no. 3 (2018): 177–185.

[37] Jonathan Fox, *A World Survey of Religion and the State* (New York: Cambridge University Press, 2008); Fox, *Political Secularism, Religion, and the State*; Jonathan Fox, *Thou Shalt Have No Other Gods before Me: Why Governments Discriminate against Religious Minorities* (New York: Cambridge University Press, 2022).

[38] Adela Suliman and Timothy Bella, "GOP Rep. Boebert: 'I'm Tired of This Separation of Church and State Junk,'" *Washington Post*, June 28, 2022, https://www.washingtonpost.com/politics/2022/06/28/lauren-boebert-church-state-colorado/.

to 2023, South America's largest country, Brazil, was led by a conservative Christian with an authoritarian bent, Jair Bolsonaro. Though a Catholic, the Brazilian leader made common cause with evangelical Christian nationalists "around a mythical representation of Brazil's past and an imagined project for its future" in the world's second largest Christian country.[39] Known as the "Trump of the Tropics," Bolsonaro came to power through the massive outpouring of support from the country's diverse Christian communities. Brazilian Christian nationalists rallied to him, owing to his perceived defense of Christian values and moral agenda. Hungary's sitting president, Viktor Orbán, has justified his authoritarian turn on the grounds that such measures are necessary to defend Hungary's "traditional Christian values" against an alien Islamic faith and creeping cultural progressivism, which are believed to threaten the Christian heritage of the landlocked central European country and eventually lead to what Orbán called a "mixed race" society.[40]

We see similar regression away from political secularism outside of Christian-majority states. Consider the world's largest Hindu and Muslim countries, India and Indonesia, respectively. India's founding principles based in secularism have given way to Hindutva, an ideology that seeks to promote Hindu cultural and political dominance. The rise of Hindutva, at both the national and state levels, has fed social polarization in India and contributed to a climate of religious intolerance, communal tensions, and violence against religious minorities, particularly Muslims and Christians. This has raised concerns about the erosion of India's secular fabric and the marginalization of minority communities. Indonesia has long been characterized by its moderate form of Islam and inclusive society. Nevertheless, a creeping form of Islamism now threatens to undo what Indonesians have worked so hard to maintain. This threat to political secularism can be clearly seen in the trial and conviction of the former governor of Jakarta, Basuki Tjahaja Purnama, a Chinese Christian popularly known as "Ahok," on fabricated blasphemy-related charges.

By contrast, countries can also become more secular over time. For example, the 2007 Nepalese Constitution recognized the landlocked

---

[39] Raimundo Barreto and João B. Chaves, "Christian Nationalism Is Thriving in Bolsonaro's Brazil," *Christian Century*, November 18, 2021, https://www.christiancentury.org/article/critical-essay/christian-nationalism-thriving-bolsonaro-s-brazil.

[40] Shaun Walker and Flora Garamvolgyi, "Viktor Orbán Sparks Outrage with Attack on 'Race Mixing' in Europe," *The Guardian*, July 24, 2022, https://www.theguardian.com/world/2022/jul/24/viktor-orban-against-race-mixing-europe-hungary.

Himalayan country as a "Hindu kingdom." The newest Constitution dropped this language and instead described Nepal as a secular state. In 2012, Norway expunged references to a state church from its Constitution. It went further in 2017, officially disestablishing the Church of Norway and legally separating it from the government. (The king of Norway, however, remains a member of the Church of Norway.)

By and large, though, political secularism may not be as robust or widespread as commonly assumed.[41] As noted earlier, even the vast majority of democracies engage in some form of religious privilege, thus undermining their secular quality.[42] How do we know if countries are secular or not in practice? If the absence of secularism is religious (or in some cases irreligious) privilege, then a good measure to gauge a state's secular quality is how it treats its religious minorities vis-à-vis religious majorities—how it manages diversity.[43] Put differently, when religious privilege is used as a basis for the restriction of minority religious practices and institutions, political secularism suffers as a result.

Political secularism has come under attack from both religious and nonreligious sources. Most obviously, secularism has been eroded by illiberal religious forces around the world, which demand privileges for their own faith tradition and their denial to others. These forces have been buoyed by a global resurgence of political religion beginning in the latter half of the twentieth century. Different movements associated with this religious resurgence seek to detach the state from secular principles and instead cultivate states grounded in the values and identity of a particular religion.

As noted at the beginning of this chapter, the preeminent example is the transformation of Iran from an imperial state to an Islamic republic. Before its religious revolution, Iran was a Western-oriented "secular" state ruled by the shah, who repressed political and religious freedoms. The 1979 revolution forced the shah to flee Iran and brought to power Ayatollah

---

[41] John T. S. Madeley, "Unequally Yoked: The Antinomies of Church-State Separation in Europe and the USA," *European Political Science* 8, no. 3 (2009): 273–288.

[42] Michael D. Driessen, "Religion, State, and Democracy: Analyzing Two Dimensions of Church-State Arrangements," *Politics and Religion* 3, no. 1 (2010): 55–80.

[43] Tariq Modood, *Church, State and Religious Minorities* (London: Policy Studies Institute, 1997); Charles Taylor, "The Meaning of Secularism," *Hedgehog Review* 12, no. 3 (2010): 23–34; Bruce J. Berman, Rajeev Bhargava, and André Laliberté, eds., *Secular States and Religious Diversity* (Vancouver: University of British Columbia Press, 2013); Charles Taylor, "How to Define Secularism," in *Boundaries of Toleration*, ed. Alfred Stepan and Charles Taylor (New York: Columbia University Press, 2014), 79–129.

Khomeini, leading to the establishment of the world's first theocratic state. Khomeini sought to enforce conservative Islamic social mores with respect to dress, gender relations, education, entertainment, and religious observance. These sweeping changes were codified into Iranian law and remain in place to this day. In the wake of Iran's revolution, Islamist movements attempted to establish their own properly Islamized governments in other Muslim-majority countries such as Afghanistan, Algeria, Bangladesh, Chad, Egypt, Pakistan, Türkiye, and Sudan.[44] Countries outside of the Muslim world to move in a less secular direction over time include Jewish-majority Israel, Buddhist-majority Sri Lanka and Myanmar, Hindu-majority India, and Christian-majority Guatemala, Samoa, the United States, and Zambia.

Interestingly, secularism can also come under attack from nonreligious forces and ideologies, including even atheistic regimes.[45] These forces do not seek to promote a properly "religious" society, but instead to put religion under the control of the state, insofar as independent religious activity is seen as a potential or actual threat to a state's regime or its prevailing ideology. For believers, obligations to the supernatural eclipse the authority of temporal states. This situation is anathema to states that claim to be the sole authority over citizens. Nonreligious threats to secularism can be seen in communist states, Arab nationalist states, and European laïcist states.

First, in some cases, state control of religion may take the form of outright hostility toward religion with the goal of eradicating religious belief in society. North Korea and the former Soviet Union, often thought of as quintessentially "secular" states, attempted to accomplish precisely this. Recall, though, that secularism should not be confused with hostility to religion. In brutally suppressing religion through a kind of forced secularization, these two states sought to replace traditional faith with a different kind of religion, a secular one deifying the state, in this way violating the most fundamental of secular principles.

In other cases, states attempt to control instead of abolish religion. They achieve this by making religion subservient to the state. Political leaders in these states believe that religion can serve a legitimating function if it can be effectively leveraged to benefit the regime. Such ends might include reducing opposition to the regime, ensuring compliance with laws, and increasing

---
[44] Gilles Kepel, *The Revenge of God: The Resurgence of Islam, Christianity, and Judaism in the Modern World* (State College: Pennsylvania State University Press, 1994).
[45] Finke, "Origins and Consequences of Religious Freedoms," 300.

morality.[46] As Mark Juergensmeyer explains, the co-optation of religion by political leaders "provides religious legitimacy for the state, and it helps to give nationalism a religious aura."[47] This model is typical of ostensibly secular states in the Arab world, such as in Algeria, Egypt, Libya, and Syria. But these states are not truly secular either in that they violate each of secularism's four essential components.

Finally, European laïcist states such as France and Belgium seek to separate religion and state by freeing the public square from all religious influence, even to the point of prohibiting religious symbols in public spaces.[48] Laïcité has its roots in the French Revolution and the overthrow of the ancient régime, an abusive monarchist government that was allied with the Roman Catholic Church. The French revolutionaries sought to emancipate the state from the enormous power of the Church and rid society of its influence in order for all French citizens to realize liberty and equality. Laïcité can be understood as hostility to public religion grounded in the assumptions that religion is a matter of personal belief and that the public expression of religion is a threat to civil society because religious claims are beyond reason. Matters of conscience must, therefore, be relegated to the private realm. Indeed, the French revolutionaries sought to convert houses of worship into "Temples of Reason." The state would be the ultimate arbiter of religious rights. Interestingly, though, although laïcist states are commonly believed to be a quintessential form of political secularism, in reality they infringe on some of its core principles. Though upholding separation of religion and state, laïcist states also have in place laws and policies that discriminate disproportionately against religious minorities, thus violating the principle of equality. Importantly, as explained in the next chapter, states justify antiminority discrimination on the basis of secularist considerations, including children's rights, animal rights, and women's rights.

In summary, political secularism finds itself in crisis around the world. It has come under siege by both religious and nonreligious forces and ideologies. An excellent indicator of how committed states are to political secularism is how they manage religious diversity. Finally, many states

---

[46] Anthony Gill, *The Political Origins of Religious Liberty* (New York: Cambridge University Press, 2008).

[47] Mark Juergensmeyer, *The New Cold War? Religious Nationalism Confronts the Secular State* (Berkeley: University of California Press, 1993), 3.

[48] Wilfred M. McClay, "Two Concepts of Secularism," *Wilson Quarterly* 24, no. 3 (2000): 54–71.

widely considered to be bastions of political secularism in reality violate its key components.

How the Crisis of Secularism Begets Religious Violence

This book argues that the global crisis of secularism is directly related to the increase in violent religious hostilities across the world since the end of the Cold War. Recall from the introduction that the preponderance of religious violence in the world is committed at the hands of religious majorities. The absence of secularism paradoxically encourages majoritarian violence by privileged religious communities more than violence by minority communities. Let us consider the logic behind this counterintuitive claim.

I propose a five-step process by which a lack of secularism in the form of religious privilege leads to religious violence: *politicization, victimization, demonization, securitization,* and *radicalization.* These should not be understood as entirely discrete processes but rather as overlapping and mutually reinforcing. Even so, the steps in the radicalization process represent a generally escalatory spiral culminating in the production of violence.

First, in contexts marked by privilege for majority faith communities, religion itself becomes politicized. Religious identity is especially prone to political manipulation by opportunistic politicians seeking to further their own political ambitions.[49] The mobilization and exploitation of religion in this manner helps create more salient and hardened religious cleavages and manufacture social polarization.[50] Political leaders justify patronage on the grounds that it is necessary for cultivating a common national identity, ensuring social stability, and protecting national security. Majoritarian religious leaders, for their part, see such alliances as a convenient way to shut out

---

[49] Paul A. Djupe and J. Tobin Grant, "Religious Institutions and Political Participation in America," *Journal for the Scientific Study of Religion* 40, no. 2 (2001): 303–314; Kenneth D. Wald, Adam L. Silverman, and Kevin S. Fridy, "Making Sense of Religion in Political Life," *Annual Review of Political Science* 8 (2005): 121–143; Robert Brathwaite and Baekkwan Park, "Deadly Influences: Evaluating the Relationship between Political Competition and Religious Violence," *Political Behavior* (2023), doi:https://doi.org/10.1007/s11109-023-09856-z.

[50] Vali R. Nasr, "International Politics, Domestic Imperatives, and Identity Mobilization: Sectarianism in Pakistan, 1979–1998," *Comparative Politics* 32, no. 2 (2000): 171–190; Nader Hashemi and Danny Postel, "Sectarianization: Mapping the New Politics of the Middle East," *Review of Faith & International Affairs* 15, no. 3 (2017): 1–13.

religious competitors.[51] Owing to their stature in society, religious leaders are able to leverage their positions of influence to mobilize support among the faithful. The politicizing of the sacred in this way creates an environment of suspicion and distrust toward those groups who in some way depart from the beliefs or identity of the dominant faith tradition, resulting in situations where dominant faith traditions believe that their de facto privileged station entitles them to treat religious minorities as second-class citizens. This naturally leads to the politicizing of minority religions as well, resulting in the hardening of religious identities across the board.

The second step in the process is *victimization*. As religion becomes politicized, faith communities come to see themselves as the victims of encroachment by other faith traditions. This sense of victimization often reflects perception rather than reality, resulting in a "persecution complex"—Christians being persecuted in Christian-majority countries, Buddhists in Buddhist-majority countries, Muslims in Muslim-majority countries, and so forth—even when no objective suppression of these religions is taking place. What matters is that these communities *feel* like they are victims. One study finds, for example, that "symbolic threat was most strongly associated with intergroup hostility."[52] Perceived victimization often results from changing religious landscapes made possible by the acceleration of global migration and the consequent increase of religious diversity. The presence of new religions is seen as threatening to the majority religious tradition, often prompting the self-segregation of the majority from the rest of society. The resulting echo chamber further reinforces the paranoia surrounding the victim narrative. In response, majoritarian religious communities, reacting to this perception of embattlement, have at times turned to (frequently illiberal) political leaders who promise to protect their rights and privileges against alien cultural forces. To take just one of a plethora of examples, consider the words of Kandiss Taylor, a former American Christian nationalist candidate for governor of the state of Georgia. "The good thing about the First Amendment is that if you're a Jew or you're a Muslim or you're a Buddhist, you still get to worship your god because you're in America. But you don't get to silence us," she declared to an approving audience.

---

[51] Anthony Gill, *Rendering unto Caesar: The Catholic Church and the State in Latin America* (Chicago: University of Chicago Press, 1998).

[52] Milan Obaidi, Jonas R. Kunst, Nour Kteily, Lotte Thomsen, and James Sidanius, "Living under Threat: Mutual Threat Perception Drives Anti-Muslim and Anti-Western Hostility in the Age of Terrorism," *European Journal of Social Psychology* 48, no. 5 (2018): 567.

Taylor went on to proclaim, "[W]e're running the state with Jesus Christ first."[53] Taylor failed to mention that the United States is a Christian-majority country where Jews, Muslims, and Buddhists *collectively* comprise only about 4 percent of the total population. Ironically, it is religious *privilege* that gives rise to this siege mentality. For those accustomed to privilege, equality often looks like oppression of the majority.

Third, the perceived victimization of one's religious tribe leads to *demonization* of religious—and nonreligious—outsiders. When this happens, majority religious groups scapegoat minorities, blaming them for their country's problems, painting them as disloyal to the nation, and claiming that the survival of their countries requires them to wrest power away from minority usurpers.[54] For example, in a 2022 speech the Republican governor of Florida, Ron DeSantis, used strongly Christian nationalist language in demonizing his perceived political and cultural opponents: "Put on the full armor of God. Take a stand against the Left's schemes. Stand firm. Stand your ground. Don't back down. . . . Let's take our country back!"[55] Christians in the audience quickly erupted in applause in response to DeSantis's first injunction, "Put on the full armor of God," recognizing the line as a well-known quotation from the biblical book of Ephesians: "Put on the full armor of God, so that you can take your stand against the devil's schemes."[56] In replacing "the devil" with "the Left," the Florida governor conveyed a clear message to this audience: the political opponents of conservative Christianity could be equated with Satan himself. Similar demonization of religious minorities has been occurring with greater frequency in Europe. In the Netherlands, for example, Dutch politician Geert Wilders has relentlessly attacked Islam, once declaring, "Our Judeo-Christian culture is far superior to Islam and we should not be afraid to say so."[57] Religious demonization, of course, is also prevalent outside of the West and has frequently preceded episodes of violence against religious minorities. In Myanmar, a militant

---

[53] Andrew Stanton, "GOP Candidate Says 'We Are the Church and We Run the State' in Viral Video," *Newsweek*, April 10, 2022, https://www.newsweek.com/gop-candidate-says-we-are-church-we-run-state-viral-video-1696729.

[54] Manish K. Thakur, "Democracy, Pluralism and the Religious Minorities: The Muslim Question in India," *Social Change* 43, no. 4 (2013): 581–594.

[55] MSNBC, "The Dangerous New Movement in Right-Wing America," YouTube, August 23, 2022, https://www.youtube.com/watch?v=tUq-h6l2W6o.

[56] Ephesians 6:12.

[57] Matthew Vadum, "Geert Wilders: I Won't Stop Warning the West about Islam," *Frontpage Magazine*, May 4, 2015, https://archives.frontpagemag.com/fpm/geert-wilders-i-wont-stop-warning-west-about-islam-matthew-vadum/.

yet popular monk named Ashin Wirathu has incited mob violence against the country's minority Muslim population through a sustained campaign of anti-Muslim demonization. "They would like to occupy our country, but I won't let them. We must keep Myanmar Buddhist," the monk dubbed the "Burmese bin Laden" once proclaimed.[58] Such sentiments have been repeated by numerous Burmese politicians. Religious demonization can also be a persistent feature of a country's culture. In Saudi Arabia, for example, school textbooks often contain passages demonizing Christians and Jews.

This sense of victimhood leads to *securitization*—the fourth step on the path to religious violence. Securitization occurs when "an issue is presented as an existential threat, requiring emergency measures and justifying actions outside the normal bounds of political procedure."[59] Applied to religion, securitization theory suggests that political and religious leaders stir up antiminority hostility among the masses by portraying minority religious communities as a threat to a country's national culture and way of life. The threat to a country's social fabric arising from the presence of religious outsiders needs to be addressed apart from normal legal and political processes, even in otherwise liberal states, if the threatened religion and a country's national culture is to survive.[60] Discriminatory laws and policies, in turn, justify antiminority bigotry and discrimination at the level of society. For example, some empirical studies have documented the considerable rise in governmental and societal discrimination against Muslims in Western democracies in the name of national security.[61] On the campaign trail in 2016, the candidate who would eventually go on to win the American presidency, Donald Trump, persistently derided Islam and Muslims. Importantly, Trump did not speak of "radical" or "extremist" Islam, but of the religion in general, proposing a "total and complete shutdown of Muslims

---

[58] Hannah Beech, "The Face of Buddhist Terror," *Time*, July 1, 2013, http://content.time.com/time/magazine/article/0,9171,214,600,000.html.

[59] Barry Buzan, Ole Wæver, and Jaap De Wilde, *Security: A New Framework for Analysis* (Boulder, CO: Lynne Rienner, 1998), 23–24.

[60] Jocelyne Cesari, *Why the West Fears Islam: An Exploration of Islam in Liberal Democracies* (New York: Palgrave Macmillan, 2013); Jonathan Fox and Yasemin Akbaba, "Securitization of Islam and Religious Discrimination: Religious Minorities in Western Democracies, 1990 to 2008," *Comparative European Politics* 13, no. 2 (2015): 175–197; Jonathan Fox and Yasemin Akbaba, "Restrictions on the Religious Practices of Religious Minorities: A Global Survey" *Political Studies* 63, no. 5 (2015): 1070–1086.

[61] Jonathan Fox, Roger Finke, and Marie Ann Eisenstein, "Examining the Causes of Government-Based Discrimination against Religious Minorities in Western Democracies: Societal-Level Discrimination and Securitization," *Comparative European Politics* 17, no. 6 (2019): 885–909; Jonathan Fox and Lev Topor, *Why Do People Discriminate against Jews?* (New York: Oxford University Press, 2021).

entering the United States until our country's representatives can figure out what the hell is going on. We have no choice. We have no choice. We have no choice."[62] In this way, Trump securitized Islam as an existential threat to the United States. Several European leaders, too, have securitized Islam in this way. In France, Marine le Pen's National Rally Party campaigned on a platform advocating the "de-Islamization" of the country, claiming Muslims posed an urgent security threat to the country. Islam has also been securitized outside of the West. In India, for example, Islam has long been securitized by Indian political leaders. In 2002, then prime minister Atal Vajpayee claimed the following about Islam: "Wherever Muslims live, they don't like to live in co-existence with others, they don't like to mingle with others; and instead of propagating their ideas in a peaceful manner, they want to spread their faith by resorting to terror and threats. The world has become alert to this danger."[63] The government thus used the logic of securitization to further crack down on the rights of Muslims following one of the worst episodes of religious violence in modern history, the Gujarat pogrom.

Finally, when all these elements are present in society, they can boil over into radicalization. The antiminority rhetoric and policies arising from political leaders indirectly—and in some cases directly—encourage acts of violent hostility against religious out-groups by providing extremists with rhetorical cover for their violence. The resulting vigilante violence is committed for the purpose of protecting a country's historically and culturally dominant faith tradition from the threat posed by religious outsiders. It is surely not happenstance that Trump's anti-Muslim rhetoric, coupled with his courting of Christian nationalists, coincided with a marked increase in violent attacks directed against American Muslims.[64] In some cases, the state may even turn a blind eye to vigilante violence in order to maintain cordial relations with the dominant religious tradition, thus perpetuating the cycle of antiminority violence. Such has been the case in India since the BJP—the political representative of Hindu nationalism—retook power in 2014. Sociologists Roger Finke and Jamie D. Harris explain that "[w]hen a religious group achieves a monopoly and holds access to the temporal power and privileges of the state, the ever-present temptation is to openly persecute

---

[62] C-Span, "Donald Trump on Muslims," YouTube, December 9, 2015, https://www.youtube.com/watch?v=-sz0KY-3PbQ.
[63] Siddharth Varadarajan, "A Stench That Is All Too Familiar," *The Hindu*, March 24, 2009.
[64] Katayoun Kishi, "Assaults against Muslims in U.S. Surpass 2001 Level," Pew Research Center, November 15, 2017, https://www.pewresearch.org/fact-tank/2017/11/15/assaults-against-muslims-in-u-s-surpass-2001-level/.

religious competitors."[65] In short, there is a powerful symbiotic relationship between antiminority rhetoric and policies from above and violent antiminority hostility from below.

The violent outgrowth of religious radicalization can occur via different mechanisms. The first mechanism is known as religious "outbidding."[66] Outbidding occurs in states where the regime derives its political authority from its commitment to upholding the beliefs of the dominant faith tradition in a country's laws and policies. Such regimes, though, are considered legitimate only to the extent that they retain their faith-based purity. If the state strays too far from the acceptable path, it may find itself at odds with ultraconservative factions that question the regime's religious bona fides. As Jonathan Fox and Jori Breslawski explain, "[S]tate support for religion often results in state control over that religion which can cause many believers to feel that the government-controlled version of their religion is inappropriate and unauthentic."[67] In these kinds of environments, religious radicals may attempt to "outbid" the regime and rival religious groups in demonstrating the zealousness of their hatred for religious outsiders and the righteousness of their claims to be the true guardians of the authentic faith. Outbidding can even involve the overthrow of the regime through violence in order to establish a more sacrosanct political order. The threat of outbidding often forces the state to become even more repressive and align itself even more closely with illiberal religious factions in order to retain its hold on power. Thus states extend patronage to certain religious communities in the belief that this support increases regime security, but in doing so end up empowering militants from those very communities. The dynamic of religious outbidding has underpinned the assassinations of various political leaders, including Sri Lanka's S. W. R. D. Bandaranaike, Egypt's Anwar Sadat, Israel's Yitzhak Rabin, and Pakistan's Benazir Bhutto. In short, in the dynamic of outbidding, militants associated with a favored religious tradition direct their wrath at a sullied state they believe has compromised its religious purity.

---

[65] Roger Finke and Jaime D. Harris, "Wars and Rumors of Wars: Explaining Religiously Motivated Violence," in *Religion, Politics, Society, and the State*, ed. Jonathan Fox (New York: Oxford University Press, 2012), 55.

[66] Toft, "Getting Religion," 103; Monica D. Toft, "The Politics of Religious Outbidding," *Review of Faith & International Affairs* 11, no. 3 (2013): 10–19; Matthias Basedau and Carlo Koos, "When Do Religious Leaders Support Faith-Based Violence? Evidence from a Survey Poll in South Sudan," *Political Research Quarterly* 68, no. 4 (2015): 760–772.

[67] Fox and Breslawski, "State Support for Religion and Government Legitimacy in Christian-Majority Countries," 1398.

In a second pathway, religious privilege encourages majoritarian violence by creating a climate of impunity through official laws and policies that favor certain religious communities over others. When states institutionalize religious favoritism, their beneficiaries may arrive at the reasonable conclusion that the state implicitly approves of discrimination, harassment, and even violence against those of nonprivileged faiths. Take laws prohibiting religious defamation, for example. In the Islamic world, so-called blasphemy laws are enforced in about half of Muslim-majority states.[68] Such laws, established for the seemingly principled goal of preventing "hate speech," criminalize words or actions considered to be in some way disrespectful of Islam. The enforcement of blasphemy codes, however, tends to be carried out by social actors instead of governmental officials. At times, extremists have violently attacked those they accuse of defamation, using the very laws enacted by their governments as legal cover for their violence.[69] In Pakistan, Islamist extremists have killed hundreds of people accused of blasphemy, including prominent politicians.[70] A climate of impunity is also produced through the removal of the deterrence effects typically associated with the possibility of holding perpetrators of violence accountable for their actions through arrest and prosecution. Often, however, the state turns a blind eye to violence carried out by adherents of the dominant faith tradition with which it has allied. In extreme cases, government agents may even participate in antiminority violence, as they have done in India, Pakistan, and Myanmar. Religious vigilantes thus feel empowered to commit acts of violence with little or no fear of governmental reprisal. In short, government laws and policies endorse, enable, and excuse the violent activities of majoritarian militants.

Finally, religious privilege can convince members of the majority community that they have a sacred duty to repel religious outsiders. As noted earlier, in countries marked by privilege, historically dominant faith communities may come to see themselves as the victims of encroachment by other faith traditions. Under these conditions, extremists from the majority may see the use of force as necessary to save their countries from impending demise.

---

[68] Paul Marshall and Nina Shea, *Silenced: How Apostasy and Blasphemy Codes Are Choking Freedom Worldwide* (Oxford: Oxford University Press, 2011).

[69] Amjad Mahmood Khan, "Pakistan's Dark Days," *Foreign Affairs*, December 21, 2014, https://www.foreignaffairs.com/articles/pakistan/2014-12-21/pakistans-dark-days.

[70] Asma T. Uddin, "Blasphemy Laws in Muslim-Majority Countries," *Review of Faith & International Affairs* 9, no. 2 (2011): 47–55; Knox Thames, "Pakistan's Dangerous Game with Religious Extremism," *Review of Faith & International Affairs* 12, no. 4 (2014): 40–48.

For example, a 2023 Public Religion Research Institute/Brookings Institution poll found that adherents of Christian nationalism in the United States are almost seven times as likely as those who reject that ideology to support political violence. A stunning 40 percent of Christian nationalism supporters believe that "true American patriots may have to resort to violence in order to save our country."[71]

Conversely, where religious actors are committed to principles of secularism, they are much more likely to reject faith-based violence.[72] Furthermore, when it is free from the control of the state, religion can naturally contribute to the common good. The command to love one's neighbors—a foundational mandate in all of the world's major religious traditions—spurs people of faith to not only reject violence but to contribute to societal flourishing. In many countries, religious institutions play an important philanthropic role by providing education, empowering marginalized communities, and managing social services, among innumerable other contributions. These initiatives, in turn, help sustain cultures of peace.

The relationship between religious favoritism and religious violence is not always unidirectional; the interactions between religious and state institutions are complex, ever evolving, and mutually reinforcing. Thus it is possible that countries' religion-state arrangements might become more entangled in response to religious conflict.[73] Majoritarian groups embroiled in conflict often look to the state for further patronage, prompting governments to further express their support for the majority religion. For this reason, the relationship between religious favoritism and violent religious conflict is best understood as a dynamic, interactive, and ongoing cycle: political elites favor a dominant religion out of perceived self-interest; such favoritism sows the seeds of conflict along religious lines; favored religious groups look to the state for further support in the midst of conflict, and states often grant it as a means to shore up their own political fortunes. While a spiral of favoritism and violence is common, a careful examination of the historical record shows that an initial religion-state arrangement of favoritism sets the stage for the various dynamics that engender conflict along religious lines. Governments might then use the realized threat of

---

[71] Public Religion Research Institute and the Brookings Institution, *A Christian Nation? Understanding the Threat to American Democracy and Culture* (Washington, DC: PRRI/Brookings, 2023), 28.

[72] Basedau and Koos, "When Do Religious Leaders Support Faith-Based Violence?"

[73] Peter S. Henne and Jason Klocek, "Taming the Gods: How Religious Conflict Shapes State Repression," *Journal of Conflict Resolution* 63, no. 1 (2019): 112–138.

religious violence as a justification for further favoritism. In short, vigilante behavior and government behavior are often interdependent. Nevertheless, it should also be noted that the state may not always support communal violence and may attempt to intervene in order to rein in violence that has spiraled out of control. In some cases, states have arrested key agitators of violence and banned militant movements following waves of violence.

One obvious rebuttal to the argument that a crisis of secularism has encouraged religious violence is the contention that secularism *itself* has been responsible for spawning a violent global backlash following the end of the Cold War. The most important proponent of this view is the renowned sociologist of religion Mark Juergensmeyer, who has argued that religious militants in places as diverse as the Middle East, South Asia, Central Asia, and Europe have fundamentally rejected ideas of secular nationalism, seeing them as illegitimate imports from the West that are intolerant of religion and lack cultural resonance in deeply religious societies.[74] In the developing world, political secularism has also given rise to failed, antireligious political ideologies and economic policies. In this sense, political secularism is seen as an all-or-nothing package imposed on countries, regardless of their own cultural traditions and unique histories. Militant religious nationalists in these places and others strive to overthrow morally bankrupt secular states and replace them with religiously faithful regimes.

Although a rejection of (Western) secularism has certainly undergirded the campaigns of many militant religious groups, this explanation for religious violence hinges on a different understanding of secularism: hostility toward religion. As detailed earlier, though, secularism, as understood here, does not entail the repression of religion. Indeed, religious repression is an infringement of secularism, not a manifestation of it. Truly secular governments protect free religious expression. Instead, secularism is degraded when government becomes *entangled with* religion—an outcome that we see in both religious and ostensibly secular states. It is often the case that ostensibly secular regimes will also attempt to co-opt the majority religion as a means to legitimate their rule and preempt religiously based challenges to their authority.[75] Put differently, religious militancy arises not just in response to the repression of religiously hostile states that seek to secularize the public square, but also in response to the attempt by states—again

[74] Juergensmeyer, *The New Cold War?*; Juergensmeyer, *Global Rebellion*.
[75] Elina Schleutker, "Discrimination against Religious Minorities," *Journal of Church & State* 61, no. 2 (2019): 282–307.

religious or secular—to co-opt dominant religious groups for political purposes, even as they repress the competitors of majoritarian religions.[76] Fox finds, for example, that "no state regulates, controls, or restricts religion without also supporting it in at least some small way."[77] When this happens, the state becomes less secular and more prone to violent religious hostilities. Thus the religious "global rebellion" Juergensmeyer writes of is actually much more acute in countries where political secularism is *in retreat*.

In the appendix, readers can access the statistical models showing the relationship between a lack of political secularism and majoritarian religious violence. The results of a statistical analysis of a unique time-series, cross-sectional data set gauging the relationship between religious privilege and attacks by religious majorities show that as privilege for majoritarian religious communities increases, so too do attacks arising from these very communities. The results of the analysis reveal that for every 1-unit increase in religious privilege, countries can expect to see anywhere from a 23 percent to a 65 percent increase in majoritarian violence. Importantly, the analysis also gauges the relative impact of various other predictors of violence in society other than privilege. Thus the statistical analysis provides robust support for the argument that a paradox of privilege lies at the heart of contemporary religious violence.

In summary, the absence of political secularism foments societal religious violence via a five-stage process: the politicization of religion, perceived victimization, demonization, securitization of minority religions, and radicalization. When religion becomes politicized, it frequently leads to a sense of victimization among those of the dominant faith community. This persecution complex, in turn, encourages demonization of out-groups, both religious and nonreligious, and generates calls for the restriction of minorities, who are deemed to threaten a country's national culture or national security. Such a toxic religious environment can give rise to vigilantes who commit physical acts of violence against religious out-groups. The violence carried out by religious militants is intended to protect a society or faith community from out-groups or deviant behaviors believed to threaten the moral norms associated with the established social order. These vigilantes are often emboldened by the quiet approval of the state. Importantly, the steps in this radicalization process should be understood not as discrete

---

[76] Gabriel A. Almond, R. Scott Appleby, and Emmanuel Sivan, *Strong Religion: The Rise of Fundamentalisms around the World* (Chicago: University of Chicago Press, 2003).
[77] Fox, *Political Secularism, Religion, and the State*, 105.

but rather as overlapping and reinforcing. Finally, religious violence occurs through three different mechanisms: outbidding, a culture of impunity, and the sense of sacred duty to protect one's faith.

Summary

This chapter has addressed the issue of political secularism. It first defined political secularism, distinguishing it from philosophical secularism. Next, it explained why political secularism is in crisis, locating the causes for its retreat in both illiberal religious and nonreligious ideologies. Finally, it theorized how the absence of secularism produces religiously motivated violence.

A core theme of this chapter concerns how the perception of religious threat stemming from changing religious demographics has led to the global rise of exclusivist narratives defining national identity in religious terms. Such narratives pose direct challenges to interreligious respect and harmony, insofar as they privilege religiously defined majoritarian communities and push minorities to the margins of public life. In extreme forms, these narratives promote systemic religious persecution and antiminority violence.

Having now set the stage by introducing the book's two core themes—religious violence and political secularism—the second part of this book examines how a lack of political secularism has encouraged contemporary violence in each of the world's major religious traditions. I begin by examining the world's largest religion, Christianity.

PART II

Chapter 2
Christianity

Christianity is the world's largest religion, consisting of around 2.4 billion believers and encompassing a little over 30 percent of the global population. The Christian religion is based on the life and teachings of Jesus Christ. At the core of Christianity can be found a great paradox: the man who suffered one of the most violent deaths ever recorded was himself a messenger of peace, one who would die for his enemies rather than slay them. Jesus placed nonviolence at the center of his most famous teaching, the Sermon on the Mount. "Blessed are the peacemakers," he taught, "for they will be called sons of God."[1] Jesus's Jewish audience would have taken for granted the morality of just retribution (lex talionis), but Jesus promulgated a new morality that rejected every form of vengeance. He instructed his listeners, "If anyone slaps you on the right cheek, turn to them the other cheek also."[2] Instead of seeking revenge, he commanded his followers to "love your enemies and pray for those who persecute you."[3] These same directives issued by Jesus would be echoed by early Christian leaders throughout the New Testament.[4]

Of course, Christianity has not always adhered to these basic tenets of the faith. Indeed, the symbol of Christianity, the cross of Christ, appeared on the armor of Christian crusaders heading off to war in the High Middle Ages. Under the banner of the cross, states engaged in the violent expulsion or murder of native inhabitants in colonial holdings. Violent racist groups set the cross ablaze as they tortured minorities. The cross was carried by the rioters who stormed the U.S. Capitol in 2021.

This chapter and the four which follow argue that religion becomes implicated in political violence when it rejects political secularism. In the case of Christian violence, it is doubly paradoxical not only that nonviolence

---

[1] Matthew 5:9.
[2] Matthew 5:39.
[3] Matthew 5:44.
[4] Romans 12:17–21, 13:4, 14:10–13; Galatians 5:19–21; 1 Timothy 3:3; 1 Peter 3:9; Titus 3:2.

God's Warriors. Nilay Saiya, Oxford University Press. © Oxford University Press (2025).
DOI: 10.1093/9780197813584.003.0003

was at the core of Jesus's moral normativity but also that he differentiated the realms of Caesar and God. The rejection of this differentiation—or secularism—directly corresponds to Christian support for and participation in violence. For the first three centuries of Christianity, the church embraced nonviolence as foundational to Christian discipleship; every major Christian thinker who addressed the topic of warfare rejected bloodshed in accordance with the example of Christ.[5] After Christianity's political empowerment—or its rejection of secularism—Christians exchanged the cross for the sword. Accordingly, throughout Christian history, those Christians who rejected the differentiation of the political and spiritual realms were the ones most likely to embrace the violence of the state or violence against it. Those who advocated the separation of church and state have also, by and large, been the least likely to support or participate in political violence.

This chapter examines contemporary Christian violence in the United States, Europe, and the developing world. It shows that the rejection of secularism and the rise of "Christian nationalism," or "Christian civilizationalism" in the case of Europe, has corresponded to an increase in violent attacks against religious minorities. It proceeds in three parts. The first explores the relationship between Christian nationalism and violence in the United States. The second examines a different antisecular ideology, Christian civilizationalism, in the European context, showing how it has fed an identitarian form of antiminority violence. The third section takes a brief look at the rise of Christian nationalism and violence in Africa and Latin America.

American Christian Nationalism and Violence

Political secularism has increasingly come under assault in various parts of the Christian world. The most direct challenge to political secularism is "Christian nationalism," a political ideology and cultural framework that seeks to amalgamate Christianity and a country's political life and calls for the privileging of a certain form of Christianity in the public square. Among advanced industrial countries, Christian nationalism is strongest

---

[5] Roland H. Bainton, *Christian Attitudes toward War and Peace* (New York: Abingdon, 1960).

in the United States. Leveraging extensive survey data, sociologists Andrew Whitehead and Samuel Perry find that those supportive of Christian nationalism ("accommodators" and "ambassadors") comprise more than half of the American population.[6] The political theology of Christian nationalism is at once both descriptive and prescriptive: Christian nationalists believe that their countries are defined by Christianity and that their governments and citizens should take steps to keep it that way.[7] For example, a survey by the Pew Research Center found that about a third of American adults who identify as politically conservative believe that being Christian is very important for being American.[8] Accordingly, the ideology of Christian nationalism threatens the principle of church-state separation, religious (and nonreligious) equality, and religious liberty. As journalist Katherine Stewart notes, Christian nationalism "does not seek to add another voice to America's pluralistic democracy, but to replace our foundational democratic principles and institutions with a state grounded on a particular version of Christianity, answering to what some adherents call a 'biblical worldview.'"[9] While the idea of Christian nationalism is not new, only recently have scholars identified it by name and begun studying its effects. The nascent scholarship on the effects of Christian nationalism has linked it to racist,[10]

---

[6] Andrew L. Whitehead and Samuel L. Perry, *Taking America Back for God: Christian Nationalism in the United States* (New York: Oxford University Press, 2020).

[7] Paul D. Miller, "What Is Christian Nationalism?," *Christianity Today*, February 3, 2021, https://www.christianitytoday.com/ct/2021/february-web-only/what-is-christian-nationalism.html.

[8] Laura Silver, "Ideological Divisions over Cultural Issues Are Far Wider in the U.S. Than in the UK, France and Germany," Pew Research Center, May 5, 2021, https://www.pewresearch.org/fact-tank/2021/05/05/ideological-divisions-over-cultural-issues-are-far-wider-in-the-u-s-than-in-the-uk-france-and-germany/.

[9] Katherine Stewart, *The Power Worshippers: Inside the Dangerous Rise of Religious Nationalism* (New York: Bloomsbury, 2020), 3.

[10] Samuel L. Perry and Andrew L. Whitehead, "Christian Nationalism, Racial Separatism, and Family Formation: Attitudes toward Transracial Adoption as a Test Case," *Race and Social Problems* 7, no. 2 (2015): 123–134; Samuel L. Perry and Andrew L. Whitehead, "Christian Nationalism and White Racial Boundaries: Examining Whites' Opposition to Interracial Marriage," *Ethnic and Racial Studies* 38, no. 10 (2015): 1671–1689; Joshua T. Davis, "Funding God's Policies, Defending Whiteness: Christian Nationalism and Whites' Attitudes towards Racially-Coded Government Spending," *Ethnic and Racial Studies* 42, no. 12 (2019): 2123–2142; Joseph O. Baker, Samuel L. Perry, and Andrew L. Whitehead, "Keep America Christian (and White): Christian Nationalism, Fear of Ethnoracial Outsiders, and Intention to Vote for Donald Trump in the 2020 Presidential Election," *Sociology of Religion* 81, no. 3 (2020): 272–293; Joshua T. Davis and Samuel L. Perry, "White Christian Nationalism and Relative Political Tolerance for Racists," *Social Problems* 68, no. 3 (2021): 513–534; Samuel L. Perry, Andrew L. Whitehead, and Joshua B. Grubbs, "Prejudice and Pandemic in the Promised Land: How White Christian Nationalism Shapes Americans' Racist and Xenophobic Views of COVID-19," *Ethnic and Racial Studies* 44, no. 5 (2021): 759–772.

nativist,[11] authoritarian,[12] homophobic,[13] conspiratorial,[14] and violent[15] views.

The United States is the world's first experiment in representative democracy and political secularism. The American commitment to political secularism, though, was far from inevitable. Many of the early American colonies had established churches, fearing that the separation of church and state would undermine public morality and religion's role in civic life. The constitutions of the Massachusetts Bay Colony and the Virginia Colony established essentially theocratic forms of government, both of which prescribed the death penalty for those guilty of committing blasphemy.

Eventually, though, arguments in favor of political secularism carried the day. Secularism would define the relationship between religion and the American state. The United States became the first country to disestablish religion, the very first clause of the first amendment to the Bill of Rights precluding the possibility of government establishing a national religion—"Congress shall make no law establishing religion"—while also prohibiting the state from interfering with religious beliefs and practice: "or preventing the free exercise thereof." Article VI of the same document prohibits religious tests for office. These laws codified political secularism by preventing the government from entering into an alliance with any particular

---

[11] Eric Leon McDaniel, Ifran Nooruddin, and Allyson Faith Shortle, "Divine Boundaries: How Religion Shapes Citizens Attitudes toward Immigrants," *American Politics Research* 39, no. 1 (January 2011): 205–233; Allyson Faith Shortle and Ronald Keith Gaddie, "Religious Nationalism and Perceptions of Muslims and Islam," *Politics and Religion* 8, no. 3 (September 2015): 435–457.

[12] Andrew L. Whitehead, Samuel L. Perry, and Joseph O. Baker, "Make America Christian Again: Christian Nationalism and Voting for Donald Trump in the 2016 Presidential Election," *Sociology of Religion* 79, no. 2 (2018): 147–171; Ramsey Dahab and Marisa Omori, "Homegrown Foreigners: How Christian Nationalism and Nativist Attitudes Impact Muslim Civil Liberties," *Ethnic and Racial Studies* 42, no. 10 (2019): 1727–1746.

[13] Andrew L. Whitehead and Samuel L. Perry, "A More Perfect Union? Christian Nationalism and Support for Same-Sex Unions," *Sociological Perspectives* 58, no. 3 (2015): 422–440.

[14] Samuel L. Perry, Joseph O. Baker, and Joshua B. Grubbs, "Ignorance or Culture War? Christian Nationalism and Scientific Illiteracy," *Public Understanding of Science* 30, no. 8 (2021): 930–946; Joseph O. Baker, Samuel L. Perry, and Andrew L. Whitehead, "Crusading for Moral Authority: Christian Nationalism and Opposition to Science," *Sociological Forum* 35, no. 3 (2020): 587–607; Andrew L. Whitehead and Samuel L. Perry, "How Culture Wars Delay Herd Immunity: Christian Nationalism and Anti-vaccine Attitudes," *Socius* 6 (2020): 2378023120977727; Katie E. Corcoran, Christopher P. Scheitle, and Bernard D. DiGregorio, "Christian Nationalism and COVID-19 Vaccine Hesitancy and Uptake," *Vaccine* 39, no. 45 (2021): 6614–6621.

[15] Samuel L. Perry, Andrew L. Whitehead, and Joshua T. Davis, "God's Country in Black and Blue: How Christian Nationalism Shapes Americans' Views about Police (Mis)Treatment of Blacks," *Sociology of Race and Ethnicity* 5, no. 1 (2019): 130–146; Miles T. Armaly, David T. Buckley, and Adam M. Enders, "Christian Nationalism and Political Violence: Victimhood, Racial Identity, Conspiracy, and Support for the Capitol Attacks," *Political Behavior* 44 (2022): 1–24.

religious tradition, ensured the equal status of all religious (and nonreligious) communities, protected religious groups from state interference, and enshrined religious freedom—America's "first freedom"—and state neutrality as the secular cornerstones governing the state's relationship with the country's myriad religious groups.[16] It is hardly coincidental that the greatest champions of American secularism were the very groups that had escaped religious persecution and discrimination in Europe and sought to live in a country where they could practice their faith freely in accordance with their conscience.[17] The American founders believed that neither Christianity nor any particular Christian denomination should enjoy special privileges from the state. This conviction that Christianity is not a privileged religion in the United States was explicitly codified in the Treaty of Tripoli of 1796, which declared that "the government of the United States of America is not in any sense founded on the Christian Religion." This treaty was negotiated by George Washington through Secretary of State Thomas Jefferson and signed by John Adams—the first three presidents of the new country.

Of course, the United States, like every other country, has at times failed to live up to its secular ideals. The ideology of Christian nationalism, in particular, has deep roots in American culture.[18] The country's high degree of religious pluralism has sometimes ignited tensions between different religious groups. Presbyterians, Baptists, Quakers, Catholics, Mormons, Jews, Muslims, Sikhs, and various other religious groups have been subjected to faith-based persecution throughout American history. Yet political secularism in the United States has stood the test of time. Persecution of religious out-groups eventually gave way to tolerance, with all religious communities being able to openly practice their faith free from the interference of the government.[19]

---

[16] Martha Nussbaum, *Liberty of Conscience: In Defense of America's Traditions of Religious Equality* (New York: Basic Books, 2008); John M. Barry, *Roger Williams and the Creation of the American Soul: Church, State and the Birth of Liberty* (New York: Viking, 2012); Nicholas P. Miller, *The Religious Roots of the First Amendment: Dissenting Protestants and the Separation of Church and State* (New York: Oxford University Press, 2012); Michael I. Meyerson, *Endowed by Our Creator: The Birth of Religious Freedoms in America* (New Haven, CT: Yale University Press, 2012).

[17] Nicholas P. Miller, *The Religious Roots of the First Amendment: Dissenting Protestants and the Separation of Church and State* (New York: Oxford University Press, 2012).

[18] Kelly J. Baker, *Gospel According to the Klan: The KKK's Appeal to Protestant America, 1915–1930* (Lawrence: University Press of Kansas, 1917); Philip S. Gorski and Samuel Perry, *The Flag and the Cross: White Christian Nationalism and the Threat to American Democracy* (New York: Oxford University Press, 2022).

[19] Diana L. Eck, *A New Religious America: How a "Christian Country" Has Become the World's Most Religiously Diverse Nation* (New York: Harper Collins, 2001).

Nevertheless, the United States today is witnessing a renewed, serious, and growing threat to its secular character. A survey by the Public Religion Research Institute (PRRI) found that 57 percent of white evangelicals prefer the United States to be a nation primarily of Christians.[20] Another survey by the Pew Research Center revealed that about 30 percent of Americans believe that public school teachers should be allowed to lead students in Christian prayers, a practice that the Supreme Court has ruled unconstitutional; about 20 percent believe that the federal government should stop enforcing the separation of church and state; roughly the same percentage hold that the U.S. Constitution was inspired by God; 15 percent think that the government should declare the United States a Christian nation.[21] Although the Pew report finds that more Americans support rather than oppose separation of church and state, it also notes that there remain large reservoirs of support for church-state integration.

The challenge to political secularism emanates primarily from a Christian movement that believes the United States is in a special relationship with God, a national divine calling it sees as being threatened by increasing religious diversity and expanding cultural progressivism—symbolized by alternative conceptions of gender, a new historiography of race, and fresh movements for social justice. The renewed American culture wars of today can be understood as a continuation of those which began in the 1970s, when a new theopolitical movement that would come to be known as the "Christian Right" burst onto the American political scene. Embodied in organizations such as the Christian Coalition and the Moral Majority, the Christian Right can be understood as a backlash to numerous seismic changes occurring in American life at the time: the women's liberation movement, the gay rights movement, the nationwide legalization of abortion, the prohibiting of teacher-led school prayer in public schools, and the war-weariness of the general public. The leaders of the Christian Right claimed that if America continued on its present path, it would bring the judgment of God upon the nation in the same way that Jerusalem was besieged in the Old Testament. They thus called for an unequivocal resurrection of "Christian values" throughout American society and politics

---

[20] Public Religion Research Institute, "Competing Visions of America: An Evolving Identity or a Culture under Attack? Findings from the 2021 American Values Survey," November 1, 2021, https://www.prri.org/research/competing-visions-of-america-an-evolving-identity-or-a-culture-under-attack/.

[21] Pew Research Center, *In U.S., Far More Support Than Oppose Separation of Church and State* (Washington, DC: Pew Research Center, 2021), 5.

in line with their specific vision of a Christian America. The strategy of the Christian Right involved using grassroots organizations, which could apply significant electoral pressure on candidates running for office. Many conservative Christians themselves ran for office, one, George W. Bush, even capturing the presidency. In this way, these Christian groups pursued Christian political privilege at the expense of political secularism.

In addition to political developments, Christian nationalism in the United States has also reacted to religious shifts. For much of its history, the United States stood out among the world's advanced industrial democracies for its uniquely high levels of religiosity. The country existed as the primary counterpoint to the so-called secularization thesis, which holds that religion loses societal influence in the presence of modernization. However, over the past thirty years the United States has witnessed a sharp increase in the number of "nones"—religiously unaffiliated Americans—from 6 percent in 1991 to 28 percent by 2024.[22] The steep decline in religiosity has been most acute in recent years.[23] Political scientist Ronald Inglehart, who until his passing in 2021 oversaw a massive research project that explored people's values and beliefs across time and space called the World Values Surveys, concluded, "Since 2007, the U.S. has been secularizing more rapidly than any other country for which we have data."[24] The religion most impacted by this decline in faith, of course, is Christianity. A 2021 Gallup poll found that church membership in the United States had fallen below the majority for the first time in nearly a century. The same poll also revealed that the number of people who said religion was very important to them had fallen to 48 percent, a new low point in the polling since 2000.[25] Christianity in the United States is shrinking—and graying.

At the same time, the United States also witnessed the increasingly visible presence of non-Christian religious traditions, a reality made possible by globalization. In some sense, the United States has always been a

---

[22] Ryan P. Burge, *The Nones: Where They Came From, Who They Are, and Where They Are Going* (Minneapolis, MN: Fortress Press, 2021); Pew Research Center, "Religious 'Nones' in America: Who They Are and What They Believe," January 24, 2024, https://www.pewresearch.org/religion/2024/01/24/religious-nones-in-america-who-they-are-and-what-they-believe/.

[23] David E. Campbell, Geoffrey C. Layman, and John C. Green, *Secular Surge: A New Fault Line in American Politics* (New York: Cambridge University Press, 2020).

[24] Ronald Inglehart, *Religion's Sudden Decline: What's Causing It, and What Comes Next?* (New York: Oxford University Press, 2021), 1.

[25] Jeffrey M. Jones, "U.S. Church Membership Falls below Majority for First Time," Gallup, March 29, 2021, https://news.gallup.com/poll/341963/church-membership-falls-below-majority-first-time.aspx.

multicultural country, symbolized by the metaphor of the "melting pot," a term often used to describe the cultural integration of immigrants to the country. Even so, the hegemony of white Protestants could always be taken for granted. That is no longer the case today.[26] Estimates from the U.S. Census Bureau show that nearly 40 percent of Americans identify with a racial or ethnic group other than white, and suggest that the decade 2010 to 2020 was the first in the nation's history in which the white population declined in numbers.[27] The increasing racial and ethnic diversity of the country has also portended an increasing religious diversity. Many of those who have immigrated to the United States over the past thirty years are not Christians, and when they arrive on American shores they do not leave their religions behind.

Combined, the rise of the nones and the religious diversification of the country means that conservative Christians—those who have always dominated American cultural and political life—no longer enjoy unquestioned social and political supremacy. These seismic shifts have fed polarization in society and created a sense of angst among some Christian communities that the country is turning its back on its Christian heritage, evoking a sense of perceived victimization.[28] For example, one study found that highly religious Christians in the United States perceive as much threat to their own identity as to those of religious minorities.[29] Accordingly, Christian nationalist rhetoric is deeply cloaked in threat narratives, prompting efforts to retain Christianity's hegemonic status.[30]

While identity has, of course, always been central to U.S. politics—particularly on the political Right—what is different today is not only the sharp decline in the white Christian majority but the widespread belief among those who remain that they are persecuted and that their entire way of life is threatened by forces of immigration and social progressivism. As these Christian nationalists scapegoat minorities for the country's ills, the changing social landscape has led to open calls for violence.

---

[26] Philip Bump, *The Aftermath: The Last Days of the Baby Boom and the Future of Power in America* (New York: Viking, 2023).
[27] U.S. Census Bureau, "National Population by Characteristics: 2010–2019," 2020, https://www.census.gov/data/tables/time-series/demo/popest/2010s-national-detail.html.
[28] Robert P. Jones, *The End of White Christian America* (New York: Simon & Schuster, 2016).
[29] Michael H. Pasek and Jonathan E. Cook, "Religion from the Target's Perspective: A Portrait of Religious Threat and Its Consequences in the United States," *Social Psychological and Personality Science* 10, no. 1 (2019): 82–93.
[30] Rosemary L. Al-Kire, Michael H. Pasek, Jo-Ann Tsang, and Wade C. Rowatt, "Christian No More: Christian Americans Are Threatened by Their Impending Minority Status," *Journal of Experimental Social Psychology* 97 (2021): 104223.

According to a 2023 survey of more than six thousand Americans, adherents of Christian nationalism are almost seven times as likely as rejectors of Christian nationalism to support political violence. Forty percent agreed with the statement "Because things have gotten so far off track, true American patriots may have to resort to violence in order to save our country."[31] Prominent Christian nationalist leaders, too, have warned of or issued calls for mass violence should Christian nationalists not get their way.[32] No longer able to rely on elections to sustain their social and political dominance, an outsized number of Christian nationalists see violence as their last hope.

American Christian nationalism is a violence-prone ideology for four reasons. First, Christian nationalists tend to also be biblical literalists who draw parallels between the ancient Israelites and present-day America. Just as the Israelites did in the Hebrew scriptures, American Christians today, a new "chosen people" operating under the same providence of God, must at times engage in sacred violence against the enemies of God, foreign and domestic. According to polling by PRRI, white Americans who agree with the statement "God has granted America a special role in human history" are more than twice as likely as those who disagree with that statement to believe that "true American patriots may have to resort to violence in order to save our country."[33]

Second, Christian nationalists believe that America's founding fathers and founding documents were divinely inspired. Consequently, they romanticize the violence of the American Revolution and glorify the American founders as agents of God, believing they themselves have a responsibility to sustain the founders' vision for the country. They frequently appeal to a quote attributed to Jefferson: "The tree of liberty must be refreshed from time to time with the blood of patriots and tyrants." They see Jefferson's "tree of liberty" as being threatened by any ideology that does not conform to their vision of a Christian America. These perils to America's founding vision must be addressed with force if necessary. Christian

---

[31] Public Research Religion Institute and the Brookings Institution, *A Christian Nation? Understanding the Threat of Christian Nationalism to American Democracy and Culture* (Washington, DC: PRRI and Brookings, 2023), 27.

[32] Benjamin Fearnow, "Pastor Rick Joyner Urges American Christians to Prepare for Civil War," *Newsweek*, March 16, 2021, https://www.newsweek.com/pastor-rick-joyner-urges-american-christians-prepare-civil-war-1576570.

[33] Public Religion Research Institute, *Competing Visions of America: An Evolving Identity or Culture under Attack* (Washington, DC: PRRI, 2021); Thomas B. Edsall, "The MAGA Formula Is Getting Darker and Darker," *New York Times*, May 18, 2022, https://www.nytimes.com/2022/05/18/opinion/christian-nationalism-great-replacement.html.

nationalists are thus disproportionately more likely to believe in the necessity of "patriotic violence." In a similar vein, America's founding documents are also believed to be divinely inspired. Accordingly, the right to bear arms found in the Constitution's Second Amendment is seen as inviolable.[34] Thus an ideology of Christian nationalism has likely contributed to skyrocketing weapons sales in the United States and associated mass killings. (White) Christian nationalist sentiments, for example, can be discerned in the mass shootings that have taken place at an African American church in Charleston, South Carolina, in 2015; at a Pittsburgh synagogue in 2018; at three different spas in the Atlanta area in 2021; and in Buffalo, New York, in 2022.

Third, a sizable number of American Christian nationalists not only see themselves as the heirs of the American Revolution but also believe in a future cosmic showdown between the forces of good and evil.[35] Nefarious supernatural powers, they believe, seek to destroy Christianity in America. Such beliefs make Christian nationalists susceptible to conspiratorial thinking. In the American context, Christian nationalists have been especially prone to the QAnon conspiracy movement alleging that a group of Satan-worshiping pedophiles controls the American government, media, and entertainment industry. The movement first emerged in the months after Donald Trump first took office in 2017. On fringe internet message boards known as 4chan, an anonymous poster going by the handle "Q" began posting secret coded messages concerning Trump's battle with the so-called deep state—a group of high-ranking officials plotting against him. The conspiracy spread rapidly on social media, many of the president's supporters latching on to the mysterious Q. Especially important is the QAnon belief in a coming "storm"—a violent future event involving the mass arrests and executions of those part of the satanic cabal running the world—which dovetails with Christian apocalyptic beliefs regarding the end of days prevalent among large swaths of evangelical Christians. A sizable portion of QAnon followers and Christian nationalists also hold virtually identical views on a number of political issues, including the conviction that the 2020 presidential election was stolen from Trump, the belief that the government used the COVID pandemic as a justification to crack down on the civil liberties of

---

[34] Andrew L. Whitehead, Landon Schnabel, and Samuel L. Perry, "Gun Control in the Crosshairs: Christian Nationalism and Opposition to Stricter Gun Laws," *Socius* 4 (2018): 1–13.

[35] Matthew Avery Sutton, *American Apocalypse: A History of Modern Evangelicalism* (Cambridge, MA: Harvard University Press, 2017).

American citizens, and antipathy toward Democratic politicians and international institutions. A 2021 survey revealed that about one-quarter of white American evangelicals believe in core QAnon tenets.[36] Many have worried that conspiracy theories animating QAnon could serve as an impetus for violence. The FBI, for example, has labeled QAnon a potential terrorist threat, and its adherents were among the most visible members of the pro-Trump mob that stormed the U.S. Capitol in 2021. Many followers of QAnon see violence as necessary to save the country.

Fourth, American Christian nationalism intersects with and accommodates other forms of exclusion, creating cross-cutting cleavages among different violent nationalist movements. The most important of these is Christian nationalism's overlap with white nationalism. Research by sociologists of religion has found that Christian nationalist views and xenophobia are very highly correlated with one another.[37] These alliances spring from the recognition that for the first time in American history, there are fewer white Christians than there are nonwhite Christians, white non-Christians, and nonwhite non-Christians. The recognition of this reality has led to the formation of cross-cutting grievances revolving around religion and race. The young white nationalist leader and former YouTube personality Nick Fuentes has suggested, for instance, that America was founded as a "Christian nation" but will cease to be so "if it loses its white demographic core and if it loses its faith in Jesus Christ."[38] James Dobson, the founder of Focus on the Family, one of the most important conservative Christian organizations in the world, expressed comparable concerns regarding the shifting ethnic and religious landscape in the United States:

> I can only report that without an overhaul of the law and the allocation of resources, millions of illegal immigrants will continue flooding to this great land from around the world. Many of them have no marketable skills. They are illiterate and unhealthy. Some are violent criminals. Their numbers will soon overwhelm the culture as we have known it, and it could bankrupt the nation. America has been a wonderfully generous and caring country since

---

[36] Jack Jenkins, "Survey: More Than a Quarter of White Evangelicals Believe Core QAnon Conspiracy Theory," Religion News Service, February 11, 2021, https://religionnews.com/2021/02/11/survey-more-than-a-quarter-of-white-evangelicals-believe-core-qanon-conspiracy-theory/.
[37] Baker, Perry, and Whitehead, "Keep America Christian (and White)."
[38] Jack Jenkins, "How the Capitol Attacks Helped Spread Christian Nationalism in the Extreme Right," Washington Post, January 22, 2022, https://www.washingtonpost.com/religion/2022/01/26/christian-nationalism-jan-6-extreme-right/.

its founding. That is our Christian nature. But in this instance, we have met a worldwide wave of poverty that will take us down if we don't deal with it. And it won't take long for the inevitable consequences to happen.[39]

At the fringes, Christian nationalism has made common cause with far-right white supremacist groups, such as the Proud Boys, the Three Percenters, and QAnon. According to polling by PRRI, white Americans who agree with the statement "God intended America to be a promised land for European Christians" are more than four times as likely as those who disagree with that statement to believe that "true American patriots may have to resort to violence in order to save our country."[40] Christian nationalist beliefs intersect with the ideology of such groups on issues relating not only to race but also to gender, patriarchy, nativism, and antigovernment ideology. Christian nationalism has thus served as a common framework uniting these far-right movements, all of which thrive on a victim narrative.

Christian nationalism reached its apex in the Trump presidencies. American Christian nationalists overwhelmingly supported Trump in the 2016, 2020, and 2024 presidential elections, one study finding Christian nationalist beliefs to be a robust predictor of voting for Trump, even after controlling for socioeconomic factors, racist and nativist views, religiosity, and political identity.[41] During the 2016 campaign, a popular chain email—later turned into a film—circulated among Christian nationalists likening Trump to Cyrus, the Persian king who allowed the Jewish people to return to their homeland. For a crucial core of Christians, Trump represented something of a salvific figure sent by God to help them reclaim America's Christian heritage—to "make America great again." Tony Perkins, president of the Family Research Council and an avid evangelical backer of Trump, offered one of the most candid explanations for Trump's support among conservative Christians. Perkins explained that Christians gave Trump a "mulligan" because they "were tired of being kicked around by Barack Obama and his leftists" and yearned for a leader "that is willing to punch the bully."[42] In other words, Perkins grounded conservative Christian support for Trump

---

[39] James C. Dobson, "Dr. Dobson's Visit to the Border," Dr. James Dobson Family Institute, July 2019, https://www.drjamesdobson.org/newsletters/dr-dobsons-july-newsletter-2.
[40] Edsall, "The MAGA Formula Is Getting Darker and Darker."
[41] Whitehead, Perry, and Baker, "Make America Christian Again"; Whitehead and Perry, *Taking America Back for God*, 62.
[42] Edward-Isaac Dovere, "Tony Perkins: Trump Gets 'a Mulligan' on Life, Stormy Daniels," *Politico*, January 23, 2018, https://www.politico.com/magazine/story/2018/01/23/tony-perkins-evangelicals-donald-trump-stormy-daniels-216498/.

in a narrative of Christian persecution, one which claimed Christians were being "kicked around" by an oppressive government, even as other religious communities fared better during the Obama presidency. Perkins had good reasons to believe that Trump would, in fact, defend and privilege Christians once in office. While on the campaign trail, the future president regularly reassured his Christian enthusiasts that Christianity would be privileged in his administration. For example, at a speech at Dordt College, a private evangelical university in Sioux Center, Iowa, he warned that "Christianity is under tremendous siege." He promised to rectify the situation as president by giving Christianity "real power" in his administration.[43] In another speech at a different Christian university, Liberty University in Lynchburg, Virginia, Trump declared, "Our country has to [rally] around Christianity."[44] In this way, Trump effectively tapped into a widespread victim narrative promulgated by conservative Christian leaders like Perkins. Trump, Perkins believed, presented American Christians with a vehicle, however unconventional, to channel their grievances.

At the same time that Trump promised to empower Christianity, he also regularly securitized Christianity's primary religious competitor, Islam, depicting the entire religion, not just Islamist extremists, as a threat to the country's national security. "I think Islam hates us. . . . There's a tremendous hatred there. . . . We're having problems with Muslims coming into the country," Trump declared in an interview with CNN. He then proceeded to securitize Islam, saying, "We have to be very vigilant. We have to be very careful. And we can't allow people coming into this country who have this hatred of the United States."[45] On the campaign trail, Trump proposed specific policies calling for the intensive monitoring of Muslim Americans, a ban on immigration from Muslim countries, a federal Muslim registry, and the torture of family members of suspected terrorists.

Once in the White House, the president's policies and rhetoric consistently undermined the country's commitment to political secularism. One of Trump's first actions as president involved the issuance of an executive order that banned citizens of seven Muslim-majority countries from entering the United States. At the same time, Trump strongly aligned himself with his

---

[43] Elizabeth Dias, "Christianity Will Have Power," *New York Times*, August 9, 2020, https://www.nytimes.com/2020/08/09/us/evangelicals-trump-christianity.html.
[44] C-SPAN, "Presidential Candidate Donald Trump at Liberty University," January 18, 2016, https://www.c-span.org/video/?403331-1/donald-trump-remarks-liberty-university.
[45] CNN, "Donald Trump: I Think Islam Hates Us," YouTube, March 10, 2016, https://www.youtube.com/watch?v=C-Zj0tfZY6o.

Christian nationalist base, regularly inviting conservative Christians to the White House for briefing sessions and prayers. On several occasions, most notably during a nationally televised presidential debate with Joe Biden, Trump refused to condemn extremist Christian/white supremacist outfits. "Stand back and stand by," he instructed the Proud Boys, a far-right hate group known for its antisemitism and Islamophobia that was founded in the midst of the 2016 presidential election campaign.[46] Trump uttered these words after several attempts by the debate moderator, Chris Wallace, to ask if he was willing to condemn white supremacists and militia groups.

In line with the argument of this book, the Trump presidency coincided with a spike in violent attacks against religious minorities. It stands to reason that the rhetoric coming out of the White House had an emboldening effect on extremist groups espousing various forms of nationalist Christianity. Christian nationalists and their allies engaged in violent clashes with Black Lives Matter protestors and Antifa groups in the streets of some American cities. Christian nationalism also figured prominently in two major episodes of violence that occurred during Trump's time as president: the 2017 Charlottesville riot and the 2021 Capitol insurgency.

Seven months into Trump's presidency, white nationalist groups organized a Unite the Right rally in Charlottesville, Virginia, in response to a decision by the Charlottesville City Council to remove a statue of Confederate general Robert E. Lee from a public park near the Downtown Mall. The rally followed smaller rallies by the Alt-Right and Ku Klux Klan in the preceding months. It turned deadly when participants violently attacked counterprotesters marching against them. A twenty-year-old man, James Alex Fields Jr., a neo-Nazi, rammed his car into a crowd of people, killing one person and injuring nineteen others. Two state police officers were also killed while monitoring the protests after their helicopter crashed. Following the rally, Trump claimed that there were "very fine people on both sides."[47]

While the two-day rally was organized by white supremacist groups, including white nationalists, neo-Confederates, neo-Nazis, and the Ku Klux Klan, it would be a mistake to overlook the role played by Christian

---

[46] CNBC, "President Donald Trump: White Supremacist Group Proud Boys Should 'Stand Back and Stand By,'" YouTube, September 30, 2020, https://www.youtube.com/watch?v=JZk6VzSLe4Y.

[47] Politico Staff, "Full Text: Trump's Comments on White Supremacists, 'Alt-Left' in Charlottesville," Politico, August 15, 2017, https://www.politico.com/story/2017/08/15/full-text-trump-comments-white-supremacists-alt-left-transcript-241662.

nationalism. Although the protestors espoused different racist ideologies, Christianity emerged as a unifying motif. The rally's organizers saw whiteness and Christianity, particularly Anglo-Saxon Protestantism, as the two primary pillars holding the country together.[48] The rally that ensued can best be described as Christian ethnonationalist, built on the symbolism of Christianity and joined with the grievance narratives of white nationalism. The St. Andrews Cross, for example, could be observed on signs and flags throughout the rally, as could Bible verses purportedly justifying racism. Interestingly, although American white supremacy seeks to make common cause primarily with Protestant Christians, journalist Katherine Kelaidis unearthed evidence that "[Eastern] Orthodoxy has become an integral part of the ideological and recruitment apparatus within some segments of the white supremacist movement," and Orthodox Christians marched at the Unite the Right rally waving "Orthodoxy or Death" banners.[49] By joining with Christian nationalists through the incorporation of Christian myths, symbols, and values, the organizers of the rally hoped to make it more appealing to Christian sympathizers who believed that their heritage, too, was under assault by the same forces threatening whites.

As terrible as the events in Charlottesville were, they would pale in comparison to what would unfold little more than three years later about one hundred miles to the north in the nation's capital. On January 6, 2021, a mob of thousands of Trump supporters descended on Washington, DC for a Save America rally, at which Trump repeated unsubstantiated claims of widespread voter fraud during the 2020 presidential election and urged his supporters to rally to his defense. "We fight like hell. If you don't fight like hell, you're not going to have a country anymore," Trump warned the crowd.[50] Following the conclusion of the rally, thousands marched to the Capitol, where the president had promised he would join them. Responding to the president's calls to action earlier that day, the crowd sought to disrupt the joint session of Congress assembled to certify the election results and formalize President-elect Biden's victory. Protestors forced their way through

---

[48] Richard Spencer, "What It Means to Be Alt-Right," AltRight, August 11, 2017, https://altright.com/2017/08/11/what-it-means-to-be-alt-right/.

[49] Katherine Kelaidis, "White Supremacy and Orthodox Christianity: A Dangerous Connection Rears Its Head in Charlottesville," *Religious Dispatches*, August 18, 2017, https://religiondispatches.org/white-supremacy-and-orthodox-christianity-a-dangerous-connection-rears-its-head-in-charlottesville/.

[50] *PBS NewsHour*, "Watch Live: Trump Speaks as Congress Prepares to Count Electoral College Votes in Biden Win," YouTube, January 7, 2021, https://www.youtube.com/watch?v=pa9sT4efsqY.

barricades, smashing windows, assaulting police officers with lead pipes and chemical agents, rampaging throughout the building, forcing the evacuation of lawmakers and their staffs, causing tens of millions of dollars' worth of property damage, and eventually taking control of the entire Capitol Complex for several hours. The riot marked the first time in over two hundred years that the building had been seized by force. Five people died either during or shortly following the riot. Many others were injured, including 138 police officers. Four officers who responded to the attack died by suicide within seven months. One week after the riot, the House of Representatives impeached Trump for incitement of insurrection.

Christian nationalism figured prominently in the Capitol insurgency, where Christian symbols and rhetoric were prevalent. Inside and outside the Capitol Building could be seen Christian flags; Christian prayer circles; Christian banners reading "Jesus Saves," "Jesus 2020," and "Proud American Christian"; placards declaring "Jesus is my Savior, Trump is my President"; pictures with Jesus wearing a MAGA hat; crosses; Bibles; and various other Christian imagery. Christian worship music blared from loudspeakers, while Christian supporters of Trump chanted "Christ is King!" Others spoke in tongues. Some Christians hailed the Proud Boys as "God's warriors."[51] Many of the rioters believed that the certification of the 2020 election results would be tantamount to America's turning its back on its Christian foundations; they thus hoped to literally—and forcefully—take America back for God. They saw Trump as a salvific figure sent by God to rescue the country from impending demise. A disproportionate number of the Christian participants identified with a charismatic form of Christianity known as the prophetic movement, a large, loosely connected group of charismatic churches and para-church organizations, many of the leaders of which had prophesied that Trump would remain in office for another four years.[52]

---

[51] Molly Olmstead, "'God Have Mercy on and Help Us All: How Prominent Evangelicals Reacted to the Storming of the U.S. Capitol," *Slate*, January 7, 2021, https://slate.com/human-interest/2021/01/trump-capitol-riot-evangelical-leaders-reactions.html; Emma Green, "A Christian Insurrection," *The Atlantic*, January 8, 2021, https://www.theatlantic.com/politics/archive/2021/01/evangelicals-catholics-jericho-march-capitol/617591/; Matthew Avery Sutton, "The Capitol Riot Revealed the Darkest Nightmares of White Evangelical America," *New Republic*, January 14, 2021, https://newrepublic.com/article/160922/capitol-riot-revealed-darkest-nightmares-white-evangelical-america.

[52] Michelle Boorstein, "For Some Christians, the Capitol Riot Doesn't Change the Prophecy: Trump Will Be President," *Washington Post*, January 14, 2021, https://www.washingtonpost.com/religion/2021/01/14/prophets-apostles-christian-prophesy-trump-won-biden-capitol/.

A group of insurrectionists made their way to the Senate chamber. Once there, activist and conspiracy theorist Jacob Angeli led them in a prayer for the country. Dressed in horns, face paint, and a fur hat, the so-called QAnon Shaman first thanked God for the opportunity to defend their "God-given unalienable rights." He continued, "Thank you for allowing the United States of America to be reborn. Thank you for allowing us to get rid of the communists, the globalists, and the traitors within our government."[53] As expressed in Angeli's prayer, the Christian rioters held decidedly anti-secular views, passionately believing that they were called by God to save Trump, thereby protecting Christian America from its usurpers. Many of the participants in the insurrection viewed the Capitol siege as a physical manifestation of a spiritual battle against the forces of evil. Stunningly, research conducted in the aftermath of the riot showed that Christian nationalists grew *more* accepting of the insurrection over time and were disproportionately more likely to believe that the participants in the riot should not be prosecuted.[54] In the end, the events of January 6, 2021 showed how an antisecular ideology can turn deadly and threaten democracy itself.

After the insurrection, Christian nationalist events were hosted at churches across the country, the most important of which was the ReAwaken America Tour, a nationwide series of rallies led by Trump's first national security advisor, Michael Flynn, and a number of other personalities devoted to a Christian nationalist, right-wing agenda. Speaking at the tour's stop in San Antonio, Texas, in November 2021, Flynn laid bare the theocratic underpinnings of American Christian nationalism: "If we are going to have one nation under God, which we must, we have to have one religion. One nation under God and one religion under God, right? All of us, working together."[55] Similarly, Sean Feucht, a worship leader and pro-Trump political activist who gained notoriety for holding public worship gatherings during the COVID-19 pandemic in defiance of governmental restrictions, did not mince words in articulating the goals of Christian nationalism: "You want

---

[53] *New Yorker*, "A Reporter's Footage from Inside the Capitol Siege," YouTube, January 18, 2001, https://www.youtube.com/watch?v=270F8s5TEKY.

[54] Samuel L. Perry and Andrew Whitehead, "January 6th May Have Been Only the First Wave of Christian Nationalist Violence," *Time*, January 4, 2022, https://time.com/6132591/january-6th-christian-nationalism/.

[55] Paul LeBlanc, "Ex-Trump Advisor Michael Flynn's Call for 'One Religion' in the US Garners Swift Condemnation," CNN, November 15, 2021, https://edition.cnn.com/2021/11/15/politics/michael-flynn-one-religion/index.html.

The Kingdom to be the government? Yes! ... You want God to come on over and take over the government? Yes! We want God to be in control of everything! ... We want believers to be the ones writing the laws! Yes! Guilty as charged."[56]

Christian nationalism's presence at the riot was not unforeseen; even before the 2020 presidential election Christian leaders had warned of a conspiracy to steal the election from Trump. In the weeks following the election, several of Trump's most prominent Christian supporters cast his efforts to discredit the election results in spiritual terms. Paula White-Cain, Trump's faith advisor and a well-known televangelist, summoned angels from Asia and Africa to "break and divide every demonic confederacy against the election, against America, against ... who you have declared to be in the White House."[57] Some of those who mobbed the Capitol had previously participated in the Jericho March, during which participants marched around the Capitol grounds seven times in the belief that doing so would keep Trump in office, in the same way that the ancient Israelites captured the city of Jericho by marching around its walls seven times.[58]

As the Unite the Right rally and the Capitol insurrection so vividly demonstrate, Christian nationalism remains the most serious threat to political secularism in the United States today and a key source of religious hostilities. There are some hopeful signs, though, that this threat is being recognized and countered. Importantly, the critique of Christian nationalism is arising internally, from within the Christian tradition itself. The most important group challenging Christian nationalism in the United States, Christians against Christian Nationalism, grounds its critique of Christian nationalism on the basis that it threatens not only American democracy but also the Christian faith itself. The conclusion of its guiding statement reads, "Whether we worship at a church, mosque, synagogue, or temple, America has no second-class faiths. All are equal under the U.S. Constitution. As

---

[56] Tim Dickinson, "MAGA Pastor Says Christians Must 'Be the Ones Writing the Laws,'" *Rolling Stone*, April 21, 2023, https://www.rollingstone.com/politics/politics-features/maga-pastor-sean-feucht-trump-christian-nationalism-1234721527/.

[57] Now This News, "Donald Trump's Faith Advisor Leads Viral Sermon after Election Day," YouTube, November 6, 2020, https://www.youtube.com/watch?v=I4daeEacIVI.

[58] Bob Smietana, "Jericho March Returns to DC to Pray for a Trump Miracle," *Christianity Today*, January 5, 2021, https://www.christianitytoday.com/news/2021/january/jericho-march-dc-election-overturn-trump-biden-congress.html; Elizabeth Dias and Ruth Graham, "How White Evangelical Christians Fused with Trump Extremism," *New York Times*, January 11, 2021, https://www.nytimes.com/2021/01/11/us/how-white-evangelical-christians-fused-with-trump-extremism.html.

Christians, we must speak in one voice condemning Christian nationalism as a distortion of the gospel of Jesus and a threat to American democracy." To date, the statement has been signed by over twenty-five thousand Christians and endorsed by some of the most influential voices in American Christianity. The organization, together with the Baptist Joint Committee for Religious Liberty and the Freedom from Religion Foundation, compiled a significant report, "Christian Nationalism and the January 6, 2021 Insurrection," detailing how Christian nationalist beliefs contributed to the events culminating in the attack on the Capitol.[59] The report was the subject of a congressional hearing on the topic.

In summary, American Christian nationalism threatens political secularism because it declares the United States is in a special relationship with God, and so Christianity must serve as the foundation for the state and the government must privilege Christianity in its laws, policies, and civic culture. True American citizenship is defined in terms of the Christian faith. Such an exclusionary ideology overlaps with other forms of marginalization, the most important being white supremacy. Christian nationalism has also been directly implicated in acts of religious violence, most notably the 2021 insurrection at the U.S. Capitol. After the Capitol riot, Christian nationalism remains a pervasive force in American society, but it is being challenged from within the Christian tradition itself.

European Christian Civilizationalism and Violence

The case of Europe presents a fascinating contrast to that of the United States. Over the past two decades, many European countries have witnessed the transformation of their religious landscapes. Two different trends have converged to catalyze this transformation. The first is the decline of Christianity. Scholars of religion have long noted that trends toward secularization appear strongest in the countries of Europe, where the church for centuries played a major role in people's lives.[60] Europe has seen the progressive secularization of society, a trend propelled by the advance of secular humanism that can be traced to the Enlightenment. Numerous polls

---

[59] Christians against Christian Nationalism, "Christian Nationalism and the January 6, 2021 Insurrection," February 9, 2022, https://www.christiansagainstchristiannationalism.org/jan6report.

[60] Hans Knippenberg, ed., *The Changing Religious Landscape of Europe* (Amsterdam: Het Spinhuis, 2005); Grace Davie, "Is Europe an Exceptional Case?," *Hedgehog Review* 8, no. 1 (2006): 23–34.

have documented the comparatively weak levels of credal Christianity and attendance at church services in this part of the world.[61]

The second trend pertains to changes in religious demography stemming from increased levels of immigration, particularly from Muslim countries. As Christianity has been steadily declining, minority faith traditions have made striking inroads into European societies that were, for most of their histories, relatively homogeneous, a development that has been compounded by a record influx of asylum seekers fleeing conflicts in Syria and other predominantly Muslim countries. Of the 450 million inhabitants of the European Union, about 9 percent are foreign-born. In Switzerland, nearly one in three residents was born outside of the country. In Iceland, the number is about one in five, and in Norway about one in six.[62] The Pew Research Center estimates that by 2050, the Muslim share of the total population of Europe could be as high as 14 percent.[63] These two simultaneous trends have together created sudden and unprecedented religious diversity, giving rise to a "post-Christian" Europe. These developments have furthermore produced a ubiquitous fear that the countries of Europe are losing their cultural identities, a fear that has been deftly exploited by right-wing parties and politicians holding xenophobic worldviews.[64]

The de-Christianization of European society, coupled with the arrival of non-European faith traditions, has led to the weakening of both confessional states *and* political secularism. Indeed, the states of Europe are less politically secular than the United States. Importantly, however, the form of religious privilege that exists in Europe is of a markedly different nature than found in the United States. Whereas Christian nationalism in the United States tends to be credal in expression—anchored in an ideology proclaiming that God has uniquely blessed the country for a divinely ordained mission in the world—Christian privilege in Europe tends to be expressed in terms of *identity* rather than belief. Here Christianity serves as a marker of communal

---

[61] Steve Crabtree, "Religiosity Highest in World's Poorest Countries," Gallup, August 31, 2010, https://news.gallup.com/poll/142727/religiosity-highest-world-poorest-nations.aspx; Pew Research Center, *Being Christian in Western Europe* (Washington, DC: Pew Research Center, 2018); Pew Research Center, *Eastern and Western Europeans Differ on Importance of Religion, Views of Minorities, and Key Social Issues* (Washington, DC: Pew Research Center, 2018).

[62] European Commission, "Statistics on Migration to Europe," April 11, 2024, https://commission.europa.eu/strategy-and-policy/priorities-2019-2024/promoting-our-european-way-life/statistics-migration-europe_en.

[63] Pew Research Center, *Europe's Growing Muslim Population* (Washington, DC: Pew Research Center, 2017).

[64] Philip Barker, *Religious Nationalism in Modern Europe* (London: Routledge, 2008).

belonging, underscoring the continent's common Christian civilizational identity. The unique form of Christian identitarianism found in Europe has given rise to what sociologist Rogers Brubaker terms "civilizationalism."[65] This secular form of Christianity is not theological in nature but instead stresses the uniquely Christian histories, identities, and cultures of European countries and the need to defend Western Christian civilization against the encroaching threat of multiculturalism in its different manifestations. Consequently, the absence of a theological foundation means that Christian privilege in Europe, unlike in the United States, is able to coexist with secular liberalism. Indeed, violent vigilantes in Europe see themselves as the defenders of Western liberal values. Christian civilizationalists take particular issue with the spread of Islam throughout Europe and visible expressions of Muslim faith in the public square, such as Muslim women donning the burqa outside the home.

Many European countries display a form of pseudo-secularity—as opposed to genuine political secularism—that is strongly discriminatory in its application.[66] Unlike American secularism, which disestablishes religion, many European states establish different sects of Christianity in their constitutions. They also display Christian privilege by disproportionately discriminating against non-Christian faiths, in this way creating an unbalanced religious playing field. States restrict minority religious practices because they are believed to contradict the secularist foundations of the state and threaten the harmony and stability of society. To be sure, the gap in rights enjoyed by majority and minority religions is not as wide as it is in other parts of the world. Nevertheless, in important areas the state's treatment of minority religious communities remains deeply problematic and has even fostered societal extremism against them.

In theory, European secularity is meant to promote social cohesion, tolerance, and pluralism by appealing to a nonreligious, universalist conception of human rights. In practice, though, it unduly discriminates against certain religious communities. For this reason, we might refer to the unique form of secularism practiced in Europe as "discriminatory secularism." Where discriminatory secularism is the governing relationship between religion and state, religious restrictions fall disproportionately on minority faith

---

[65] Rogers Brubaker, "Between Nationalism and Civilizationism: The European Populist Moment in Comparative Perspective," *Ethnic and Racial Studies* 40, no. 8 (2017): 1191–1226.
[66] Fox, "Civilizational Clash or Balderdash?"; Jonathan Fox, "What Is Religious Freedom and Who Has It?," *Social Compass* 68, no. 3 (2021): 321–341.

traditions, especially Islam. For example, the French government takes particular aim at public displays of the Muslim faith, such as women wearing the hijab, burqa, and beach burkinis outside the home, as well as public prayer and halal aisles in supermarkets. Laïcité—the uniquely French form of secularism—has been weaponized to legitimize Islamophobia and discriminatory governmental practices toward the French Muslim population. French president Emmanuel Macron once justified anti-Muslim policies on the grounds that Islam, and in particular the religion's proneness to separatism, undermined French values.[67] Accordingly, in 2021 the Council of Ministers enacted the Law Reinforcing Respect of the Principles of the Republic, which strengthened the state's ability to monitor mosques and Islamic organizations.

Elsewhere, European political leaders such as Hungarian president Viktor Orbán and Dutch parliamentarian Geert Wilders, along with various right-wing political parties—Austria's Freedom Party, Germany's Alternative and PEGIDA parties, Greece's Golden Dawn, Hungary's Fidesz, Italy's Brothers of Italy, Poland's Law and Justice Party, Slovenia's Democratic Party, and Switzerland's People's Party—have decried the threat to Christian civilization stemming from the presence of Islam in Europe. They have supported measures such as banning the public wearing of Islamic dress, prohibiting Muslim immigration, and repatriating Muslims to their countries of origin. Indeed, research by Jonathan Fox on global minority religious discrimination reveals that "non-Orthodox Western and European democracies" engage in antiminority discrimination with far more frequency and intensity than democracies found in other parts of the world.[68] The Pew Research Center similarly documents that Europe has seen some of the largest increases in restrictions on religious minorities, with its religious restriction score doubling over a ten-year period.[69]

How European discriminatory secularism results in the restriction of rights for minority faith communities manifests in a number of different areas, including restrictions on the wearing of religious garb in public,

---

[67] Myriam Francois, "France's Treatment of Its Muslim Citizens Is the True Measure of Its Republican Values," *Time*, December 8, 2020, https://time.com/5918657/frances-muslim-citizens-republican-values/.

[68] Fox, "What Is Religious Freedom and Who Has It?," 331.

[69] Jeff Diamant, "Europe Experienced a Surge in Government Restrictions on Religious Activity over the Last Decade," Pew Research Center, July 29, 2019, https://www.pewresearch.org/fact-tank/2019/07/29/europe-experienced-a-surge-in-government-restrictions-on-religious-activity-over-the-last-decade/.

prohibitions on ritual animal slaughter as performed in the Jewish kosher and Muslim halal traditions, and the regulation of male infant circumcision.[70] All three sets of these restrictive laws and policies fall disproportionately on minority religious communities, namely Jews and Muslims, and are justified on the basis of (philosophically) secular ideological belief. Let us take a closer look at each of these.

First, certain European countries, or particular regions within countries, prohibit or restrict Muslim women from wearing Islamic face coverings such as the niqab and burqa in public, which some Muslims consider a religious obligation.[71] Austria, Belgium, Bulgaria, Denmark, France, the Netherlands, and Switzerland all have in place full or partial restrictions on the veil. Croatia, Italy, Malta, Norway, and Spain prohibit the wearing of the veil in certain regions or towns. In 2021, the European Court of Justice, reaffirming and expanding on a decision it had reached in 2017, ruled that European companies can, under certain conditions, legally ban the wearing of religious dress and symbols such as Islamic headscarves in the workplace. While laws against face veiling in these countries do not mention Islam or Islamic headgear by name in order to avoid violating legal antidiscrimination provisions, they are widely believed to be targeted at Muslims and, accordingly, are often referred to by their supporters as "burqa bans."[72] Supporters of these policies ground their opposition to the public wearing of Islamic face coverings on explicitly (again philosophically) secularist grounds, especially a secularist conception of women's rights, which sees Islamic head coverings as a symbol of female oppression and as dehumanizing to women. As political scientist Federiga Bindi explains, the veil "goes against the most basic Western principle: looking into someone's eyes as the way to build trust."[73] In defending proposed legislation outlawing burqas, former French president Nicolas Sarkozy castigated public veiling as a violation of "women's dignity" and a sign of "subservience and debasement."[74] Thus proponents of public veil bans believe that these laws empower Muslim women by freeing them from

---

[70] Cesari, *Why the West Fears Islam*; Fox, *Thou Shalt Have No Other Gods before Me*, 140, 155–156.
[71] Valerie Behiery, "Bans on Muslim Facial Veiling in Europe and Canada: A Cultural History of Vision Perspective," *Social Identities* 19, no. 6 (2013): 775–793.
[72] Nilay Saiya and Stuti Manchanda, "Do Burqa Bans Make Us Safer? Veil Restrictions and Terrorism in Europe," *Journal of European Public Policy* 27, no. 12 (2020): 1781–1800.
[73] Judy Dempsey, "Judy Asks: Is the Burka Compatible with Integration?," Carnegie Europe, August 31, 2016, https://carnegieeurope.eu/strategiceurope/64432.
[74] Angelique Chrisafis, "Nicholas Sarkozy Says Islamic Veils Are Not Welcome in France," *The Guardian*, June 22, 2009, https://www.theguardian.com/world/2009/jun/22/islamic-veils-sarkozy-speech-france.

the bondage of traditional cultural mores, which inhibit their participation in public life. However, a strong case can be made that these restrictions on Islamic dress themselves constitute violations of political secularism in their discriminatory targeting of Muslim minorities and their violations of religious freedom—two of the four essential components of political secularism discussed in the previous chapter.

Second, discriminatory European states restrict the practice of ritual animal slaughter in the Muslim halal and Jewish kosher traditions.[75] In these faiths, the ritual slaughter of animals is considered mandatory for food production purposes and has been practiced for centuries in the case of Islam and for millennia in the case of Judaism. Ritual slaughter practices forbid the stunning of animals before they are killed. Opponents of ritual animal slaughter, however, believe that the un-stunned killing of animals amounts to an act of senseless cruelty and ground their opposition to ritual slaughter in animal rights.[76] In 2020, the European Court of Justice ruled that states are permitted to prohibit halal and kosher slaughter. To date, Belgium, Denmark, Germany, Greece, Iceland, Norway, Sweden, and Switzerland have in place laws restricting the ritual slaughter of animals.[77] Other countries are presently considering similar legislation. Again, we see that a religious restriction grounded in a commitment to philosophical secularism falls solely on religious minorities.

Third, several European states regulate the circumcision of infant males, a practice central to both Islam and Judaism that finds its origins in the ancient covenant between God and Abraham as recorded in the book of Genesis. Opponents of infant circumcision, though, appeal to children's rights in decrying the practice, claiming that the act of circumcision inflicts great pain on an unwilling participant and is irreversible. A German court ruled in 2012 that a "child's right to physical integrity trumps religious and parental rights." (The federal government later passed legislation allowing for male infant circumcision following protests by Jewish and Muslim groups.) Fox notes that most European countries do not ban infant male circumcision outright, but some do regulate it heavily, as seen in Denmark, Norway, and Sweden.[78] The circumcision issue has also been

---

[75] Gerhard van der Schyff, "Ritual Slaughter and Religious Freedom in a Multilevel Europe: The Wider Importance of the Dutch Case," *Oxford Journal of Law and Religion* 3, no. 1 (2014): 76–102.

[76] Carla M. Zoethout, "Ritual Slaughter and the Freedom of Religion: Some Reflections on a Stunning Matter," *Human Rights Quarterly* 35, no. 3 (2013): 651–672.

[77] Fox, *Thou Shalt Have No Other Gods before Me*, 155.

[78] Fox, *Thou Shalt Have No Other Gods before Me*, 155.

hotly debated in Belgium and Finland, though restrictions on infant male circumcision ultimately did not pass.

In all three cases—restrictions on the public wearing of the veil, on ritual animal slaughter, and on infant male circumcision—apply solely to religious minorities, and in particular, Jews and Muslims. Those belonging to majority Christian populations do not wear face coverings (though some Christian women do cover their hair), practice ritual animal slaughter, or require baby boys to be circumcised. It is thus the case that the discriminatory secularism found in many parts of Europe is highly prejudiced in nature and that restrictions on the rights of minority communities are justified on the basis of secularist commitments: women's rights, animal rights, and children's rights. It is also important to note that the specific ways in which European states restrict the rights of minority religious communities are highly unusual and generally do not exist outside of this context.

The context of discriminatory secularism prevalent throughout Europe has worked to produce a climate of hostility toward minority out-groups. As discriminatory secularism has risen, so too have attacks on religious minorities. The Pew Research Center documents that Europe's level of social hostilities involving religion increased by a factor of 4 from 2007 to 2018.[79] Twenty-eight countries in Europe (62 percent) had higher levels of violent religious hostilities in 2018 than they did in 2007. In numerous cases—Belgium, Denmark, Finland, France, Germany, Italy, the Netherlands, Norway, Poland, Spain, Sweden, Ukraine, and the United Kingdom—violent religious hostilities increased significantly, largely the result of majority-on-minority violence.[80] The rise in hate crimes also comes amid a surge in popularity for far-right political parties. Jewish and Muslim communities, in particular, have encountered rising levels of xenophobia, discrimination, and physical attacks. This antiminority culture is sustained by various groups and individuals associated with majoritarian communities, including secular politicians, right-wing extremists, and Christian civilizationalists, all of whom consider the presence and practices of minority religious communities threatening to their countries' national cultures and identities. Attacks against Jews and Muslims and their holy places have been sharply increasing in various European countries, especially following major international

---

[79] Diamant, "Europe Experienced a Surge in Government Restrictions on Religious Activity over the Last Decade."

[80] Pew Research Center, *Globally, Government Restrictions on Religion Reached Peak Levels in 2021, While Social Hostilities Went Down* (Washington, DC: Pew Research Center, 2024), 67–68.

crises such as the 2008 global financial recession, the COVID-19 pandemic, the October 7, 2023 Hamas attack against Israel, and Israel's reprisal war against Hamas in Gaza. This increased antiminority violence is partly the result of a culture created by official laws and policies that are discriminatory toward minority out-groups. For example, in France, state policies grounded in laïcité have served to alienate Muslim communities from the fabric of French life, give rise to an increasingly influential radical right political movement, promote discrimination against Muslims, and provide a fertile breeding ground for attacks against French Muslim communities.[81]

Violence against religious minorities in Europe arises from three different sources. First, it can stem from self-professing Christians who consider the presence of religious outsiders a threat to the Christian heritage of their countries. Consider the case of Anders Breivik, a Christian terrorist who in 2011 killed or injured nearly four hundred people in separate attacks in Oslo, Norway, in the single worst episode of violence in that country since World War II. Most of the carnage occurred at an annual summer camp held by the Norwegian Labour Party's youth organization. Breivik's 1,500-page manifesto, *2083: A European Declaration of Independence*, which he distributed electronically shortly before his attacks, detailed the killer's grievances. Essentially, Breivik held that Christianity, the cornerstone of Western civilization, was under siege from mass immigration, particularly from the Islamic world, and that this demographic shift was contaminating "monocultural Christian Europe." He decried "the ongoing Islamic invasion through Islamic demographic warfare against Europe," believing that the changing religious landscape "justified every military action against our enemies." Accordingly, Breivik vehemently opposed the pro-multicultural policies of the Norwegian Labour government, believing they polluted the "pure" Christian European culture. He declared that "multiculturalism (protolegitimized moral relativism) must be deconstructed and delegitimized."[82]

Second, violence can stem from extremist secular groups such as neo-Nazis and other white supremacist outfits. Unlike Christian civilizationalists, these groups are more likely to appeal to racist rather than religious arguments in justifying violence against religious minorities. For example, groups such as Blood and Honour, Combat 18, Feuerkrieg Division,

---

[81] Denis Leven, "Hate Crimes Spike in France," *Politico*, March 20, 2024, https://www.politico.eu/article/hate-crimes-racial-tension-booming-france/.

[82] Anders Breivik [Andrew Berwick], *2083: A European Declaration of Independence*, 2011, 1404, 1329, 1404.

Generation Identity, National Action, Nordic Resistance Movement, and Order of Nine Angels have gained prominence for their commitment to ethnic purity. Groups such as these promote hatred against minorities and have been increasingly involved in violent attacks in recent years. They are largely motivated by the theory of the "Great Replacement," "the process by which the Indigenous European population is replaced by non-European migrants."[83] Jewish communities, in particular, have experienced mounting episodes of antisemitic violence carried out by hate groups in various countries, including France, Germany, Italy, and the United Kingdom. Attackers have targeted Jewish individuals, cemeteries, synagogues, and kosher restaurants. Antisemitic demonstrations in Europe have featured the burning of Israeli flags in front of synagogues and community centers, threats of violence, physical assaults, and vandalism.[84] In these cases, Christian privilege and the degrading of political secularism encourages violence against religious minorities stemming from nonreligious sources.

Third, antiminority violence can stem from a general culture of hostility toward religious minorities. In this case, antiminority attacks are not associated with any particular group or ideological movement but originate instead from lay elements within society. For example, paramilitaries and street patrols have arisen throughout Europe in response to the migration crisis and the perceived Islamization of European society.[85] Acts of violence are often unplanned and constitute what are commonly referred to as "hate crimes"—transgressions motivated by hatred toward specific groups.[86] It is often the case that these attacks are indirectly or directly promoted by the incendiary rhetoric of far-right politicians and religious leaders who manufacture a fear of minorities. Among the many examples are Dutch parliamentarian Wilders's campaign against the Islamic takeover of European civilization, French president Macron's expressed desire to shut down certain Islamic societal and educational organizations, former Austrian chancellor Sebastian Kurz's proposed legislation to ban political Islam, and Hungarian prime minister Orbán's belief that Muslim migration embodies

---

[83] Counter Extremism Project, "European Ethno-Nationalist and White Supremacy Groups," 2022, https://www.counterextremism.com/content/european-ethno-nationalist-and-white-supremacy-groups.

[84] U.S. Commission on International Religious Freedom, *Antisemitism in Europe* (Washington, DC: USCIRF, 2021).

[85] Jussi Rosendahl and Tuomas Forsell, "Anti-Immigrant 'Soldiers of Odin' Raise Concern in Finland," Reuters, January 13, 2016, https://www.reuters.com/article/us-europe-migrants-finland-idUSKCN0UR20G20160113.

[86] Nathan Hall, *Hate Crime* (London: Routledge, 2013).

a national security threat. Far-right political parties like Germany's Alternative, Greece's Golden Dawn, Hungary's Jobbik, Italy's Northern League, and the United Kingdom's Britain First have been able to garner substantial popular support by promising to defend their respective countries against the cultural attacks stemming from Muslim minorities. These leaders and parties securitize the religion of Islam, presenting it as an existential threat to European culture. The antiminority rhetoric arising from political and religious leaders provides extremists with a ready-made rhetorical cover for targeting minorities.

In summary, many European states violate core principles of political secularism by creating a religious landscape in which religious minorities suffer from a climate of discrimination. Unlike in the United States, the European privileging of the majority religious tradition, Christianity, is not credal but identitarian and secularist in nature. It can be seen in laws and policies regulating acceptable religious dress, the ritual slaughter of animals, and infant male circumcision. The undermining of political secularism in this way serves to create a culture of hostility against religious minorities, making attacks against them more likely. Violence against minorities in these cases is often justified on the basis that the practices of minority groups undermine the secular foundations of the state and threaten social cohesion. The rise in antiminority violence comes amid a surge in popularity for far-right political parties across the continent.

Christian Nationalism and Violence in the Developing World

Calls for the integration of Christianity and the state are not just a problem confronted by Western countries. Increasingly, violent forms of Christian nationalism, again in myriad forms, are manifesting in the developing world. This section takes a snapshot of two cases in Africa, Uganda and Central African Republic, and two in Latin America, Brazil and Mexico. These are arguably the most important countries in the developing world where Christian violence has unfolded in recent years. As in the West, Christian violence in Africa and Latin America has coincided with secularism retreats.

First, the intersection of Christian privilege, Christian nationalism, and antiminority violence has gripped the region of Central Africa, especially the countries of Uganda and Central African Republic, where political leaders have manipulated Christian identity to mobilize support for their political or ethnic agendas. Uganda, a country historically known for its cultural and religious diversity, has taken a theocratic turn, especially with respect to gender and sexuality. At the behest of Christian pastors, the government has sanctioned a "morality crusade" against sexual depravity, including homosexuality.[87] In 2023, Uganda's Parliament passed the Anti-Homosexuality Act, one of the world's strictest anti-LGBTQ bills. The law, which received strong support from churches and Christian nationalist politicians, mandates the death penalty for certain same-sex acts and a twenty-year sentence for "promoting" homosexuality. The sponsor of an earlier version of the bill, David Bahati, declared his intention "to kill every last gay person." Bahati argued, based on an interpretation of Romans 13, that he had been given this authority by God for the good of Uganda.[88] President Yoweri Museveni provided strong support for the bill.

Uganda's antisecular turn has paved the way for religious conflict, empowering majoritarian vigilantism (and more recently a violent minority backlash). The Pew Research Center determined that in 2021, Uganda had one of the highest rates of social hostilities involving religion in the world.[89] Even before the passage of the Anti-Homosexuality Act of 2023, LGBTQ Ugandans had frequently encountered discrimination, harassment, and physical attacks. Rights groups now claim that the passage of the law has unleashed a new wave of abuses and violence against gender and sexual minorities.[90] A report by a group called Convening for Equality documented hundreds of cases of violence based on the victims' sexual orientation and gender identity.[91] A report by the Kampala-based Human Rights Awareness and Promotion Forum similarly noted that the bill sparked a wave of violence against LGBTQ people; about 70 percent of people surveyed reported "some form of negative treatment or action targeting individuals because of their presumed Sexual Orientation, Gender Identity, and Expression" in the

---

[87] Deborah Kintu, *The Ugandan Morality Crusade: The Brutal Campaign against Homosexuality and Pornography under Yoweri Museveni* (Jefferson, NC: McFarland, 2018).

[88] Jeff Sharlet, "Straight Man's Burden: The American Roots of Uganda's Anti-Gay Persecutions," *Harper's*, September 2010, https://harpers.org/archive/2010/09/straight-mans-burden/.

[89] Pew Research Center, *Globally, Government Restrictions on Religion Reached Peak Levels in 2021, While Social Hostilities Went Down*, 70.

[90] Stephen Kafeero, "New Report Paints Violence Surge Post Anti-Homosexuality Law Enactment," *Monitor*, September 29, 2023, https://www.monitor.co.ug/uganda/news/national/new-report-paints-violence-surge-post-anti-homosexuality-law-enactment-4383532.

[91] Reuters, "Uganda's Anti-Gay Law Causing Wave of Rights Abuses, Activists Say," September 28, 2023, https://www.reuters.com/world/africa/ugandas-anti-gay-law-causing-wave-rights-abuses-activists-say-2023-09-28/.

weeks following the law's passage.[92] It appears that the law has radicalized the public against Uganda's LGBTQ community.

Political secularism has also come under attack elsewhere in the region. Since 2012, the government and sectarian forces have been locked in an intermittent but catastrophic struggle in the small, impoverished, landlocked country of Central African Republic. Christian nationalism has figured prominently in the civil conflict that has killed or displaced approximately one in four residents. For much of its postindependence history, relations between Christians and Muslims were relatively harmonious. Many towns and villages were mixed, and interreligious marriage was common. Why did a country with relatively harmonious interreligious relations suddenly witness a descent into conflict and strife? As in Uganda, the hostilities appear to have been, at least in part, the product of a reversal in political secularism, namely the development of a close alliance between Christianity and the state during the presidency of François Bozizé.[93] The president deliberately cultivated an anti-Muslim political narrative that weaponized Christianity against the country's minority Muslim population, which subsequently suffered from social shame, discrimination, political marginalization, and religion-based socioeconomic inequalities, all of which contributed to their status as second-class citizens.[94] This situation directly fed majority-on-minority violence. Christian militias known as the Antibalaka have waged a religious war against the country's minority Muslim population, forcing the exile of entire Muslim communities to the neighboring states of Cameroon, Chad, Niger, Nigeria, and Sudan.[95] The government has also employed Russian-backed mercenaries who "raped, tortured, and killed Muslim civilians" in a 2021 massacre at a mosque.[96] The victims of the violence appear to have been targeted solely on the basis of their religious identity. The human rights watchdog Amnesty International referred to the situation in Central African Republic as a clear-cut case of ethnic cleansing.[97]

---

[92] Human Rights Awareness and Promotion Forum, *Increasing Violence and Violations: The First 21 Days of the Antihomosexuality Act, 2023* (Kampala: HRAPF, 2023).

[93] Saiya, *The Global Politics of Jesus*, 111–114.

[94] Henry Kam Kah, "Anti-Balaka/ Séléka, 'Religionisation' and Separatism in the History of the Central African Republic," *Conflict Studies Quarterly* 9, no. 4 (2014): 38.

[95] Human Rights Watch, "Central African Republic: Muslims Forced to Flee: Christian Militias Unleash Waves of Targeted Violence," February 12, 2014, https://www.hrw.org/news/2014/02/12/central-african-republic-muslims-forced-flee.

[96] Pew Research Center, *Globally, Government Restrictions on Religion Reached Peak Levels in 2021, While Social Hostilities Went Down*, 33.

[97] Amnesty International, "Central African Republic: Ethnic Cleansing and Sectarian Killings," February 12, 2014, https://www.amnesty.org/en/latest/news/2014/02/central-african-republic-ethnic-cleansing-sectarian-violence/.

Finally, secularism has been in retreat in the Catholic-majority region of Latin America. In Latin America's largest country, Brazil, Christian nationalism thrived during the presidency of Jair Bolsonaro, a conservative Catholic who claimed to govern with the guidance of God in accordance with the Judeo-Christian tradition. Running on a campaign platform of "Brazil before everything, and God above all," Bolsonaro easily won the 2018 presidential election, owing in large part to the widespread support he received from Brazil's evangelical population.[98] In Mexico, home to the world's second-largest Catholic population after Brazil, a decline in political secularism has accompanied the growth of Protestantism and a majoritarian backlash to this growth, despite guarantees of church-state separation and religious freedom found in the Constitution.

The Pew Research Center has documented that both Brazil and Mexico have seen "high" levels of religious hostilities in recent years.[99] Once Bolsonaro was in power, Brazil witnessed a noticeable increase in acts of violent religious hostility. The majority, though not all, of these incidents were perpetrated by radical Pentecostal groups that, in the quest for Christian political privilege, have violently attacked non-Christians, especially followers of Afro-Brazilian religions such as the Macumba, Umbanda, and Candomblé.[100] In the year following Bolsonaro's election, a neo-Pentecostal group calling itself the Soldiers of Jesus unleashed a campaign of violence throughout the country. The group has been accused of killing Candomblé priests, stoning children, destroying religious artifacts, and forcibly shutting down non-Christian houses of worship.[101] Some Christian extremist groups have joined forces with drug traffickers and paramilitary forces in waging a holy war against non-Christian faiths.[102] On June 8, 2023—nearly two years to the day after the Capitol insurrection in the United States—Christian rioters stormed the presidential palace, capitol, and supreme court

---

[98] Catherine Osborn, "Bolsonaro's Christian Coalition Remains Precarious," *Foreign Policy*, January 1, 2019, https://foreignpolicy.com/2019/01/01/bolsonaros-christian-coalition-remains-precarious-brazil-brasil-president/.

[99] Samirah Majumdar and Virginia Villa, *Globally, Social Hostilities Related to Religion Decline in 2019, While Government Restrictions Remain at Highest Levels* (Washington, DC: Pew Research Center, 2021), 64.

[100] Virginia Garrard, "Hidden in Plain Sight: Dominion Theology, Spiritual Warfare, and Violence in Latin America," *Religions* 11, no. 2 (2020): 640.

[101] Terrence McCoy, "'Soldiers of Jesus': Armed Neo-Pentecostals Torment Brazil's Religious Minorities," *Washington Post*, December 9, 2019, https://www.washingtonpost.com/world/the_americas/soldiers-of-jesus-armed-neo-pentecostals-torment-brazils-religious-minorities/2019/12/08/fd74de6e-fff0-11e9-8501-2a7123a38c58_story.html.

[102] Kristina Hinz, Doriam Borges, Aline Coutinho, and Thiago Cury Andries, "The Rise of Brazil's Neo-Pentecostal Narco-Militia," Open Democracy, May 6, 2021, https://opendemocracy.net/en/democraciaabierta/rise-narco-militia-pentecostal-brazil-en/.

buildings after Bolsonaro lost his presidential reelection bid.[103] Like their American counterparts, they hoped to prevent the peaceful transfer of power from Bolsonaro to Brazil's newly elected president, Luiz Inácio Lula da Silva. Brazil's Christian extremists see themselves as waging a spiritual war against satanic forces for the soul of the country. The political empowerment of Christianity, they believe, can keep these malevolent powers at bay.

Mexico has rapidly become one of the world's most violent countries. A general climate of societal violence has targeted religious leaders, both Protestant and Catholic. Increasingly, the violence has taken on a religious dimension. Some Catholic groups have sought to shut out their Protestant competition through intimidation—cutting off water and electricity and preventing Protestant children from attending school—and sometimes violence, including beatings, forced displacement, mob attacks, and assaults on property. Christian Solidarity Worldwide, a human rights watchdog focusing on the global persecution of Christians, reported that local Mexican authorities frequently overlook or even excuse such incidents by claiming that under the Law of Uses and Customs, Mexican Catholics have the right to protect their culture.[104] This situation has created a culture of impunity in certain Mexican states conducive to religious conflict and violence.

In summary, despite media and scholarly portrayals, violent forms of Christian nationalism are not just a problem encountered in the Anglophone world. In the developing world as well we see Christian nationalist violence occurring in the Christian-majority countries of Central Africa and Latin America, namely Uganda, Central African Republic, Brazil, and Mexico. Of course, the specific forms that this violence takes vary from country to country and are driven by complex sociopolitical factors unique to each context. However, one consideration that remains constant across the cases involves the politicization and weaponization of the Christian faith for political gain. Political leaders have used religious rhetoric and identity to mobilize support or suppress dissent, thus exacerbating tensions and creating a fertile ground for violence. In the end, these cases illustrate the main argument of the book, that the political privileging of majoritarian religious communities corresponds to religious violence committed by extremists from these very communities.

---

[103] Eduardo Campos Lima, "Christians Represented Significant Faction of Capital Rioters in Brazil," Religion News Service, January 17, 2023, https://religionnews.com/2023/01/17/christians-represented-significant-faction-of-capital-rioters-in-brazil/.

[104] Christian Solidarity Worldwide, "A Culture of Impunity: Religious Discrimination in Mexico," 2020, https://www.csw.org.uk/2020-mexico-report.

Summary

This chapter has surveyed the relationship between the antisecular ideology of Christian nationalism—the belief that a certain form of Christianity should be privileged in a country's laws, policies, and civic life—and antiminority religious hostility. Contrary to essentialist accounts that consider Christianity to be a uniquely secular faith owing to the teachings of Christ and the first apostles on the separation of spiritual and temporal power, political secularism is, in fact, confronting threats across the Christian world. This secularism recession has corresponded to increasing antiminority violence.

Importantly, the cases of Christian violence discussed in this chapter are cases of violence dispensed by Christians in *Christian*-majority countries; it is the violence of the majority and not the minority. Christian violence can be understood as a majoritarian backlash to a changing religious landscape that is perceived to be shifting in favor of minority and nonreligious groups. Increasing pluralism, demands for equal rights by traditionally marginalized groups, and declining Christian populations, at least in the West, have combined to trigger feelings among Christian majorities that they are losing their historically dominant positions in society. This reality has reinforced in-group solidarity among Christian communities and increased hostility toward out-groups. Fringe elements from these "threatened" communities undertake violence as a means of reasserting their control over society.

The cases in this chapter show that Christian nationalism is not merely an academic concern that has little relevance in the real world. Christian nationalism is a global problem, plaguing both Western and non-Western countries alike. It is also a problem found in each of Christianity's major branches.

Having explored the relationship between religious privilege and violence in the world's largest faith tradition, Christianity, the next chapter turns to the world's second-largest religion, Islam.

Chapter 3
Islam

When one considers the relationship between faith and violence in the modern world, the religion of Islam—the world's second-largest religion with nearly 2 billion global followers—is likely the first to spring to mind. The spectacle of three commercial airliners hijacked by nineteen Muslim extremists crashing into two of the most recognizable buildings in the world is permanently etched in many memories. Since the terrorist strikes of September 11, 2001, attacks by Islamist extremists have claimed the lives of countless innocent civilians. Among the most prominent attacks are the 2002 Bali bombings, the 2004 Madrid train bombings, the 2004 Beslan school siege in Russia, the 2004 murder of Dutch filmmaker Theo van Gogh, the 2005 London bombings, the 2006 and 2008 Mumbai bombings, the 2011 Christmas Day bombings in Nigeria, the 2013 Boston Marathon bombings, the 2014 Peshawar school massacre, the 2015 attack at the headquarters of the satirical French magazine *Charlie Hebdo*, the 2016 Bastille Day attack in France, the 2017 attack on a Turkish nightclub, the 2019 Easter Sunday bombings in Sri Lanka, the 2021 Kabul school bombing, the 2022 mosque attack in Peshawar, and the 2023 attack by Hamas against Israel. Beyond these specific attacks, Islam has featured prominently in the internecine fighting in various Middle Eastern countries, the genocide of Yazidis, and the kidnaping of hundreds of schoolchildren in Nigeria, among other atrocities.

Indeed, religious violence today is far more prevalent in Islam than in any other of the world's religions. The world's deadliest militant organizations of the twenty-first century—al Qaeda, ISIS, Boko Haram—all claim to be acting in the name of Islam. As noted in the introductory chapter, this reality has led many pundits to conclude that Islam is inherently prone to violence. They argue that extremism is not marginal to Islam, as it is in other religions, but rather embedded in it. To support their contention, they highlight various violent passages in the Qur'an that appear to condone, if not command, violence against the enemies of Islam.[1] They cite the example of Islam's prophet, Muhammad, who waged wars against non-Muslims. They point to the prevalence of repression and violence—terrorism, civil wars, and hate crimes—in the Muslim world today. For contemporary critics of Islam, violence is simply hardwired into the religion. As I show in this chapter, however, the uniquely high levels of religious violence in Muslim-majority countries are not the product of Islamic texts or foundational doctrines, as commonly claimed; rather, they stem from a distinctively large political secularism deficit in the Islamic world. In other words, politics and not theology lies at the root of religion-related violence in Muslim-majority countries.

This chapter explores why there is a deficit of political secularism in the Muslim world, how this deficit encourages majoritarian violence, and if it can be overcome. It proceeds in three parts. The first section takes a bird's-eye view of how political secularism is compromised in the Muslim world. Importantly, it contends that attacks on political secularism stem from two sources: Islamist regimes and "pseudo-secularist" regimes. While the Islamist sources of Muslim privilege have long been recognized, equally important are the pseudo-secularist sources. Whereas Islamist regimes seek to establish Islamic law as the law of the land, pseudo-secularist regimes, in an attempt to withstand challenges to their rule, attempt to co-opt an amenable form of Islam through financial, legal, and social privileges not granted to non-Muslims. In this way, secular regimes hope to make Islam dependent on and beholden to the government. The second part of the chapter homes in on one particularly important way in which the rejection of political secularism promotes antiminority religious violence, namely the presence of so-called blasphemy codes in about half of Muslim-majority countries. These laws prohibiting acts or speech insulting to Islam are exploited as a legal basis for extremists to persecute those whose beliefs and activities, both non-Muslims and heterodox Muslims, fail to conform to the beliefs of the majority. As a result, Muslim-majority countries having in place and enforcing blasphemy codes experience much higher levels of religious violence than Muslim-majority countries not having or enforcing these laws. The third part of the chapter asks if political secularism—an idea that is highly controversial in the Muslim world—can take root in Muslim-majority countries.

---

[1] Qur'an 2:191, 9:5, 8:12.

How Political Secularism Is Undermined in the Muslim World

Recall from the first chapter that political secularism—encompassing the separation of religion and state, state neutrality in religious affairs, equality of faith communities, and religious liberty—becomes corrupted when the state treats certain religious groups better than others. The Muslim world, defined here as the approximately fifty countries where Muslims constitute the majority of the population, is the least politically secular group of countries in the world today. Political scientist Daniel Philpott finds that nearly three-quarters of Muslim-majority countries are religiously unfree.[2] This section takes a look at two general ways by which many Muslim-majority states undermine political secularism: Islamism and "pseudo-secularism."

The first and most obvious way the Islamic world has rejected political secularism owes to the ideology of Islamism or political Islam, the belief that Islam should serve as the foundation for all spheres of life, including law, politics, family, education, and society at large.[3] Central to Islamist thought is the identification of *jahiliya*—the state of ignorance or barbarism that exists apart from Islam—brought on by a godless form of Westernization and secularism. Islamists therefore equate political secularism with religious hostility and the removal of Islamic influences from public life and see it as an extension of Western imperialism by Christian states.[4] They reject the idea that human laws can be superior to Islamic law and that Islam can be relegated to the private realm with no application to public, including political, life. Their solution involves a political and social program that reclaims the sovereignty of God in every area of life and seeks to replace political systems entrenched in secularism with systems grounded in Islam. Islamism advocates using the laws of the state, and even the use of force, to uphold a rigid interpretation of Islam in both public and family life. In this way, Islamic civilization can flourish once again as it did prior to Western colonialism.

Present-day Islamist states can be understood as a continuation of a political system developed in the eleventh century that fused Islam and military and political power. This system manifestly rejected political secularism, declaring unorthodox and dissenting Muslims to be apostates.[5] Islamism, in both its Sunni and Shia expressions, experienced a major resurgence

---

[2] Daniel Philpott, *Religious Freedom in Islam: The Fate of a Universal Human Right in the Muslim World Today* (New York: Oxford University Press, 2019).

[3] Jocelyn Cesari, *What Is Political Islam?* (Boulder, CO: Lynne Rienner, 2017).

[4] Abdullah Saeed, "Secularism, State Neutrality, and Islam," in *The Oxford Handbook of Secularism*, ed. Phil Zuckerman and John R. Shook (Oxford: Oxford University Press, 2017), 188.

[5] Ahmet T. Kuru, *Islam, Authoritarianism, and Underdevelopment: A Global and Historical Comparison* (New York: Cambridge University Press, 2019).

during the 1970s and 1980s as part of a general global religious renaissance. The laws, policies, and beliefs that came with this Islamic awakening have remained part and parcel of many Muslim societies. In Muslim theocracies—the most extreme version of Islamism—sharia is the law of the land, and it is defined and applied by Muslim scholars and jurists who operate within the government itself. Today about half of Muslim-majority states can be broadly classified as "Islamist."[6]

In their attempt to impose a specific form of Islam, Islamist regimes suppress religious minorities and heterodox believers in the majority faith who depart from the official religious doctrine. Antiminority repression, sometimes involving outright bans on the practice of nonofficial faiths, is justified on the grounds that the visible presence and expression of minority religions risks undermining the unity of the Muslim community and provoking social instability. Consider Pakistan and Iran, two archetypal Islamist states. Article 2 of Pakistan's Constitution establishes Islam as the official religion of the country and permits no law "repugnant to Islam." Similarly, the Islamic Republic of Iran, according to Article 2 of its Constitution, is a system based on the beliefs in "the One God . . . His exclusive sovereignty and the right to legislate, and the necessity of submission to His commands." In Iran, the Council of Guardians has the power to vet parliamentary candidates and veto legislation, and another religious body, the Council of Experts, directly selects the supreme leader, the highest political office in the land. The constitutional and legal partiality shown to Islam in Islamist countries results in situations where the state either promotes the objectives of the favored religion through legislation and judicial powers or, as in the case of Iran, allows certain religious groups to hold special prerogatives in the government, such as standing titles, offices, or legal privileges in appointing state officials or vetoing government decisions.

Islamism, however, is not the only way that political secularism in the world of Islam has been undermined. In many cases, genuine political secularism has been usurped by a form of religious co-optation I call pseudo-secularism. These types of regimes are not religious; they are instead characterized by a commitment to secular nationalism, the creation of institutions tasked with monitoring Islamic institutions and cultivating an Islamic moderatism and, contrary to their Islamist counterparts, the repression or prohibiting of conservative forms of Islam. Pseudo-secular regimes simultaneously favor and repress Islam.

---

[6] Philpott, *Religious Freedom in Islam*, 114–148.

Pseudo-secularism, unlike Islamism, does not arise from a commitment to Islam but is rather an import of the West—a legacy of singularly Western developments such as the Enlightenment and the French Revolution. In the Muslim world, local secular elites were frequently placed into positions of power by colonial authorities as a way to maintain colonial rule. Pseudo-secular regimes would take root in several Muslim-majority countries whose political leaders sought to emulate the economic development, scientific advancement, social equality, and national unity found in Western states. Islam, they believed, was an impediment to the realization of these goals, insofar as it redirected the loyalty of Muslim citizens away from the temporal ambitions of the state and toward a higher power.

The legacy of pseudo-secularism in the Muslim world harks back to the fall of the Ottoman Empire following World War I. In Türkiye, Mustafa Kemal Atatürk led a political and cultural revolution based in the explicit rejection of religion in government. Atatürk asserted that Islam should have no religious, legal, or educational prerogatives in governing the state; instead he embraced a Western-oriented modernization program that entailed the abolishment of the caliphate, the Islamic court system, religious educational institutions, the public wearing of traditional Islamic garb, and the political expression of religion. Following the Second World War, Atatürk's secularist aspirations captured the imaginations of many political leaders across the Islamic world, particularly in Arab Middle Eastern and North African states, where secularist leaders hoped to reform Islam from the top down, making it dependent on and serviceable to the state.[7] Algeria, Chad, Egypt, Iraq, (pre-revolutionary) Iran, Jordan, Libya, Morocco, Syria, Tunisia, and all of the Muslim-majority states of Central Asia would follow in Türkiye's footsteps. For the leaders of these countries, Islam represented the past, secularization and modernization the future.

Today an imported form of secularism remains the guiding principle for a little less than half of Muslim-majority states. Most of these states, however, are not truly secular. Philpott explains that they "proffer a political theology of secularism, rooted in the West, holding that the public influence of Islam ought to be stifled so as to make way for nationalism, economic modernization, and modernity in general."[8]

---

[7] Scott W. Hibbard, *Religious Politics and Secular States: Egypt, India, and the United States* (Baltimore: Johns Hopkins University Press, 2010), 49–79.

[8] Philpott, *Religious Freedom in Islam*, 50.

Control over Islam is seen as necessary to ensure national security and social cohesion. Understanding that religious institutions serve as potential platforms for mobilization against the regime by providing disgruntled citizens with a ready-made venue to air grievances—yet also recognizing the profound importance of religion to the vast majority of their citizens—secularist leaders hope to lessen the likelihood of violent religious hostilities by artificially undercutting the supply of religion.[9] They do this by monitoring and sharply controlling mosques, schools, seminaries, universities, publications, broadcasting, and sometimes dress. Most of these countries have a Ministry of Religious Affairs dedicated to this very purpose. At times, the management of Islam has involved brutal suppression, including the jailing, torturing, and killing of Islamic leaders believed to be preaching an antistate message.

Yet repression is only one side of pseudo-secularism. Such states are simultaneously repressive of Islam *and* supportive of it. Both aspects of pseudo-secularism—religious repression and religious privilege—undermine genuine political secularism. Yet secularist political leaders see both as necessary for keeping Islam's power in check.

On the one hand, ostensibly secular leaders in the Muslim world view Islam as a potential threat to their rule. They thus seek to curtail its political influence, keeping a watchful eye on religious individuals and organizations, sometimes exploiting fear of an Islamist takeover to justify authoritarian measures against Islamic parties and institutions. For example, after the Islamic Salvation Front (FIS) won the first round of parliamentary elections in Algeria in 1992, defeating the ruling National Liberation Front, the military government intervened, nullifying the results and canceling the next round of elections. It further outlawed the FIS, arrested thousands of its members, and declared martial law. Similarly, the Turkish military repeatedly overthrew Islamist governments throughout the twentieth century in keeping with Atatürk's vision of a secular nation. In 2016, a faction of the Turkish military attempted a coup against sitting president Recep Tayyip Erdoğan. Unlike past coups, however, this one failed.

Secular autocrats may also offer some limited protections for non-Muslim minorities in the hopes of undercutting conservative Islam in their societies and maintaining a reservoir of loyalty. Such was the case in Saddam

---

[9] Gizem Arikan and Pazit Ben-Nun Bloom, "Religion and Political Protest: A Cross-Country Analysis," *Comparative Political Studies* 52, no. 2 (2019): 246–276.

Hussein's Iraq, Hosni Mubarak's Egypt, Muammar Qaddafi's Libya, and Bashar Assad's Syria, all of which offered support to Christians in the belief that Christian communities could help keep Islamism at bay. This strategy, though, has proven to be a double-edged sword for non-Muslim minorities. On the one hand, they receive some protection from the state; on the other, perceived support for these groups feeds into the narrative of a war against Islam, thereby leaving non-Muslim minority communities, perceived to be allies of secular, corrupt, and brutal regimes, even more vulnerable to societal hostilities. Importantly, though, the protection offered to non-Muslim minorities is always limited, and for some groups nonexistent. When the protection of non-Muslim minorities was seen as detracting from the goal of achieving stability, autocrats often looked the other way when minorities were harassed or assaulted by majoritarian Muslim groups.

At the same time, political leaders in the Muslim world have realized that the best way to keep Islam's political power under control is not by trying to eliminate it but by co-opting a moderate strain of Islam while simultaneously suppressing conservative forms. This approach to religion is particularly evident in the states of the Middle East and North Africa. For example, in the ostensibly secular state of Egypt, the Constitution "affirms that the principles of Islamic Sharia are the principal source of legislation" and declares Islam to be the "religion of the state." Morocco's Constitution similarly proclaims Islam to be the "religion of the state." Article 1 of Libya's Constitution declares Islam to be the religion of the country and "Islamic Sharia" to be the "main source of legislation." Algeria's Constitution describes the country as the "land of Islam" and Islam as the "religion of the state." The presidential oath requires the leader of Algeria to "glorify the Islamic religion." In these countries, fear of and support for Islam are inextricably intertwined. At times, pseudo-secularist leaders may even attempt to portray themselves as defenders of Islam to bolster their image among their devout populations. Iraq's Saddam Hussein, for example, undertook a Return to Faith campaign in 1993 as a means of brandishing his Islamic bona fides among Sunni Muslims. Yet even in these cases, the goal of advancing a secular nationalist vision of society remains firmly intact, and religion is seen as merely a tool toward this end.

Secular state leaders believe that such patronage is necessary for fostering a common identity, ensuring social stability, and protecting national security, all of which are believed to be threatened by unfettered religious actors.[10] These leaders also believe that through their support for a dominant form of Islam, they can bolster their domestic standing among their religious constituencies.[11] The religious majority, in turn, legitimates the authority of the government. Co-optation of Islam in this manner entails privileging a compliant form of Islam over other faith traditions, while conservative forms most likely to challenge the political status quo are presented as enemies of the nation intent on destroying the fabric of society. This strategy is grounded in the logic that a religion that enjoys the privilege of the state will be less likely to rebel against it. So long as Islam serves the interests of the state by promoting social cohesion and obedience to the regime, it continues to receive the support of the state. However, if it begins to acquire an independent base of power and challenge the regime, the state intervenes to keep the favored form of Islam in its proper place. Jonathan Fox contends that "supporting religion is among the most effective strategies to make religious institutions dependent on the government, and thereby more subject to its control."[12]

In summary, nowhere is the global crisis of secularism more evident than in Muslim-majority countries. Political secularism has come under attack from two different forces in the Islamic world: Islamism and pseudo-secularism. In both cases, authoritarian leaders, both Islamist and pseudo-secularist, have pursued religion-related policies that they believe can bolster their regimes. Privileging religion is believed to make the task of governing easier—and safer. Pseudo-secularism can be understood as a political strategy employed by secular leaders in Muslim-majority countries to keep religion's public power in check. This strategy involves coopting a moderate strain of the predominant faith tradition, making it dependent on and beholden to the government, while suppressing, sometimes brutally, nonprivileged religions, especially those believed to pose the greatest danger to the ruling regime. Islamism, by contrast, can be understood as a backlash against pseudo-secularism. This antisecular response is reflected most clearly in Islamist states that gain their legitimacy by propagating a particular Islamic ideology in virtually every aspect of social and political life. In contrast to pseudo-secular states,

---

[10] Jonathan Fox, Roger Finke, and Marie Ann Eisenstein, "Examining the Causes of Government-Based Discrimination against Religious Minorities in Western Democracies: Societal-Level Discrimination and Securitization," *Comparative European Politics* 17, no. 6 (2019): 885–909.

[11] Jonathan Fox, *The Unfree Exercise of Religion: A World Survey of Discrimination against Religious Minorities* (New York: Cambridge University Press, 2016).

[12] Fox, *Political Secularism, Religion, and the State*, 105.

Islamist states are characterized by their promotion of a conservative form of Islam through official religious institutions, their adherence to Islamic law, and their antipathy toward non-Muslims. That political secularism finds itself under attack on *two* fronts helps explain why the Muslim world is the least secular part of the world today. As discussed in the following section, these mutually reinforcing forces have also contributed to the uniquely high levels of violence prevalent throughout the Islamic world.

Muslim Privilege and Islamist Violence

It was not always the case that Muslim-majority countries were uniquely prone to violence. Until about the mid-twentieth century, minorities lived peaceably under Muslim rule. In the 1950s and 1960s, decolonization marked a transition from colonial governance and compliant local leaders to sovereign and independent states, free for the first time to chart their own course. The early postindependence leaders in the Middle East and North Africa yearned to transform their countries into modern, developed societies—to become like the West. Early on, there was reason for optimism: women enjoyed rights; artists and musicians could practice their crafts; journalists and authors could write freely. Yet political leaders ultimately proved to be uninterested in freedom and democracy; they turned out to be ruthless, corrupt, unaccountable, and deeply unpopular dictators intent only on securing their own rule. This aspiration required squashing dissent and throttling civil society. Most of all, as noted earlier, it meant reining in any form of independent Islam—from which the most serious threats to their dominance over society could arise—through a blend of co-optation and repression. Ordinary people longed for a simpler and purer alternative. They turned to Islam, which provided a robust source of empowerment. Islam became the language of resistance to despotic regimes, the Iranian Revolution forever changing the secularist trajectories of these countries. After Iran's revolution, the world of Islam became locked in a perpetual struggle between the forces of repressive secularism and the forces of Islamism.

Both Islamist and pseudo-secularist regimes in the Islamic world have encouraged violent religious hostilities, especially violence dispensed by religious majorities against minorities. This section takes a snapshot of several cases where the presence of Muslim privilege has emboldened violent vigilantes to take up the gun against minorities. It reveals similar dynamics underpinning violent religious hostilities in both Islamist and pseudo-secularist states in the Muslim world.

The most obvious examples of this dynamic can be witnessed in the Muslim world's major theocratic states, namely Saudi Arabia, Iran, and Afghanistan. In each case, the official alignment of mosque and state has emboldened Muslim extremists through cultures of impunity. Let us briefly consider each of these.

The Kingdom of Saudi Arabia thoroughly fuses Islam and the state to such an extent that it is arguably the least politically secular country in the world. According to its Constitution, the Kingdom of Saudi Arabia exists as a "sovereign Arab Islamic State," its system of government "established on the foundation of justice, Shoura (collective decision making), and equality in compliance with the Islamic Shari'ah (the revealed law of Islam)." The Saudi educational system "aims at the inculcation of the Islamic creed in the young generation." The two clauses of Article 23 mandate, "The State shall protect the Islamic Creed and shall cater to the application of Shari'ah" and "The State shall enjoin good and forbid evil, and shall undertake the duties of the call to Islam." A religious police force, the Committee for the Promotion of Virtue and the Prevention of Vice, enforces proper religious observance in public life. Those who depart from acceptable religious practices face a range of sanctions, including fines, deportation, and even execution. The government prohibits non-Muslims from worshiping in public or building houses of worship. The alliance between mosque and state in the kingdom harks back to a partnership between the Al Saud ruling family and a puritanical sect of Islam known as Wahhabism. The government's support, enforcement, and exportation of Wahabism has been enabled by its abundant oil wealth.

The kingdom's thoroughgoing fusion of Islam and the state has rendered religious minorities second-class citizens and encouraged violence against them. Shias, for example, the country's largest minority group at about 12 percent of the population, endure harsh governmental persecution. Since 2011, Saudi Arabia has executed scores of Shia participants in antigovernment protests. The state's ruthlessness toward its Shia population has inflamed existing sectarian tensions and produced periodic violent clashes between Sunnis and Shias. State-supported Sunni clerics have exploited their positions of prominence to incite hostility against

Shias. Terrorist outfits such as al Qaeda and ISIS have seized on hate speech by prominent clerics to justify anti-Shia violence, including attacks on Shia mosques that have resulted in the deaths of dozens of civilians.[13] When Saudi Shias are assaulted, they can expect little by way of justice from the legal system. While religious hostilities have diminished in recent years in the kingdom itself, the government continues to fuel religious conflict abroad in places like Yemen and Iraq—conflicts wherein some long-standing minority communities have been nearly eradicated. The continued culling of political secularism in the kingdom will likely prolong cycles of violence domestically and abroad, contributing to further regional instability.

While Saudi Arabia is a Sunni Muslim theocracy, Iran, the kingdom's Persian neighbor across the Gulf, is a Shia theocracy. The Iranian Constitution stands out as the only one among Muslim-majority countries to specify a specific branch of Islam, namely Twelver (Ja'afari) Shiism, as the country's official religion. As recounted earlier in the book, the Iranian Revolution of 1978–1979 brought to power an Islamist government following the overthrow of the secular Pahlavi dynasty. The Islamization of Iranian society quickly ensued, turning Iran into an official Islamic republic. The preamble to the Constitution opens with the following words: "In the Name of Allah, the Compassionate, the Merciful ... The Constitution of the Islamic Republic of Iran sets forth the cultural, social, political, and economic institutions of Iranian society on the basis of Islamic principles and norms, which represent the earnest aspiration of the Islamic Ummah (community of believers)." Article 2 grounds the system of governance in belief in the "One God," "Divine revelation," "the return to God in the hereafter," "the justice of God in creation and legislation," the "continuous leadership" of clerics, and the exalted dignity of man in accordance with "responsibility before God." The law criminalizes "corruption on Earth," "insulting the sacred," and "enmity against God." In 2021, Iranian president Hassan Rouhani amended the country's penal code to punish those guilty of "insulting Islam" and conducting "deviant activity" that contradicts Islam.[14]

---

[13] Adam Coogle, "Anti-Shia Bias Driving Saudi Arabia Unrest," Human Rights Watch, August 24, 2017, https://www.hrw.org/news/2017/08/24/anti-shia-bias-driving-saudi-arabia-unrest.

[14] U.S. Commission for International Religious Freedom, *2022 Annual Report* (Washington, DC: USCIRF, 2022), 22–23.

While some Iranian minorities may not be quite as imperiled as they are in Saudi Arabia—the Iranian Constitution designates Christians, Jews, and Zoroastrians as "people of the book"—Iran still exhibits a very high level of religious persecution made possible by its theocratic religion-state arrangement. In the Islamic Republic, the government bans conversion from Islam, imprisons those who proselytize other religions, and arrests those who attend underground non-Muslim houses of worship or print and distribute non-Muslim religious literature. Those convicted of blasphemy face possible execution. Even the so-called people of the book endure governmental discrimination and sharp restrictions on their religious practices. Importantly, as in the other Islamist states, the government does not restrict its persecution to religious minorities but targets all who do not conform to the prescribed religious path, including atheists and humanists. The government actively persecutes members of the LGBTQ community, putting to death those found to have engaged in same-sex relations.

The government's persecution of religious minorities has spawned majoritarian forms of violence. No minority group has suffered more than Baha'is, Iran's largest religious minority. One of the world's newer religious traditions, the Baha'i faith rejects an exclusivist rendering of religion and instead teaches that God reveals himself through different prophets, including the Buddha, Jesus, Mohammed, and the Baha'i faith's central figures, the Báb and Bahá'u'lláh. Baha'is stress the unity of humankind and of the world's different religions and question the finality of Muhammad's prophethood. Accordingly, Baha'i beliefs are deemed incompatible with traditional Islamic beliefs, and Baha'is frequently face persecution by those who believe that they are heretics and apostates. Baha'is are barred from holding leadership positions in the government, required to send their children to Islamic schools, banned from obtaining higher education, and forbidden to own property.[15] They have had their institutions disbanded, villages raided, properties confiscated, and holy sites desecrated.[16] The state frequently violates the physical integrity rights of Bahai's, subjecting them to arbitrary detention, solitary confinement, torture, and forced disappearance. Since the Islamic Revolution, hundreds of Baha'is have been executed

---

[15] Philpott, *Religious Freedom in Islam*, 125.
[16] Firuz Kazemzadeh, "The Baha'is in Iran: Twenty Years of Repression," *Social Research* 67, no. 2 (2000): 537–558; Siyyamak Zabihi-Moghaddam, "State-Sponsored Persecution of Baha'is in the Islamic Republic of Iran," *Contemporary Review of the Middle East* 3, no. 2 (2016): 124–146.

by the state. The government's maltreatment of Baha'is has created a societal climate of impunity in which Bahai's and those who advocate on their behalf endure regular physical attacks at the hands of Muslim extremists. Bahai's regularly see their cemeteries vandalized, their homes destroyed, their meeting places ransacked, their children abused, and their leaders beaten.[17] The societal violence against Bahai's is bolstered by a legal system that treats them as enemies of the state. According to one Baha'i advocate, "[T]he attackers are well aware that they will go unpunished."[18] That the Baha'i faith is one of the world's most peaceful religions, owing to its total rejection of violence, makes its violent persecution all the more ironic and tragic.

Afghanistan, too, is an Islamic republic, with the "sacred religion of Islam" being enshrined in its Constitution as the country's official religion. Article 3 of the document precludes the possibility of any form of political secularism emerging: "No law shall contravene the tenets and provisions of the holy religion of Islam in Afghanistan." The Afghan government does not recognize any non-Sunni religious communities. Upon assuming office, the president swears the following Oath of Allegiance: "In the name of God, Most Gracious, Most Merciful, I swear by the name of God Almighty that I shall obey and protect the Holy religion of Islam, respect and supervise the implementation of the Constitution as well as other laws, safeguard the independence, national sovereignty and territorial integrity of Afghanistan, and, in seeking God Almighty's help and support of the nation, shall exert my efforts towards the prosperity and progress of the people of Afghanistan."

In 2001, a U.S.-led military coalition attacked Afghanistan following its refusal to hand over the mastermind of the 9/11 attacks, Osama bin Laden. At the time, Afghanistan was ruled by a theocratic regime known as the Taliban. Following a war that lasted two decades, the Taliban retook control of Afghanistan in 2021, two decades after being removed from power by Washington. Despite concerns over Kabul's vulnerability to the Taliban absent foreign support, American president Joe Biden announced that all American forces would leave the country by September 11—exactly two decades after the 9/11 attacks. Following the American withdrawal, the Taliban swiftly and

---

[17] Baha'i International Community, *Violence with Impunity: Acts of Aggression against Iran's Baha'i Community* (New York: Baha' International Community, 2013).
[18] Bahá'í World News Service, "Increasing Violence against Iranian Baha'is Engineered by Government," BWNS, March 6, 2013, https://news.bahai.org/story/942/.

systematically retook parts of the country, ultimately capturing the capital of Kabul. The situation for religious minorities had been grave during the twenty-year war, as the Taliban and American troops fought a bloody war that claimed hundreds of thousands of lives. Even before the Taliban recaptured power in 2021, it was illegal to convert from Islam, and those who did so faced imprisonment, violence, and even death. Minorities endured persecution not only from the government but also from Islamist militants who targeted them in the name of Islam.

While the situation of Afghanistan's religious minorities was certainly perilous during the war, it grew considerably worse following the withdrawal of American troops. After retaking power, the Taliban, despite assurances that they had reconsidered some aspects of their Islamist ideology, imposed a harsh interpretation of sharia that has made life exceedingly difficult for minorities.[19] They reestablished their Ministry for the Promotion of Virtue and Prevention of Vice, a notoriously violent policing body that investigates and sanctions behavior deemed un-Islamic. Since its reconstitution, the ministry has banned certain behaviors, including Western-style haircuts, Western dress, most music, and dancing. Those who fail to faithfully comply with the Taliban's strict and brutal interpretation of Islam risk ostracization, torture, or even death. The rule of the Taliban since retaking power has been reminiscent of its brutal reign before the war.

This book has argued that religious favoritism by the state encourages extremist elements from the majority religious group to undertake vigilante violence, owing, in part, to the presence of a culture of impunity. However, Afghanistan represents a case where the rebels themselves have assumed power. That the leader of al Qaeda, Ayman al-Zawahiri, was assassinated in a 2022 drone strike by the United States in Afghanistan suggests that he, like his predecessor bin Laden, was being sheltered by the Taliban. Exacerbating the plight of minorities has been internal fighting between the Taliban and extremist Islamist groups like ISIS–Khorasan Province, which has left minorities caught in the middle. So precarious has the situation of minorities become that most belonging to Hindu, Sikh, Christian, Baha'i, Shia, and Ahmadiyya communities have fled the country or practice their

---

[19] Kanika Gupta, "Afghanistan Minorities Fear for Future Despite Taliban Assurances," *Nikkei Asia*, July 24, 2022, https://asia.nikkei.com/Politics/International-relations/Afghanistan-turmoil/Afghanistan-minorities-fear-for-future-despite-Taliban-assurances.

faith in secret.[20] These groups now teeter on the verge of extinction.[21] The only known Afghan Jew, Zebulon Simentov, fled the country in September 2021.[22] Those who remain face daily hardships. Shia Hazaras, for example, have been forcibly evicted from their homes and have had their properties seized.[23] The postwar culture of impunity has seen several massacres of Hazaras, attacks on Shia mosques during Friday prayers, and the vandalization and ransacking of Hindu temples and Sikh gurdwaras.[24] Hence minority communities are left with no safeguards against violent persecution, making them more vulnerable to violence than perhaps anywhere else in the world.

Theocracies such as Saudi Arabia, Iran, and Afghanistan are not the only Islamist countries where we see the symbiotic relationship between Muslim privilege and religious violence. The same can be seen, to varying extents, in Islamist *democracies*, including Pakistan, Nigeria, and Bangladesh—countries where electoral democracy coexists with governmental laws and policies that accord privilege to dominant forms of Islam but also repress non-Muslims and dissenting Muslims.

Arguably the most problematic Islamist democracy with respect to Muslim privilege and attendant religious violence is Pakistan, officially an Islamic republic whose capital city is Islamabad. The Pakistani Constitution declares Islam to be the "State religion of Pakistan" and the governance of the country to be based on "Islamic principles of social justice." Article 31 delineates a social context steeped in Muslim privilege, including state funding for Islamic educational institutions, the compulsory teaching of the Qur'an, the mandatory learning of the Arabic language, the observance of Islamic moral standards, and the funding of mosques. The Islamization of Pakistani society in this manner, however, stands in stark contradiction to the vision of a religiously plural and harmonious country laid out by Pakistan's founder,

---

[20] David Curry, "One Year after Withdrawal, Afghanistan Christians Are in Hiding or on the Run," Religion News Service, August 31, 2022, https://religionnews.com/2022/08/31/one-year-after-withdrawal-afghanistan-christians-are-in-hiding-or-on-the-run/; Associated Press, "Attacked at Home, Afghan Sikhs Find Community on Long Island," *NBC News*, September 1, 2022, https://www.nbcnews.com/news/asian-america/attacked-home-afghan-sikhs-find-community-long-island-rcna45688.

[21] Hafizullah Emadi, "Minorities and Marginality: Pertinacity of Hindus and Sikhs in a Repressive Environment in Afghanistan," *Nationalities Papers* 42, no. 2 (2014): 307–320.

[22] *VOA News*, "Taliban Say No Christians Live in Afghanistan; US Groups Concerned," May 16, 2022, https://www.voanews.com/a/taliban-say-no-christians-live-in-afghanistan-us-groups-concerned/6575680.html.

[23] Rhea Mogul, "Afghanistan's Religious Minorities Live in Fear of Taliban, Brace for Persecution," *NBC News*, August 29, 2021, https://www.nbcnews.com/news/world/afghanistan-s-religious-minorities-live-fear-taliban-brace-persecution-n1277249.

[24] U.S. Commission for International Religious Freedom, *2022 Annual Report*, 12–13.

Mohammed Jinnah. In his 1947 speech to the Constituent Assembly, Jinnah envisioned a country founded not on religious hierarchy and privilege but on diversity, tolerance, and harmony:

> You are free; you are free to go to your temples, you are free to go to your mosques or to any other place of worship in this State of Pakistan. You may belong to any religion or caste or creed—that has nothing to do with the business of the State. . . . We are starting in the days where there is no discrimination, no distinction between one community and another, no discrimination between one caste or creed and another. We are starting with this fundamental premise that we are all citizens, and equal citizens of one State. . . . I think that we should keep that in front of us as our ideal and you will find that, in course of time, Hindus would cease to be Hindus and Muslims would cease to be Muslims, not in the religious sense, because that is the personal faith of each individual, but in the political sense as citizens of the state.[25]

Pakistan has strayed far from Jinnah's hopeful vision. Less than a decade after the nation's establishment, the Constitution of 1956 prohibited the enactment of laws contrary to the Qur'an and Hadith. The Islamization of the Pakistani state continued apace over the next twenty years and took an extreme turn during the presidency of General Zia ul-Haq. After seizing power in a coup, Zia instituted a number of Islamist measures, including the compulsory collection of Zakat, the codification of *hudood* ordinances (punishments for violating Islamic law), the banning of alcohol, the bolstering of madrassas, the empowering of the Islamist movement Jamaat-e-Islami, the establishment of federal sharia courts, the creation of a religious advisory council known as the Majlis-e-Shoora, and the strengthening of the antiblasphemy law.[26] "Pakistan," Zia claimed, "was created in the name of Islam [and] will continue to survive only if it sticks to Islam. . . . [The] Islamic system [is] an essential prerequisite for the country."[27] Subsequent leaders would follow in Zia's Islamist footsteps.

---

[25] "Muhammad Ali Jinnah's First Presidential Address to the Constituent Assembly of Pakistan," August 11, 1947, http://www.columbia.edu/itc/mealac/pritchett/00islamlinks/txt_jinnah_assembly_1947.html.

[26] Shahid Javed Burki, Craig Baxter, Robert LaPorte, and Azfar Kamal, *Pakistan under the Military: Eleven Years of Zia ul-Haq* (Boulder, CO: Westview, 1991), 36–37.

[27] As quoted in William L. Richter, "The Political Dynamics of Islamic Resurgence in Pakistan," *Asian Survey* 19, no. 6 (1979): 555.

Zia's Islamization program would have catastrophic consequences for Pakistan's minority communities, especially Ahmadis, Shias, and Christians. During and following Zia's reign, several militant Islamist organizations came into existence, including Jamiat al-Mujahedin, Hizbul Mujahedin, and Abu Nidal. Muslim minorities, including Shias, Sufis, and Ahmadis, endured attacks perpetrated by these and other Islamist Sunni groups—including assassinations, mob violence, lynchings, terrorism, kidnapings, rapes, and vandalism of places of worship—all of which became an endemic feature of Pakistani life. Majoritarian violence has also been directed against non-Muslim minorities. Vigilante Muslim groups and individuals have been empowered by a state that has consistently demonstrated its willingness to turn a blind eye to antiminority crimes committed by privileged Sunnis, including militant Islamist groups.[28] Rare have been the cases where perpetrators of violence have been brought to book for their crimes. As discussed in the following section, Pakistan's blasphemy culture has encouraged numerous attacks upon those charged with insulting Islam. Mere charges of blasphemy have been enough to incite mob violence against people of faith who depart from the predominant Sunni expression of Islam.

In 1971, East Pakistan fought a war for independence against Islamabad. The new country, Bangladesh, like its parent state, was not founded as an Islamist country. That status changed only in 1981, when General Hussain Muhammad Ershad declared the country to be an Islamic republic, though a milder one than that of its erstwhile enemy. The Bangladeshi Supreme Court has upheld important aspects of political secularism and rejected blasphemy codes. Still, Muslim privilege is present at the local level, where clerics issue fatwas and enforce sharia. Recent times have seen the increasing passage of laws supportive of Muslim privilege. Militant Islamists in Bangladesh draw encouragement from official laws and policies that privilege Islam and protect extremists, but in some cases they believe that this support does not go far enough. Thus Islamist extremists have targeted both the government and minorities. My analysis of religious violence reveals, somewhat surprisingly, that Bangladesh ranks among the world's worst countries in per capita violent religious hostilities.

---

[28] Hannah Ellis-Peterson and Shah Meer Baloch, "Family of Pakistani Journalist Await Truth of His Death in Sweden," *The Guardian*, May 14, 2020, https://www.theguardian.com/world/2020/may/14/family-of-pakistani-journalist-await-truth-of-his-death-in-sweden.

Africa's most populous country, Nigeria, is a third example of an Islamist democracy. Although the Constitution provides for a secular state, including assurances of religious freedom, the country has also seen the rapid Islamization of society and expansion of sharia, especially in the north of the country. State authorities in Kano State, for example, have charged and convicted many individuals for blasphemy. These developments have coincided with a surge in religion-related hostilities, particularly between Muslims and Christians. Violent Muslim vigilantes have interpreted Islamist laws and policies as a sign of approval from the state to harass, intimidate, threaten, coerce, and attack non-Muslims. Further emboldening extremists is the fact that Nigeria is a failed state that is essentially incapable of protecting its citizens.[29] Local-level sharia and national state failure have colluded to produce a breathtaking culture of impunity with few consequences for perpetrators of violence. It was in this milieu that Boko Haram, once the world's deadliest terrorist group, gained traction. Its name meaning "Western education is sin" (*Jama'tu Ahlis Sunna Lidda'awati wal-Jihad*), Boko Haram gained international infamy for its kidnaping of schoolchildren, indiscriminate attacks on civilians, and the extensive use of children and women as suicide bombers. The group has also carried out extensive attacks against the country's minority Christian population. Beyond attacks by Boko Haram, charges of blasphemy and proselytizing to Muslims have encouraged mob violence against religious minorities.[30] Attacks on minority houses of worship, sacred sites, and religious leaders, abetted by a government that has frequently failed to take a stand against violent actors, remain a serious concern for Nigeria's minority religious communities.

Several smaller Muslim-majority states can also be characterized as Islamist, including the small countries forming the coastline of the Arabian Peninsula (Bahrain, Kuwait, Oman, Qatar, United Arab Emirates, and Yemen), three sub-Saharan African states (Comoros, Mauritania, and Sudan), and the archipelagic country of Maldives. In these countries can be seen similar patterns of Muslim privilege and majoritarian violence but generally to lesser degrees than seen in the preceding cases. All these Islamist states, both theocratic and democratic, demonstrate how Muslim privilege begets Muslim violence in Islamist states. Yet secularist regimes, too, like their Islamist counterparts, engender violence. Here we see at work

---

[29] Robert I. Rotberg, "Nigeria Is a Failed State," *Foreign Policy*, May 27, 2021, https://foreignpolicy.com/2021/05/27/nigeria-is-a-failed-state/.

[30] U.S. Commission for International Religious Freedom, *2022 Annual Report*, 24–25.

the dynamic of outbidding discussed in the first chapter. Two of the most prominent examples include Egypt and Algeria.

Though Algeria is widely understood to be a country rooted in secular nationalism, its laws privilege Islam. Article 2 of the Constitution declares Islam to be the "religion of the State," while Article 10 prohibits "infringing [against] Islamic morals." The presidential oath mandates the leader of the country to serve as head of the High Islamic Council and "glorify the Islamic religion." Algerian authorities have been increasingly prosecuting cases pertaining to blasphemy and attempted conversion of Muslims. The government has also cracked down on the ability of minority groups such as Christians and Ahmadi Muslims to worship collectively and of agnostic groups and individuals to exercise a public voice.[31] Nevertheless, the guiding philosophy of the Algerian government has remained resolutely secular, adopting a version of laïcité introduced by the French during its colonial occupation of the country.[32] The state has repressed conservative forms of Islam, at times through brutal force—mass imprisonment, torture, and summary executions—even as it has sought to promote an acceptable, moderate form of Islam from above through the control of religious education, the construction and governance of mosques, and the regulation of religious publications.

The actions of the Algerian government in 1992—canceling the elections in which Islamists had prevailed, conducting mass incarcerations, and declaring martial law—prompted former FIS members to form militant organizations such as the Armed Islamic Group and the Armed Islamic Movement. These extremist outfits carried the country into a decade-long civil war, which produced extreme violence and brutality, resulting in the deaths of between 100,000 and 200,000 people. Entire neighborhoods and villages were massacred. Although the bloodshed was carried out by Sunni Muslims fighting against the Algerian government, religious minorities also suffered greatly as they encountered groups committed to the imposition of sharia. Among the minority groups caught in the violence was Algeria's Ahmadi community, which was seen as a threat to the majority Sunni faith. Religious hostilities remain a persistent problem in the country.

Another North African country, Egypt, became embroiled in a brutal Islamist insurgency in the 1990s. A country widely believed to be governed

---

[31] U.S. Commission for International Religious Freedom, *2022 Annual Report*, 42–43.
[32] Michael D. Driessen, *Religion and Democratization: Framing Religious and Political Identities in Muslim and Catholic Societies* (New York: Oxford University Press, 2014), 135–179.

according to secular principles, the historical religion-state arrangement in Egypt, as in Algeria, can be better understood as a combination of support for and repression of Islam—pseudo-secularism. Since its independence, a series of Egyptian leaders, to greater and lesser extents, have worked to co-opt Islam for their own political gain. For example, even under ostensibly secular governments, the Constitution always acknowledged Islam to be the religion of the state and the principles of sharia to be the primary source of legislation. Egypt's first postindependence leader, Gamal Abdel Nasser, promoted a co-opted moderate form of Islam through support for religious broadcasting on state-run television, regulation of religious education in school curricula, and appointment of clerics. He even participated in the *hajj* in order to brandish his Islamic bona fides. This deference to Islam can be understood as an attempt to appease the Egyptian population, which always remained strongly religious in identity, belief, and practice. At the same time, Egyptian leaders have repressed conservative forms of Islam, in particular the Muslim Brotherhood, and exercised broad control over the entire religious landscape, including mosques, religious programming and publications, religious education, and clerics and imams.

The government's crackdown on Islamists intensified by magnitudes following an assassination attempt on Nasser. The repression of the Muslim Brotherhood in Egypt—and especially the brutal treatment of its spiritual leader, Sayyid Qutb—contributed to the radicalization of conservative Islam and the appeal of extremist ideas holding that the Islamic and Western worlds were locked in a perpetual spiritual struggle. Simultaneously, the state's crackdown on civil liberties among the broader population increased the credibility of these claims among the constituencies of radical groups. Eventually, these persecuted movements morphed into the world's deadliest transnational organizations.[33] While the co-opted "moderate" form of Islam remained quiescent in the face of increasing governmental repression as it continued to enjoy privileges from the Egyptian state, the non-co-opted, conservative, and repressed forms of Islam grew increasingly discontent. While Egypt experienced sporadic attacks in the 1980s, by the 1990s mass discontent among Islamists gave way to a prolonged insurgency throughout much of the decade, led by the militant groups al-Gama'a al-Islamiyya

---

[33] Lawrence Wright, *The Looming Tower: Al Qaeda and the Road to 9/11* (New York: Alfred Knopf, 2007), 52.

and al-Jihad. Because the violence was carried out by those who espoused a fundamentalist interpretation of Islam, it naturally targeted not only the Egyptian government but also those within Egyptian society who did not faithfully adhere to their teachings and vision for the country. Religious minorities in particular, especially Sufis, Coptic Christians, and Baha'is, suffered greatly at the hands of Islamist extremists. After about fifteen years of relative calm, the violence escalated again, this time with far more frequency than even the insurgency of the 1990s. As of this writing, violent religious hostilities remain a significant problem in Egypt. Coptic Christians continue to experience mob attacks and church destruction at the hands of actors in society. A branch of ISIS active in the Sinai Peninsula continues to stage attacks on Coptic Christians in rural areas. A rash of suspicious church fires across Egypt in 2022 suggests that Coptic Christians remain targets for militant Islamists. Exacerbating antiminority violence have been "persistent imbalances in the treatment of perpetrators from the Muslim majority and their Coptic victims." The government, for instance, has relied on extrajudicial "reconciliation councils" to mediate religious conflicts between Christians and Muslims, which rarely provide justice for victims of attacks.[34]

In summary, because both Islamist and secular governments in the Muslim world ally with and privilege Islam over other faith traditions, they inspire societal religion-related violence. Although embattled minorities have at times turned to the gun as a means to remedy their grievances, far more prevalent has been violence by groups representative of the religious majority directed against religious minorities, including non-Muslims and nonconformist Muslims. The widespread belief that Islam should enjoy special privileges from the state has contributed to the emergence of antiminority violence in both Islamist and pseudo-secularist states. Both types of states have contributed to cultures of impunity not only by failing to protect religious minorities from majoritarian violence but also by failing to hold perpetrators of antiminority violence accountable for their actions. The following section shifts attention to one of the most important ways by which the rejection of political secularism has fostered majority-on-minority violence in the Muslim world, namely the passage and enforcement of blasphemy codes.

---

[34] U.S. Commission for International Religious Freedom, *2022 Annual Report*, 42–43.

The Problem of Blasphemy Codes

To further understand the relationship between Muslim privilege and majoritarian violence, let us consider one very specific and important way by which political secularism is compromised in the world of Islam, namely through legal codes banning criticism of Islam, Islamic beliefs, Islamic figures, and Islamic institutions.[35] Known as "blasphemy laws" or "religious insult laws," these statutes are enacted for the ostensibly noble purposes of defending Islam and promoting communal harmony. Proponents of blasphemy laws believe that Islam requires punishment, including death, for the sin of blasphemy. Among the many purported blasphemers are the novelist Salman Rushdie, whose book *The Satanic Verses* earned him a fatwa by Iran's Ayatollah Ruhollah Khomeini calling for his death; Dutch filmmaker Theo van Gogh, whose short film critical of Islam, *Submission*, resulted in his murder at the hands of an Islamist extremist; and Pakistani Christian Aasia Bibi, whose purported insulting of the Prophet Muhammad led to her becoming the first woman to be sentenced to death under Pakistan's blasphemy code. (Bibi's sentence was commuted by the Pakistani Supreme Court in 2018, but only after she had already served nine years on death row.) About half of Muslim-majority countries have in place and enforce blasphemy codes.[36]

Ironically, however, despite the prevalence of blasphemy codes in the Islamic world, Islam's holy book, the Qur'an, never mentions blasphemy, much less mandate any punishment for insulting Islam or the Prophet Muhammad. In fact, a strong case can be made that in Islam acts of sacrilege should be met with restraint, peaceful admonition, and rational dialogue.[37] The erroneous belief that Islam prescribes punishment for blasphemy likely stems from the existence of blasphemy codes throughout much of the Islamic world. Historically, authoritarian leaders—both secular and Islamist—have exploited religious sensibilities as a shrewd way to gain and maintain power. By supporting blasphemy codes, these leaders hope to silence criticism of their regimes, redirect attention away from failed policies, foster national cohesion, co-opt Muslim leaders, and undercut detractors, in these ways

---

[35] Leonard W. Levy, *Blasphemy: Verbal Offense against the Sacred, from Moses to Salman Rushdie* (New York: Knopf, 1993).
[36] Angelina E. Theodorou, "Which Countries Still Outlaw Apostasy and Blasphemy?," Pew Research Center, July 29, 2016, www.pewresearch.org/fact-tank/2016/07/29/which-countries-still-outlawapostasy-and-blasphemy/.
[37] Qur'an 9:47, 15:7, 16:102, 17:48, 33:58–59, 73:10.

entrenching their own rule.[38] Though they may not personally be very religious, these leaders are often backed by Islamists who regard defamation of Islam as heresy.[39] By branding their opponents "apostates," "blasphemers," or "enemies of Islam," political elites can strengthen their domestic standing by claiming that they are defending Islam. For example, in Pakistan blasphemy laws were greatly strengthened during the presidency of General Zia, who used them as a way to fuse religion and nationalism, gain the support of conservative Islamist forces, silence moderates and liberals, and weaken opponents.[40]

Laws against religious defamation violate religious equality and religious freedom, two fundamental aspects of political secularism. Paul Marshall and Nina Shea write that blasphemy codes "punish independent and innovative thinking, leading to the curtailment of other freedoms."[41] What constitutes blasphemy is defined by those in positions of religious and political power who claim to represent the proper view of Islam, leaving minorities and dissenters vulnerable. Accordingly, blasphemy laws legalize discrimination against minority religious groups and codify the existing reality of religious persecution in society.[42] Human rights organizations aver that laws criminalizing blasphemy open the door to repression of heterodox religious communities or nonbelievers by the state, which sometimes imprisons or punishes in other ways those charged with defaming religion.[43]

Importantly, laws prohibiting the defamation of religion are centrally related to violence in the Islamic world. Blasphemy laws naturally encourage majoritarian violence by creating a culture of vigilantism in which extremists, claiming to be the defenders of Islam, attack those they believe are guilty of heresy. Research shows that countries enforcing blasphemy laws suffer disproportionately from communal violence, including terrorism and mob violence.[44]

---

[38] Ron E. Hassner, "Blasphemy and Violence," *International Studies Quarterly* 55, no. 1 (2011): 26.

[39] Olivier Roy, *Secularism Confronts Islam*, trans. George Holoch (New York: Columbia University Press, 2013).

[40] Burki et al., *Pakistan under the Military*.

[41] Paul Marshall and Nina Shea, *Silenced: How Apostasy and Blasphemy Codes Are Choking Freedom Worldwide* (Oxford: Oxford University Press, 2011), 6.

[42] Grim and Finke, *The Price of Freedom Denied*, 32.

[43] Jo-Anne Prud'homme, *Policing Belief: The Impact of Blasphemy Laws on Human Rights* (Washington, DC: Freedom House, 2010); Human Rights First, *Blasphemy Laws Exposed: The Consequences of Criminalizing "Defamation of Religions"* (New York: Human Rights First, 2012).

[44] Pew Research Center, *Rising Restrictions on Religion* (Washington, DC: Pew Research Center, 2011), 67–73; Nilay Saiya, "Blasphemy and Terrorism in the Muslim World," *Terrorism and Political Violence* 29, no. 6 (2017): 1087–1105.

This dynamic unfolds in the following way. Proponents of blasphemy believe that there is a single, correct interpretation of Islam, that this understanding of the faith should be protected by law, and that those who insult the acceptable practice of Islam should face sanctions. Religious defamation laws thus preclude the development of a multiplicity of views within Islam and between Islam and other faith traditions. Instead, the prevention of peaceful dialogue and the lack of intellectual diversity stifle the healthy exchange of ideas and insulate radical theologies by smothering open debate and discourse regarding the proper construal of the Qur'an and Hadith, instead of allowing for the exposing of logical inconsistencies and incorrect interpretation by extremists.[45] In essence, acceptable and unacceptable ideas about Islam and its interpretation are decided a priori. As religious liberty attorney Asma Uddin explains, "Armed with ... blasphemy laws, the state determines which interpretation of a given religion is 'correct' and worth preserving and, thus, interferes with the autonomy of individuals and religious organizations to decide theological matters for themselves."[46] Where laws against blasphemy exist, radicals do not have their views challenged and critiqued in the marketplace of ideas, so they are not forced to defend them from competing views.[47] Reformers (including those of the majority faith who disagree with blasphemy codes) are silenced. Thus the moderation that accompanies the proliferation of doctrines, interpretations, and practices has little room to flourish.[48] The standards for blasphemy are often highly subjective, largely dependent on one's own religious convictions and how another's beliefs and practices are construed. In this way, blasphemy codes prevent the open debate that allows a healthy political secularism to flourish, one that protects all of a country's citizens regardless of their personal religious convictions.

Rarely do Muslim governments execute those accused of blasphemy. A much more dire threat comes from the extralegal enforcement of blasphemy codes by mobs, vigilantes, and terrorists. In countries with blasphemy codes, those who dare to criticize or insult the dominant interpretation of Islam

---

[45] Prud'homme, *Policing Belief*, 3–4.

[46] Asma T. Uddin, "Blasphemy Laws in Muslim-Majority Countries," *Review of Faith & International Affairs* 9, no. 2 (2011): 52.

[47] Toft, Philpott, and Shah, *God's Century*, 121–73; Grim and Finke, *The Price of Freedom Denied*, 61–87.

[48] Timothy Samuel Shah, *Religious Freedom: Why Now? Defending an Embattled Human Right* (Princeton, NJ: Witherspoon Institute, 2012), 65–68.

are accused of blaspheming against the "one true faith." Charges of religious defamation work to kindle passions against those slandering Islam, motivate vigilantes, and justify acts of violence. As attorney Amjad Mahmood Khan argues, "The [blasphemy] codes thus provide legal cover for terrorists to commit atrocities in the name of protecting Islam's integrity based on their warped view of the faith."[49] Violent vigilantes have attacked with impunity individuals and the homes, places of worship, and businesses of those believed to be blasphemers, using the very laws passed by the state to justify their violence. In turn, the state commonly turns a blind eye to violence carried out by adherents of the dominant Islamic tradition, on whose behalf it ostensibly proscribes blasphemy in order to retain its good standing with that religious group. Violent nonstate actors thus feel empowered to commit acts of vigilantism with little or no fear of governmental reprisal because blasphemy laws, in effect, lend the authority of the state to extremists. Rather than control the forces of extremism, blasphemy laws appease and encourage them. The result, expectedly, is that states that attempt to curry favor with radicals embolden them to take matters into their own hands.

Importantly, both Islamist and pseudo-secular countries have in place blasphemy codes. Pakistan, an example of the former, has arguably the world's most draconian blasphemy law. Found in Section 295 C of the legal code, it reads as follows: "Use of derogatory remarks etc. in respect of the Holy Prophet: Whoever by words, either spoken or written, or by visible representation, or by any imputation, innuendo, or insinuation, directly or indirectly, defiles the sacred name of the Holy Prophet Muhammad (peace be upon him) shall be punished with death, or imprisonment for life and shall also be liable to fine."

In 1987, Pakistan's Federal Shariah Court ruled that the only acceptable punishment for blasphemy was death. However, the vagueness of the language concerning blasphemy allowed radicals to interpret the code in very loose ways and openly persecute those they believed to be guilty of defiling, in any way, "the sacred name of the Holy Prophet Muhammad." Charges of blasphemy often involve fabricated or petty accusations used to prompt violence against those accused or the larger communities to which

---

[49] Amjad Mahmood Khan, "Pakistan's Dark Days: Terrorism and the Blasphemy Laws," *Foreign Affairs*, December 21, 2014, http://www.foreignaffairs.com/articles/142711/amjad-mahmoodkhan/pakistans-dark-days.

they belong.⁵⁰ For example, in 2013 an accusation of blasphemy against a Christian ignited a wave of attacks on the predominantly Christian neighborhood of Lahore known as Joseph Colony, resulting in the destruction of at least 150 Christian homes, businesses, and churches. Hundreds of Christians were forced to flee for their lives.

Those who speak out against Pakistan's blasphemy culture or represent those accused of blasphemy invite retaliation and are sometimes themselves killed, as in the cases of Punjab governor Salman Taseer and Minorities Minister Shahbaz Bhatti—outspoken politicians who courageously took a public stand against the country's blasphemy laws and specifically against the death sentence of Aasia Bibi. The international outcry surrounding Bibi's sentence and her eventual release did not prompt an about-face, however, as demonstrated by the brutal murder of a Sri Lankan factory worker who allegedly insulted Islam by removing posters inscribed with verses from the Qur'an, the vicious beating of a Christian nurse accused of blasphemy by her coworkers, and the mob attack of a Hindu temple in retaliation for an alleged instance of blasphemy by an eight-year-old child.⁵¹ Though the government has publicly denounced such violence, it has done little to protect minority communities.⁵² The courts, likewise, have done little to provide justice to victims of blasphemy-related violence.

Beyond Pakistan, blasphemy codes exist in other Islamist states. In Nigeria, charges of blasphemy have generated mob violence, leading to the deaths of hundreds and the strengthening of militant groups like Boko Haram. Similar dynamics have played out in Saudi Arabia, Iran, Afghanistan, and various other countries with blasphemy laws. In these countries, charges of blasphemy have resulted in the deaths of filmmakers, satirists, artists, journalists, novelists, and heterodox Muslim believers. In the end, these cases demonstrate how blasphemy codes weaken reform-minded moderate Muslims, silence members of minority faiths and political dissidents, and promote extremism and antiminority violence.

---

⁵⁰ Ishtiaq Ahmed, "The Spectre of Islamic Fundamentalism over Pakistan," in *Pakistan in Regional and Global Politics*, ed. Rajshree Jetly (London: Routledge, 2009), 150–80.

⁵¹ U.S. Commission for International Religious Freedom, *2022 Annual Report*, 28–29.

⁵² Amnesty International, "Pakistan: Authorities Must Ensure Protection of Minority Christian Community," August 16, 2023, https://www.amnesty.org/en/latest/news/2023/08/pakistan-authorities-must-ensure-protection-of-minority-christian-community/; Human Rights Watch, "Pakistan: Mob Attacks Christian Settlement," August 22, 2023, https://www.hrw.org/news/2023/08/22/pakistan-mob-attacks-christian-settlement.

Blasphemy laws can also exist in ostensibly secular countries. For example, in Egypt, a country with laws against insulting "heavenly religions," the renowned liberal thinker Farag Foda was murdered in 1992 by those claiming he was "an apostate who deserved to die."[53] Several bloggers have been detained for blasphemy-related offenses in accordance with Article 98(f) of the Penal Code. These cases have involved not only Egyptians but also foreign nationals. Critics allege that Egypt's blasphemy law disproportionately affects religious minorities and can be exploited to persecute individuals who express divergent religious beliefs or criticize majoritarian religious interpretations. There have been calls from domestic and international human rights organizations to reform or repeal these laws to ensure greater protection of freedom of speech and belief in Egypt.

In summary, blasphemy codes are among the most important ways by which political secularism is compromised in the world of Islam. These laws prohibiting defamation of religion are often promoted as a way to protect Islam from being "insulted," safeguard the integrity of religious communities and traditions, preserve social harmony and morality, and reduce religious hostilities. In reality, however, blasphemy codes do not increase respect for Islam and Muslims—the very thing they are supposed to do—but instead punish religious minorities who hold unorthodox beliefs, coerce religious conformity, silence opposing religious views, and weaken the forces of moderation. Not only do blasphemy codes promote intolerance and increase the political salience of religion, in restricting the limits of acceptable discourse, they also promote a culture of vigilante justice in the countries where they exist, in this way encouraging majority-on-minority violence. This occurs because blasphemy laws, instead of protecting religion from insult or offense, provide extremists with a pretext for attacking those believed to be guilty of religious defamation. Thus the application of blasphemy laws serves to prompt and exacerbate violent religious hostilities rather than prevent them.

Can Muslim-Majority Countries Accept Political Secularism?

The discussion thus far, especially the case of blasphemy codes, reveals that the contemporary Muslim world exhibits uniquely high levels of religious privilege and attendant majoritarian violence. Does this mean that Islam

---

[53] Marshall and Shea, *Silenced*, 74.

inherently rejects political secularism? Critics of Islam have long noted that whereas Jesus, the founder of Christianity, drew a sharp distinction between the temporal and spiritual realms of authority in his command to "render unto Caesar the things that are Caesar's and to God the things that are God's," the Prophet Muhammad functioned as both a spiritual and a military leader, amalgamating the spheres of authority that Jesus had separated. Whereas Christianity remained separate from and often suppressed by the state during the first three centuries following the crucifixion of Jesus, Islam, by contrast, *was* the state and thus associated with the exercise of temporal authority from the beginning of its existence.[54] According to this view, the lack of political secularism in Muslim-majority countries, including the paucity of minority rights, mosque-state separation, and religious liberty, stems from Islam's foundational doctrines, sacred texts, and legacy of military conquest.[55] The hardwired antipathy toward political secularism has produced unchecked political authority, few cross-cutting cleavages within Muslim societies, and little tolerance for religious diversity. The eighteenth-century French philosopher Montesquieu wrote in his classic work *The Spirit of the Laws* that "moderate government" (read "secular") "is better suited to the Christian religion, and despotic government to Mohammedanism."[56] Political secularism is thus seen as a uniquely Western mode of governance that has little resonance in the Muslim world. At first blush, it appears that the cynicism of the skeptics is justified. Indeed, the fusion of Islam and the state in many parts of the Muslim world has resulted in a major deficit of political secularism, resulting in the open persecution of religious minorities.

To make matters worse, the concept of political secularism carries connotations in the world of Islam very different from those in the West. Political secularism in the West is often associated with a set of positive attributes: democracy, development, human rights, modernity, and freedom. In the Islamic world, however, political secularism tends to be viewed in a much more negative light, associated not with democracy, freedom, and human

---

[54] Bernard Lewis, *The Political Language of Islam* (Chicago: University of Chicago Press, 1991), 15; Bernard Lewis, *Islam and the West* (Oxford: Oxford University Press, 1993), 135; Huntington, *The Clash of Civilizations*, 70.

[55] Elie Kedourie, *Democracy and Arab Culture* (Washington, DC: Washington Institute for Near East Policy, 1992).

[56] Charles de Secondat Baron De Montesquieu, *Montesquieu: The Spirit of the Laws*, ed. Anne M. Cohler, Basia Carolyn Miler, and Harold Samuel Stone (Cambridge: Cambridge University Press, 1989), 461.

rights but with oppression, corruption, economic stagnation, colonialism, and Westernization.[57] Thus, for different reasons, both critics of Islam and Islamists arrive at the same conclusion: Islam and political secularism cannot coexist. Islamic skeptics aver that Islam inherently rejects secularism owing to its foundational texts and doctrines; Islamists believe that Islam rejects political secularism because it is an undesirable import of the West.

There are at least three reasons to think, though, that the argument that Islam inherently rejects political secularism may be exaggerated: variation in Islamic thought about political secularism across time, variation in levels of political secularism across space, and the Quranic basis for political secularism. The first reason concerns Islam's acceptance and subsequent rejection of political secularism over time. Essentialist renderings of Islam contend that political secularism is theologically incompatible with Islam. However, a number of scholars of Islam have argued, contrary to this view, that the separation of Islam and power is not inconsistent with even early Islamic history. Although religious and political power were united under Muhammad's leadership of the early ummah, between the eighth and eleventh centuries several premodern Islamic polities exhibited some degree of separation of spiritual and political authority, even if they did not conform to post-Enlightenment views of political secularism. This shift was made possible when political power began to be wrested from caliphs and transferred to secular sources of authority. At the same time, Islamic scholars (ulema) began to value their independence from political authorities, believing that funding from the state would serve to corrupt the message of Islam. Because the ulema believed that the state should not be in a position to determine or enforce Islamic doctrine, they created the doctrine of the charitable trust (waqf) to support Islamic institutions and activities apart from state support, thus retaining Islam's independence from political rulers and upholding the integrity of Islamic teachings as an independent source of moral authority. Accordingly, Muslim scholars typically rejected state appointments, which they believed would compromise their integrity and the message of the Prophet. Political scientist Ahmet Kuru notes that both the founders of the four major branches of Sunnism and early Shia leaders endured persecution owing to their refusal to serve as instruments of the state.[58] To be sure, these ancient polities remained officially Islamic, but Islam began to develop its

---

[57] Nader Hashemi, *Islam, Secularism, and Liberal Democracy: Toward a Democratic Theory for Muslim Societies* (New York: Oxford University Press, 2009).
[58] Kuru, *Islam, Authoritarianism, and Underdevelopment*, 71–116.

own hierarchies separate from those of the political orders that ruled them.[59] Scholars of Islam have long noted how Islamic civilization flourished during this period in the areas of science, medicine, architecture, literature, and mathematics.

The widespread Islamism one sees today has never been an intrinsic part of Islam, Kuru argues, and emerged only in the eleventh century in the form of a new ulema-state alliance, a partnership between religious and political authorities that has shaped many Muslim-majority countries to this day. Nevertheless, even after the eleventh century, a commitment to political secularism existed in parts of the Muslim world. For example, political secularism could be found in the early modern Mughal Empire in South Asia, especially under the reign of its third emperor, Abu Akbar, who believed that all religions should be respected and treated equally. Akbar included in his government many Hindus, terminated the tax (*jizya*) that had been imposed on non-Muslims, and allowed non-Muslims to be ruled in accordance with their own customs and laws. During the age of colonialism, Islamic modernist thinkers argued against the inseparability of religion and state and advocated for political secularism as a necessary way to *strengthen* Islam and resist Western imperialism. In the nineteenth century through the first half of the twentieth, Muslim thinkers such as Ali Abdel Raziq, Muhammad Abduh, Abd al-Rahman al-Kawakibi, Rashid Rida, Taha Hussein, and Mohammed Taga maintained that political secularism, including tolerance for minorities, not only did not violate the tenets of Islam but was actually more consistent with Islamic history than an Islamic state. They argued that the separation of Islam and state was foundational to the message of the Prophet Muhammad. The existence of Muslim thinkers such as these belies the claim that Islam inherently rejects political secularism.

Beginning in the mid-twentieth century, however, a decidedly antisecular movement began to reemerge across the Islamic world. The Islamist resurgence can be traced to ideologues such as Sayyid Qutb and Sayed Abul A'la Maududi and the groups they founded, namely Qutb's Muslim Brotherhood and Maududi's Jamaat-e-Islami.[60] Seeing Islam subjugated by pro-Western, corrupt "secular" regimes, they reasoned that the problems confronting the Muslim world resulted from Muslims collectively turning their backs on God. Secularism, they believed, had shackled traditional

---

[59] Ira M. Lapidus, "The Separation of State and Religion in the Development of Early Islamic Society," *International Journal of Middle East Studies* 6, no. 4 (1975): 363–385.
[60] Sayyid Qutb, *Al-Adala al-Ijimaiyya fi-I Islam* (Beirut: Dar al-Kitab al-Arabi, 1979).

Islamic morality and unmoored society from the truth of Islam. Healthy Islamic polities could be sustained only if they embraced Islamic norms and values and rose up against their colonial masters. The solution thus required an unequivocal return to Islamic principles that would thoroughly infuse law, politics, economics, and culture. Properly Islamized states, they believed, would fuse state power and Islam and be ruled in accordance with sharia. Such states, according to Maududi, endeavor to "mould every aspect of life and activity in consonance with its moral norm and programmes of social reform. In such a state, no one can regard any field of his affairs as personal and private."[61] He declared that those who participated in secular politics were in rebellion against Allah and Islam.[62] The global Islamist movement enjoyed a major boost following the Iranian Revolution in 1979, with some of the most ostensibly secular of Muslim-majority countries—Egypt, Algeria, Türkiye—witnessing a major resurgence of political Islam. In Türkiye, political Islamists have held power since the beginning of the twenty-first century, reversing decades of top-down secularization. Even some putatively secular leaders like Iraq's Saddam Hussein invoked Islam in defense of their domestic and foreign policy goals.[63] Islamic revivalism also paved the way for a massive explosion of violence that would engulf large parts of the Islamic world in the following decades. The ideas of Qutb and Maududi would be taken up by some of the world's most dangerous ideologues, including bin Laden and al Zawahiri.

This Islamist resurgence being recognized, the fact that attitudes among Muslim intellectuals toward political secularism have fluctuated over time, coupled with the relative recentness of Islamist revivalism, suggests that Islam does not inherently reject political secularism. Indeed, some scholars of Islam have argued that a secular state built on equality and minority rights is more consistent with Islamic history than the Islamist regimes of today. In fact, through much of history, the Muslim world, including the lands of the Middle East, was hospitable to religious minorities at the same time that Christian Europe was killing or expelling them. Muslims and non-Muslims had extensive and intimate contacts that involved social as well as intellectual association. The reciprocal partnership that developed between Islam and the state is not intrinsic to Islam but rather is historically constructed

---

[61] Abul A'la Maududi, *Islamic Law and Constitution* (1960; New Delhi: Taj, 1986), 144–145.
[62] Ashgar Ali Engineer, "Islam and Secularism," in *The Blackwell Companion to Contemporary Islamic Thought*, ed. Ibrahim M. Abu-Rabi (Oxford: Blackwell, 2006), 338.
[63] Lewis, *Islam and the West*, 184.

and whose legacy persists across many Muslim-majority countries today. Modern Islamism should be understood as a product of its times, namely a response to the modern world. The Sudanese scholar Abdullah Saeed concludes that despite negative historical experiences with political secularism, the Islamic world can accept its basic principles.[64]

The second reason to question the incompatibility of Islam and political secularism concerns variation across space. Although the Muslim world today displays the highest levels of religious privilege in the world, sites of political secularism can still be found. On the western and eastern margins of the Islamic world we find seeds of political secularism: West Africa (Burkina Faso, Gambia, Guinea, Mali, Niger, Senegal, and Sierra Leone) and Southeast Asia (Malaysia and Indonesia). In these regions, Islamic privilege is lower than in the Arab world. Moreover, whereas authoritarian leaders in the Middle East keep Islamic institutions on a short leash, major religious organizations in Southeast Asia, including the world's largest Muslim organization, Indonesia's 90-million-member Nahdlatul Ulama, and in West Africa exist independently of the state.

Consider the case of Indonesia. At first blush, Indonesia, the world's largest Muslim state and fourth most populous country, appears to be a weak case for the possibility of political secularism in Islam. Its guiding philosophy is Pancasila (Godly Nationalism). Of Pancasila's five undergirding principles, *Ketuhanan yang Maha Esa* (Belief in the Almighty God) is at the top of the list. Furthermore, the government offers official recognition to six belief systems: Buddhism, Catholicism, Confucianism, Hinduism, Islam, and Protestantism. Critics of Pancasila point out that these aspects of Indonesia's unique religion-state arrangement violate in some way all of the principles of political secularism. For example, the International Humanist and Ethical Union, an atheist group, has criticized the government's approach to religion because it does not include a right to reject religion. The group argued that this enables a culture of repression against atheists and anyone else who does not subscribe to one of the belief systems officially recognized by the state.[65] A closer look, though, complicates the picture.

---

[64] Saeed, "Secularism, State Neutrality, and Islam," 188.
[65] Kate Hodal, "Indonesia's Atheists Face Battle for Religious Freedom," *The Guardian*, May 3, 2012, https://www.theguardian.com/world/2012/may/03/indonesia-atheists-religious-freedom-aan; Humanists International, "Secular Groups Criticise 'World Statesmen Award' for Indonesian President," May 10, 2013, https://humanists.international/2013/05/secular-groups-criticise-world-statesmen-award-indonesian-president/.

Owing to the commitment to equality and freedom displayed by a succession of Indonesian presidents—Abdurrahman Wahid, Megawati Sukarnoputri, Susilo Bambang Yudhoyono, and Joko Widodo—Indonesia never became a fertile breeding ground for extremism as other Muslim-majority countries have. Moreover, although illiberal Islamist groups are present and allowed to operate, they must contend with the uniquely tolerant version of Islam that has been present in Indonesia since the thirteenth century and is now embodied in the country's largest Muslim organizations—Nahdlatul Ulama and Muhammadiyah—both of which offer the theological resources and social presence to support an inclusive and moderate understanding of Islam.[66] According to political scientists Daniel Finnbogason and Isak Svensson, the region of Southeast Asia stands out for not having experienced a single jihadist civil war from 1975 to 2015. Even today the countries of the region have few links to pan-jihadist movements.[67] For a country with a population numbering around 270 million, Indonesia has been remarkably free from religious violence, averaging around five identifiable religion-related attacks annually since 9/11—nearly five times lower than the average for all countries in the Islamic world.[68] Unfortunately, reversals in a commitment to political secularism have coincided with growing extremism in recent years, but if Indonesia can reaffirm its commitment to inclusivity, tolerance, and freedom for all, the threat of religious violence will likely wane accordingly.

Islamic privilege and violence have been similarly absent in Muslim West Africa. In the Muslim-majority countries of Burkina Faso, Gambia, Guinea, Mali, Niger, Senegal, and Sierra Leone, governments have historically refused to impose a certain kind of Islam upon society as in Islamist or pseudo-secularist regimes, but instead have promoted the inclusion of religious minorities, including the Ahmadiyya and Sufi forms of Islam that frequently elicit repression elsewhere.[69] They protect the right to religious freedom not just on paper but in practice. Unlike in Muslim Southeast

---

[66] Robert W. Hefner, *Civil Islam: Muslims and Democratization in Indonesia* (Princeton, NJ: Princeton University Press, 2000); Jeremy Menchik, *Islam and Democracy in Indonesia: Tolerance without Liberalism* (Cambridge: Cambridge University Press, 2016).

[67] Daniel Finnbogason and Isak Svensson, "The Missing Jihad: Why Have There Been No Jihadist Civil Wars in Southeast Asia?," *Pacific Review* 31 (2018): 96–115.

[68] Nilay Saiya, "Why Freedom Defeats Terrorism," *Journal of Democracy* 32, no. 2 (2021): 107.

[69] Alfred Stepan, "Rituals of Respect: Sufis and Secularists in Senegal in Comparative Perspective," *Comparative Politics* 44, no. 4 (2012): 383–384; Mamadou Diouf, ed., *Tolerance, Democracy, and Sufis in Senegal* (New York: Columbia University Press, 2013); Philpott, *Religious Freedom in Islam*, 51–66.

Asia, some countries' constitutions in Muslim West Africa even declare their government to be officially secular. The very first line of the first article of Senegal's Constitution, for example, declares the country to be "secular, democratic, and social," assuring the "equality before the law of all citizens, without distinction of origin, of race, of sex, and of religion." Although the Senegalese motto proclaims "One Faith," this appears to be more of a reference to a secular "civil religion" than an allusion to any particular religious tradition, insofar as the government does not recognize as official any religion. While the government does play a role in religious affairs, cultivating good relations with religious leaders and encouraging peaceful coexistence between faiths, religion and state remain institutionally separated and the government's involvement in religion does not take on a discriminatory character. The Constitution provides robust protections for religious freedom. Similar promises of political secularism, religious equality, and religious tolerance are present in neighboring countries.

As in Muslim Southeast Asia, in many West African countries orthodox Muslims coexist peacefully with both non-Muslims and heterodox Muslims. The most politically secular of these states, Senegal and Sierra Leone, have suffered from no identifiable Islamist attacks, largely as a result of the interreligious harmony that has been made possible by a commitment to secular principles.[70] By contrast, the countries most ravaged by religious violence in the Muslim world—Afghanistan, Iraq, Nigeria, Pakistan, Somalia, Syria, and Yemen—are among the least politically secular Muslim-majority countries, pitting Islam, or a favored Islamic tradition, against other religions. In these countries, the state co-opts Islamic leaders and marginalizes religious minorities, while Islamist groups seek to take over the state or use it to further a religiously informed agenda against other religious communities.

Although neither region of West Africa or Southeast Asia can be objectively classified as fully secular—they do after all feature governments that directly support religious activities and, in this way, undermine core aspects of political secularism, and both have witnessed rising religious hostilities—their commitment to religious pluralism and general respect for religious freedom position them closer to the secular end of the political secularism spectrum than the rest of the Muslim world.

---

[70] Leonardo A. Villalóon, *Islamic Society and State Power in Senegal: Disciples and Citizens in Fatick* (Cambridge: Cambridge University Press, 1995); Donal B. Cruise O'Brien, "The Senegalese Exception," *Africa* 66, no. 3 (1996): 458–464.

The third reason to think that Islam and political secularism can coexist concerns the theology of Islam itself. While it is true that Muhammad functioned as both a spiritual and a political leader, one can point to Quranic passages that appear to support the idea of political secularism. The Qur'an portrays Muhammad as a messenger of Allah sent to convey to the people of the world the message of Islam, not to impose it on the unwilling.[71] Perhaps the most famous verse supportive of political secularism declares that "there is no compulsion in religion."[72] Another is "To you be your religion and to me my religion."[73] These verses comport with the notion that God did not desire humanity to comprise "one nation."[74] Some have referred to the Covenant of Medina as an essentially secular constitution. On the other hand, of course, Quranic verses seemingly supportive of secularism need to be tempered by the actual historical record of Muhammad's use of the sword against nonbelievers. At the same time, however, although one can find similar verses condoning the violent repression of pagans in the Bible, much of the Christian world has, by and large, nevertheless come to embrace political secularism today. Might the same happen in Islam as well?

In summary, those who claim that Islam and political secularism cannot coexist point to the example of the Prophet Muhammad, who served as a religious and political leader, the early unification of Islam and political power, and the existence of contemporary Islamist regimes as evidence that confirms their verdict. Interestingly, both Islamists and critics of Islam, for entirely different reasons, arrive at this same conclusion. Both groups see Islam and the secular state as incompatible. They hold a static and essentialist view of religion that fails to acknowledge the constant evolution—and devolution—of political theology, often in response to contextual pressures. While we must indeed acknowledge the dearth of political secularism in the world of Islam today—and the violence it has produced—variation in attitudes toward political secularism over time among Muslim intellectuals, differences in contemporary political regimes in the Muslim world across space, and the political theology of Islam itself all suggest that opposition to political secularism may not be hardwired into the religion, as both the critics of Islam and Islamists charge. Accordingly, essentialist claims that Islam intrinsically rejects political secularism should be rejected. This reality

---

[71] Qur'an 42:6.
[72] Qur'an 2:256.
[73] Qur'an 109:1–6.
[74] Qur'an 5:48.

leads Kuru to aptly conclude, "If Muslims decide to separate their religious and governmental institutions, they do not have to search for models exclusively in the West. They can find inspirational examples in their own early history."[75]

Summary

In Muslim-majority countries exhibiting a high level of religious privilege, the authority of the dominant form of Islam and the authority of the state are profoundly intertwined, often to the detriment of religious minorities, thus creating an unbalanced religious playing field.[76] In the Muslim world, this privilege comes in two general forms. The first is found in Islamist states, where political elites gain their legitimacy by promoting a conservative form of Islam throughout politics and society. The second is found in pseudo-secularist countries whose governments, though guided by ideologies grounded in antipathy to the public practice of religion, nevertheless grant dominant forms of Islam special favors not bestowed upon minorities and dissidents in the hopes of fostering stability and precluding threats to their regimes.

Religious privilege remains a serious problem in the Muslim world. Advocates for political secularism can still be found, but their influence remains marginal, owing, in large part, to the belief, widespread among both Islamists and critics of Islam, that Islam does not separate the spiritual and political spheres. This chapter has argued that the integration of religion and state in the Muslim world has corresponded to uniquely high levels of violence. Laws and policies privileging Islam and suppressing non-favored religious groups encourage extremists and vigilantes from the very communities favored by the state to attack those from communities that do not enjoy this privilege. For some, a repudiation of political secularism is embedded in Islam. However, variation across time in the thought of Muslim intellectuals with respect to political secularism, variation across space in the practice of political secularism, and the theological basis for political secularism in the Qur'an itself argue against the incompatibility of Islam and secularism.

---

[75] Ahmet T. Kuru, "Islam, Catholicism, and Religion-State Separation: An Essential or Historical Difference?," *International Journal of Religion* 1, no. 1 (2020): 101.
[76] Grim and Finke, *The Price of Freedom Denied*, 22–24.

Beyond the religious hostilities and social upheaval that are part and parcel of religious privilege, there is another reason for Muslims to reject political privilege: it is bad for Islam itself. Somewhat paradoxically, research has consistently shown that state interference in religious affairs, and especially religious privilege, has a profoundly *negative* impact on the vitality of the favored religious group.[77] Although it might make intuitive sense that the best way to protect one's religion is to remove competition from other religions, this appears not to be the case. Religions are strongest when they have to compete with other religions on an equal playing field. Contexts of pluralism strengthen individual religions by forcing adherents to possess a deep knowledge of their faith and to defend it with persuasive arguments in the marketplace of ideas. Just as iron sharpens iron, competition hones religion. Conversely, political privilege has the opposite effect. When majoritarian religions see the presence of minorities as threatening and look to the state to give them advantages over the competition, they end up becoming enervated and apathetic, dependent on the state for their subsistence.[78] In the Muslim world, we see evidence supporting this claim in Iran, for example, where secularization appears to be increasing dramatically and Islam is losing adherents.[79] It is hardly coincidental that Iran features one of the world's strongest fusions of religion and state. In Iran, Islam has necessarily become implicated in the failure of the state to deliver on the promises of the Islamic Revolution. Perhaps counterintuitively, the best way for Muslims to keep Islam strong is to separate it from political authority and to level the religious playing field for all religious groups in society.

The discussion in this chapter carries important policy implications. Combating violence in the name of Islam requires more than ratcheting up military campaigns against jihadi groups. It also obliges countries to address the cultures of impunity that incubate violent religious hostilities. If political and religious leaders in the Islamic world are serious about ridding themselves of the scourge of violence afflicting their countries, they

---

[77] Laurence R. Iannaccone, "Religious Markets and the Economics of Religion," *Social Compass* 39, no. 1 (1992): 123–131; Laurence R. Iannaccone, Roger Finke, and Rodney Stark, "Deregulating Religion: The Economics of Church and State," *Economic Inquiry* 35, no. 2 (1997): 350–364; Roger Finke and Rodney Stark, "Religious Economies and Sacred Canopies: Religious Mobilization in American Cities, 1906," *American Sociological Review* 53, no. 1 (2005): 41–49.

[78] Anthony Gill, "Government Regulation, Social Anomie and Religious Pluralism in Latin America: A Cross-National Analysis," *Rationality and Society* 11, no. 3 (1999): 287–316.

[79] Ammar Maleki and Pooyan Tamimi Arab, "Iranians' Attitudes toward Religion: A 2020 Survey Report," GAMAAN, 2020, https://gamaan.org/wp-content/uploads/2020/09/GAMAAN-Iran-Religion-Survey-2020-English.pdf.

must be willing to take a close look at their penal codes that criminalize religious defamation, choke freedom of religion, and empower extremism. They must further be willing to provide protection for vulnerable populations (particularly religious minorities) and prosecute known extremists.

This chapter and the previous one have examined the relationship between religious privilege and religion-related violence in the world's two largest religions: Christianity and Islam. Both also happen to be monotheistic faiths. The following chapter turns to the world's largest polytheistic and third-largest religion: Hinduism. Whereas the previous chapter on Christianity and the present one on Islam have taken a cross-national approach to understanding the relationship between religious privilege and majoritarian violence, the next chapter focuses on a single country, India. Despite the clear theological differences between Hinduism and the Abrahamic traditions, we nevertheless observe the same relationship between the rejection of political secularism—this time in the form of Hindu privilege—and violent religious hostilities.

Chapter 4
Hinduism

Hinduism, considered by many scholars to be the world's oldest living religious tradition, boasts a substantial global following of more than 1.2 billion adherents, making it the world's third-largest religion and the largest non-Abrahamic/monotheistic faith tradition. Despite this impressive number and the fact that Hindus can be found on every continent, it comprises the majority religious tradition in only three countries—India, Mauritius, and Nepal—with about 94 percent of the world's Hindus living in India alone.

As a "natural religion," Hindu philosophies and practices are considered universally accessible through study, reason, and experience apart from special revelation. Central to Hindu spirituality is karma, the law of cause and effect. Everyone has a duty, dharma, to pursue that which is right in accordance with one's place in society. Hindus believe in reincarnation (samsara), the idea that upon death one's soul enters into a new bodily form, depending on the moral quality of one's previous life. Those who follow their dharma accrue good karma, sending their soul upward in the next life. It is possible to live such a good life that one is freed from the cycle of reincarnation altogether (*moksha*). These beliefs make Hinduism conducive for peace (*shanti*), a virtue that builds positive karma. The Upanishads, the earliest of the *Vedas* (Hindu philosophical teachings) and arguably the most important teachings in the Hindu traditions, say virtually nothing about violence between peoples and groups or coercion of non-Hindus, but they contain numerous prayers or chants for peace (*shanti* mantras). Thus India's most ancient scriptures contain formulations of what we know today as tolerance and pluralism. Violence can be found in the *Vedas*, but it is attributed to the various deities, who engaged in continual acts of slaughter. Hindus interpret these stories not as promoting bloodshed but as metaphorical depictions of the human struggle to overcome the inner tendencies that veil the truth and enslave humanity in ignorance. Inaction or the unwillingness to fulfil one's dharma is considered unrighteousness. Essentially, the *Vedas* concern the quest of human beings to find peace (*ahimsa*) within themselves and with the universe. Accordingly, Hindu societies have historically been among the most inclusive and tolerant.

This depiction of Hinduism as a religion of peace belies contemporary realities, however. In India, Hinduism has become weaponized in internecine political and interreligious violence. The 1984 Sikh massacre involved a series of organized pogroms against Sikhs following the assassination of Indira Gandhi by her Sikh bodyguards. Independent sources estimate the number of resulting deaths to be over thirty thousand.[1] In 2002, large-scale intercommunal violence broke out in the western state of Gujarat and other parts of India. Described as a pogrom by many pundits and scholars, the violence resulted in the deaths of over two thousand people, the vast majority of whom were Muslims. In 2008, another round of intercommunal violence occurred, this time in the eastern state of Odisha (formerly Orissa). The violence between Hindus and Christians there produced deaths in excess of thirty-five hundred. Since the election of Narendra Modi as the country's prime minister in 2014, Hindu violence against minorities witnessed another resurgence in various parts of the country, including in states that had previously experienced little by way of religious conflict.

This chapter argues that Hindu violence in India has been abetted by the country's repudiation of its secular founding principles. India's postindependence leaders believed that the country's remarkable ethnic and religious diversity required a foundation of secular nationalism. They understood that the embryonic country could survive only if all of India's diverse communities believed they had a place in it free from bigotry and discrimination. Quickly, though, the dedication to political secularism began to wane. Both the federal government and various state governments co-opted Hinduism for political purposes, seeking to "saffronize" the country in the face of religious diversity. Hindu nationalists have grown increasingly bold in their interactions with religious minorities.[2]

This chapter proceeds as follows. The first section describes the situation of political secularism in India. It notes that India's extraordinary level of religious belief, coupled with its unparalleled religious diversity, requires a commitment to political secularism in order for the country to flourish. Although India's postindependence leaders understood this reality, the

---

[1] Paul Joseph, ed., *The Sage Encyclopedia of War: Social Science Perspectives*, vol. 1 (Thousand Oaks, CA: Sage, 2017), 433.
[2] Thomas Blom Hansen, *The Saffron Wave: Democracy and Hindu Nationalism in Modern India* (Princeton, NJ: Princeton University Press, 1999).

state's commitment to political secularism quickly began to wane. Today, a ubiquitous decline in political secularism has coincided with the resurgence of the Hindu nationalist Bharatiya Janata Party (BJP). The second section argues that the decline of political secularism has abetted Hindu nationalist violence against minorities. Although antiminority hostility has been a consistent feature of India's postindependence history, attacks against minorities often fluctuate in response to the political empowerment of Hindu nationalism. The third section considers one of the most important ways political secularism is undermined in India, namely through the passage of "anticonversion laws," and how these bills encourage militant Hindus to attack minorities. The fourth section concludes by considering the future of secularism in the world's largest democracy.

Political Secularism in India

India's unique religious constellation has created distinctive background conditions for the development of its unique version of political secularism. India is a deeply religious and religiously diverse country, the birthplace of a number of the world's religious traditions: Hinduism, Buddhism, Jainism, and Sikhism. Although India's nearly 1 billion Hindus comprise about 80 percent of the population, numerous minorities also call India home, including over 200 million Muslims, nearly 30 million Christians, and over 20 million Sikhs. These figures demonstrate that India is home to the world's largest Hindu and Sikh communities, second largest Muslim community, and twentieth largest Christian community. As remarkable as these numbers are, India also contains sizable numbers of Jains, Buddhists, and nonbelievers.

Throughout Indian history, different faith traditions—Islam, Christianity, Hinduism, Sikhism, Jainism, Buddhism, and various smaller faiths—coexisted with one another; pluralism, tolerance, and interreligious trust were considered natural to the Indian experience. This natural condition remained largely intact until the arrival of colonialism, when religious identities became weaponized as a political tool to define national communities. After independence, though, India's early leaders envisioned a return to the natural harmony that had formed the basis of interreligious relations. This would be made possible through a form of political secularism distinct to the Indian experience. The state would remain equidistant from all religious traditions and grant universal religious freedom. Unlike in the West, however, the state also reserved the right to intervene in the religious realm should relations between or within religious groups sour or if religion was being used to undermine human rights.[3] Furthermore, the government reserves the right to address illiberal social practices emerging from particular religious traditions.[4] But it does not necessarily interfere in every religion's objectionable customs equally. For example, while the state has intervened to remedy illiberal cultural practices in Hinduism, it has not similarly intervened to address illiberal practices in Islam. Another difference between Western secularism and Indian secularism concerns the latter's emphasis on the rights of groups in contrast to the former's preoccupation with the rights of individuals. However, as political philosopher Timothy Shah notes, this has sometimes led to systemic and arbitrary government regulation of majoritarian Hindu communities, including extensive control over Hindu temples.[5] Accordingly, the "wall" separating religion and state in the United States does not exist in India. Instead, the Indian Constitution envisions a "principled distance" between religion and the state, wherein the state welcomes all of the country's myriad religious traditions without extending special privileges to any particular religion.[6]

Historically, political secularism in India has been buoyed by a number of factors: a secular and inclusive constitution that endows citizens with religious freedom and prohibits religiously based discrimination; broad religious representation in society and politics; autonomous bodies, such as the National Human Rights Commission of India, tasked with protecting religious minorities; and the grassroots work of nongovernmental organizations (NGOs) seeking to promote communal harmony. Owing to these features designed to hold together what is an incredibly multicultural population, India has managed to sustain its status as the world's largest secular democracy for almost all of its postindependence history, despite the presence of astonishing cultural, linguistic, ethnic, and religious diversity.

---

[3] Thomas Pantham, "Indian Secularism and Its Critics: Some Reflections," *Review of Politics* 59, no. 3 (1997): 523–540.

[4] Lauren Frayer, "India's Supreme Court Orders Hindu Temple to Open Doors to Women, but Devotees Object," NPR, December 22, 2018, https://www.npr.org/2018/12/22/675548304/indias-supreme-court-orders-hindu-temple-to-open-doors-to-women-but-devotees-obj.

[5] Timothy S. Shah, "India's Other Religious Freedom Problems," *Religions* 12 (2021): 490.

[6] Bhargava, "What Is Secularism For?," 504.

Nevertheless, despite auspicious founding conditions and secular safeguards, political secularism has been steadily eroded. Religious privilege is nothing new in India. Hinduism has long been politicized by elites, predating even colonial times.[7] In the prepartition princely states, kings entered into a quid pro quo with priests (brahmins) in which the state backed Hinduism with material resources and assurances of safety in return for its legitimization of political rulers.[8] The age of British colonial rule further exacerbated communal conflict. The "divide and conquer" approach being part and parcel of colonial rule, as seen in the 1909 Moreley-Minto Reforms and the 1919 Montagu-Chelmsford Reforms, pitted Indians against each other as the British sought to consolidate their rule. This strategy precipitated the breakdown of communal harmony, manufactured communal difference, and stoked conflict between Hindus and Muslims by politicizing religious identity. In this way, the British hoped to awaken and leverage Muslim consciousness as a means of countering emerging anti-British nationalism among Hindus.[9] The politicizing of religion in this way gave rise to contending religious nationalisms, ultimately leading to the division of the subcontinent into predominantly Hindu India and predominantly Muslim Pakistan. Thereafter political leaders associated with the family of Hindu nationalist organizations known as the Sangh Parivar, fearing declining Hindu political and economic power, directly or indirectly supported violence against religious minorities in the hopes of winning or holding onto power by consolidating the Hindu vote.[10] The resurgence of Hindu nationalism in the 1980s and 1990s prompted numerous India analysts to fear that the country had descended into a "crisis of secularism."[11]

---

[7] C. A. Bayly, "The Pre-History of 'Communalism'? Religious Conflict in India, 1700–1860," *Modern Asian Studies* 19, no. 2 (1985): 177–203.

[8] Peter van der Veer, *Religious Nationalism: Hindus and Muslims in India* (Berkeley: University of California Press, 1994); Susan Bayly, *Saints, Goddesses and Kings: Muslims and Christians in South Indian Society 1700–1900* (Cambridge: Cambridge University Press, 2003); Peter Friedlander, "Hinduism and Politics," in *Routledge Handbook of Religion and Politics*, ed. Jeffrey Haynes (London: Routledge, 2016), 70–71.

[9] Suranjan Das, "Communal Violence in Twentieth Century Colonial Bengal: An Analytical Framework," *Social Scientist* 18, nos. 6–7 (1990): 21–37; Bipan Chandra, *Communalism in Modern India* (New Delhi: Har-Anand, 2008).

[10] Paul R. Brass, *The Production of Hindu-Muslim Violence in Contemporary India* (New Delhi: Oxford University Press, 2003); Steven I. Wilkinson, *Votes and Violence: Electoral Competition and Ethnic Riots in India* (Cambridge: Cambridge University Press, 2006); Martha Nussbaum, *The Clash Within: Democracy, Religious Violence, and India's Future* (Cambridge, MA: Harvard University Press, 2009).

[11] Sumit Ganguly, "The Crisis of Indian Secularism," *Journal of Democracy* 14, no. 4 (2003): 11–25; Anuradha Dingwaney Needham and Rajeswari Sunder Rajan, eds., *The Crisis of Secularism in India* (Durham, NC: Duke University Press, 2007).

In 2014, India experienced a watershed moment with respect to its commitment to political secularism when Narendra Modi, a Hindu nationalist politician who had previously served as the chief minister of the state of Gujarat, was elected as the country's prime minister.[12] A resurgent strain of militant Hindu nationalism helped bring Modi's BJP—a right-wing, Hindu nationalist political party that explicitly rejects the principle of political secularism—back to power after a ten-year hiatus. The BJP is animated by a political ideology called "Hindutva"—the belief that India should be a country for Hindus alone—which it inherited from the Rashtriya Swayamsevak Sangh (RSS), a Hindu nationalist volunteer organization whose goal is to create a Hindu Rashtra (nation) to the exclusion of religious minorities.[13] As explained by the originator of the term, Vinayak Damodar Savarkar, Muslims, Jews, Parsis, and Christians, unlike those subscribing to faith traditions indigenous to India (Hindus, Buddhists, Jains, Sikhs), could never be considered legitimate citizens of the Indian nation because "Their Holyland is far off in Arabia or Palestine. Their mythology and Godmen, ideas and heroes are not the children of this soil. Consequently, their names and their outlook smack of a foreign origin. Their love is divided."[14] Savarkar thus believed that these "foreign" religious groups for whom India was not a "Holyland" (*punyabhoomi*) should either be converted to Hinduism or be excluded from social life.

The BJP, steeped in ideas of Hindutva, ran on a platform calling for an explicit alliance between Hinduism and the state. It lambasted the Congress Party, the political party that had governed India for most of its postindependence history, for its accommodation and opportunistic political mobilization of Muslims, Christians, and other religious minorities at the expense of the Hindu majority.[15] Echoing Savarkar, Rajeshwar Singh, a leader in the

---

[12] Angana P. Chatterji, Thomas Blom Hansen, and Christophe Jaffrelot, eds., *Majoritarian State: How Hindu Nationalism Is Changing India* (New Delhi: Harper Collins, 2019); Christophe Jaffrelot, *Modi's India: Hindu Nationalism and the Rise of Ethnic Democracy* (Princeton, NJ: Princeton University Press, 2021).

[13] Tanika Sarkar, *Hindu Wife, Hindu Nation: Community, Religion, and Cultural Nationalism* (Bloomington: Indiana University Press, 2001); Christophe Jaffrelot, ed., *Hindu Nationalism: A Reader* (Princeton, NJ: Princeton University Press, 2007); Wendy Doniger and Martha C. Nussbaum, eds., *Pluralism and Democracy in India: Debating the Hindu Right* (New York: Oxford University Press, 2015); Thomas Blom Hansen and Srirupa Roy, eds., *Saffron Republic: Hindu Nationalism and State Power in India* (Cambridge: Cambridge University Press, 2022).

[14] Quoted in A. G. Noorani, "What Is Hindutva?," *Dawn*, December 10, 2016, https://www.dawn.com/news/1301496.

[15] Paul R. Brass, *The Politics of India since Independence* (New York: Cambridge University Press, 1994), 233.

BJP and a close confidant of Modi, baldly declared the goal of the Hindu nationalist movement: "Our target is to make India a Hindu Rashtra by 2021. The Muslims and Christians don't have any right to stay here. So they would either be converted to Hinduism or forced to run away from here."[16]

The 2014 election saw the BJP, capitalizing on a major economic downturn and corruption allegations against the Congress Party, capture more than 30 percent of the popular vote and win 282 out of 543 possible seats in the legislature, thus becoming the first party to gain a majority of seats in the lower house of India's bicameral parliament, the Lok Sabha, since 1984. (The same election saw the lowest number of Muslim MPs elected since India's independence and the Congress Party's worst performance in history.) Modi's BJP would go on to win the 2019 and 2024 general elections. The BJP also began to expand its footprint at the local level, making inroads even into states beyond its traditional strongholds in the "cow belt" of North Central India. As of this writing, the BJP and its allies control governments in over half of Indian states. From 1989 to 2014, India had been ruled by a succession of coalition governments—including one led by the BJP itself—many of which were not even able to complete their full terms. Today, the BJP enjoys a popular mandate unparalleled in recent history.

The resurgence of the BJP in Indian politics, sometimes referred to as the "BJP 2.0" in order to distinguish it from its ideological predecessor, marked a pointed shift in Indian politics toward a militant brand of Hindu nationalism, as Hindu nationalist politicians exploited their newfound political power to systematically dismantle the country's secular foundations and target minorities. The BJP's victory marked the onset of a politics characterized by majoritarianism and exclusion of minorities.[17] Although Hindus comprise about 80 percent of the population, BJP leaders have nevertheless proven adroit at manufacturing a widespread perception of threat to Hinduism's dominant position in Indian society, demonstrated by its success in consolidating the Hindu vote in electorally important states. While the immediate goal of the BJP is, of course, to win elections, its larger agenda centers upon the cultural transformation of the country in order to reflect its Hindu character. A report by the New Delhi Television Network

---

[16] Piyush Srivastava, "Dharm Jagran Samiti Leader Vows to Create Hindu Rashtra by 2021," *India Today*, December 19, 2014, https://www.indiatoday.in/india/story/dharm-jagran-samiti-leader-vows-to-create-hindu-rashtra-by-2021-231854-2014-12-19.

[17] Amrita Basu, *Violent Conjunctures in Democratic India* (New York: Cambridge University Press, 2015); Achin Vanaik, *The Rise of Hindu Authoritarianism: Secular Claims, Communal Realities* (London: Verso, 2017).

documented a fivefold increase in the employment of "hateful and divisive" language in statements made by high-ranking politicians from 2014—the first year Modi's BJP took power—to 2018.[18]

Moreover, the creation of a Hindu Rashtra necessarily entails the suppression of religious diversity and the expulsion of foreign influences. Citing the Foreign Contribution Regulation Act of 1976, a law regulating access to foreign funding, the Modi administration enacted a series of severe restrictions on foreign religious entities operating in India and canceled or suspended the registration of tens of thousands of NGOs, including minority faith-based organizations such as the Christian social service NGOs Compassion International and the Missionaries of Charity, groups working for the betterment of marginalized religious communities and those of lower castes. (Following international outcry, the Missionaries of Charity's license was renewed in early 2022.) These moves appear to have been motivated by a desire to shut down organizations critical of the Indian government or believed to be promoting foreign religions. The central government also pursued policies that targeted Muslims specifically. In August 2019, it revoked the special status of India's only Muslim-majority state, Jammu and Kashmir, thereby annulling its degree of autonomy and self-government afforded it by the Constitution and integrating it into the Indian Union. In the process, the government jailed dozens of its political and civil society leaders without due process. The entire state was further subjected to a prolonged internet shutdown. In December of the same year, the government passed the Citizenship Amendment Act (CAA), which effectively prevented foreign-born Muslims from the surrounding Muslim-majority states of Pakistan, Bangladesh, and Afghanistan from becoming Indian citizens, while at the same time providing a fast track to citizenship for non-Muslim migrants. The CAA came into force following comments by the home minister, Amit Shah, comparing illegal immigrants to "termites . . . eating the food that should go to our poor." He vowed to "find each and every one and send them away."[19] These moves sparked protests and counterprotests, resulting in several days of prolonged violence in Delhi. In the state of Assam, tensions over the CAA led to violent clashes between security forces and Muslim

---

[18] Nimisha Jaiswal with Sreenivasan Jain and Manas Pratap Singh, "Under Modi Government, VIP Hate Speech Skyrockets—by 500%," NDTV, April 19, 2018, https://www.ndtv.com/india-news/under-narendra-modi-government-vip-hate-speech-skyrockets-by-500-1838925.

[19] Deepshikha Ghosh, "Amit Shah 'Termite' Remark on Immigrants Unwanted, Says Bangladesh," NDTV, September 24, 2018, https://www.ndtv.com/india-news/amit-shah-termite-remark-on-immigrants-unwanted-says-bangladesh-1921088.

villagers. The government also renamed towns, streets, airports, and train stations having Islamic names with Hindu-centric ones, in this way "Hinduizing" the public square.[20] For example, the government renamed the city of Allahabad to Prayagraj. Behind the name change was Yogi Adityanath, a Hindu priest, self-styled monk, prominent member of the BJP, Hindutva firebrand, and chief minister of India's largest state, Uttar Pradesh. Some Hindu nationalist leaders have spoken openly about the need to Hinduize the Constitution, schools, universities, and prestigious institutions such as the Indian Council for Historical Research and the National Council for Educational Research and Training.[21] The purpose of these laws and policies is to protect the dominant Hindu community from perceived threats posed by other faith traditions, especially Islam and Christianity. All these specific developments should be considered in light of a broader context in which Hindu nationalists seek to purify India of non-Hindu influences. The decline in Indian secularism deepened following Modi's reelection in 2019 and the government's response to the coronavirus pandemic in 2020.

The empowerment of Hindu nationalism at the national level has also unleashed it at the local level. In some BJP-controlled states, including Gujarat, Rajasthan, and Maharashtra, local governments have moved to rewrite school textbooks in an attempt to valorize the Hindu contribution to India's history and development, while downplaying or neglecting altogether the contributions made by non-Hindus.[22] Several state governments have also passed or strengthened legal statutes banning the slaughter of cows and prohibiting the conversion of Hindus to minority religions.

In summary, India has strayed far from its secular founding ideals. Proponents of Hindutva, in contrast to Nehru and Gandhi and the rest of India's founders, envision the country not as a multicultural state but as a majoritarian one. The coming to power of a right-wing, Hindu nationalist political party, the BJP, animated by an ideology of Hindutva that sees India as a land for Hindus, crystallized a new phase of majoritarianism and exclusivism in

---

[20] Lauren Frayer, "India Is Changing Some Cities' Names, and Muslims Fear Their Heritage Is Being Erased," NPR, April 23, 2019, https://www.npr.org/2019/04/23/714108344/india-is-changing-some-cities-names-and-muslims-fear-their-heritage-is-being-era.

[21] Heewon Kim, "Understanding Modi and Minorities: The BJP-led NDA Government in India and Religious Minorities," *India Review* 16, no. 4 (2017): 357–376.

[22] Anubhuti Maurya, "Rewriting 'Old History' for a New India," *The Hindu*, July 27, 2022, https://www.thehindu.com/opinion/op-ed/rewriting-old-history-for-a-new-india/article65567906.ece; Kavita Chowdhury, "School Social Science Textbook Revisions in India Kick Up Controversy," *The Diplomat*, July 27, 2022, https://thediplomat.com/2022/07/school-social-science-textbook-revisions-in-india-kick-up-controversy/.

Indian politics and society.[23] Supporters of Hindutva decry religious pluralism as a threat to India's Hindu identity. They see minorities not just as outsiders but as irreconcilable enemies who must be assimilated into the country's Hindu culture or expelled altogether. The BJP-led government, together with leaders at the national, state, and local levels, have extended state patronage to a collection of Hindu nationalist groups (Sangh Parivar) to further the Hindutva cause. They have advocated, implemented, and enforced sectarian policies intended to maintain the country's Hindu character. The resurgence of the BJP has had the effect of bringing Hindutva into mainstream discourse at the same time that popular support for political secularism has been waning. If the BJP is being rewarded for its brand of Hindu supremacism, it has no incentive to moderate its approach to minorities. The success of the BJP has also served to push more secular-minded bodies and parties, fearful of jeopardizing their share of the Hindu vote bank, in the direction of Hindu nationalism. Consequently, India is arguably a less politically secular country today than at any point since independence.

Hindu Nationalism and Violence

Although the legal measures undermining political secularism in India are of great concern, especially for minorities, of even greater concern are the social consequences that flow from these measures. Some right-wing Hindu groups have seized on official laws and policies as a means to weaken religious minority communities. With increasing frequency and intensity, Hindu extremists have deployed vigilante violence against minorities to administer existing laws they believe are being insufficiently enforced by the state.

Curiously, despite its status as the world's largest democracy, the ideals of religious liberty and equality set forth in its Constitution, and religious minorities' long-standing presence in the country, India ranks among the world's worst countries in terms of antiminority hostility. According to the Pew Research Center, in 2021 India had the second-highest rate of religious hostilities in the world, and the highest levels of social hostilities in the Asia-Pacific region.[24] Communal violence has been a problem in India

---

[23] Chatterji, Hansen, and Jaffrelot, *Majoritarian State*.
[24] Pew Research Center, *Globally, Government Restrictions on Religion Reached Peak Levels in 2021, While Social Hostilities Went Down* (Washington D.C.: Pew Research Center, 2024), 35.

since the days of the British Raj. It has, however, experienced a significant and troubling increase in recent years, an escalation that has coincided with the empowerment of Hindu nationalism.[25]

Hindu nationalism has paved the way for the strong intensification of antiminority hatred, especially toward Muslims and Christians.[26] To be sure, antiminority violence in India has a long and disturbing history, with major riots targeting minorities occurring in places like New Delhi in 1984, Ayodhya in 1992, and Gujarat in 2002—massacres for which most perpetrators were never brought to justice and in which law enforcement officials either participated or to which they turned a blind eye.[27] In the case of Gujarat, critics allege that its chief minister, none other than the man who would eventually become India's fourteenth prime minister, Modi, allowed the anti-Muslim violence to continue unabated for three days, leading to over a thousand fatalities. The Delhi, Ayodhya, and Gujarat pogroms, however, occurred in response to local developments that later engulfed other parts of India. With the election of the BJP, a culture of antiminority discrimination now exists not only at the state level but at the federal level as well. Consequently, violence directed at India's minority communities has increased greatly, especially in states containing large numbers of minorities.

Data reveal a breathtaking increase in levels of antiminority violence since 2014.[28] One report found that in just the first three months of the Modi administration, minorities suffered more than six hundred attacks.[29] Another study found that the total number of hate crimes against religious minorities, including Muslims, Christians, and Sikhs, increased by a factor

---

[25] Veena Das, ed., *Mirrors of Violence: Communities, Riots, and Survivors in South Asia* (New Delhi: Oxford University Press, 1990); Ashutosh Varshney, *Ethnic Conflict and Civic Life: Hindus and Muslims in India* (New Haven, CT: Yale University Press, 2002); Gyanendra Pandey, *Routine Violence: Nations, Fragments, Histories* (New Delhi: Permanent Black, 2006); Amartya Sen, *Identity and Violence: The Illusion of Destiny* (New York: W. W. Norton, 2006).

[26] Paul R. Brass, *Theft of an Idol* (Princeton, NJ: Princeton University Press, 1997); Ornit Shani, *Communalism, Caste, and Hindu Nationalism: The Violence in Gujarat* (Cambridge: Cambridge University Press, 2007); Chad M. Bauman, *Pentecostals, Proselytization, and Anti-Christian Violence in Contemporary India* (New York: Oxford University Press, 2015); Chad M. Bauman, *Anti-Christian Violence in India: History, Theory, Interpretation* (Ithaca, NY: Cornell University Press, 2020).

[27] Human Rights Watch, "We Have No Orders to Save You: State Participation and Complicity in Communal Violence in Gujarat," April 30, 2002, www.hrw.org/report/2002/04/30/wehave-no-orders-save-you/state-participation-and-complicity-communal-violence.

[28] C. J. Werleman, "Rising Violence against Muslims in India under Modi and BJP Rule," *Insight Türkiye* 23, no. 2 (2021): 39–50.

[29] John Dayal, *100 Days under the New Regime: The State of Minorities: A Report* (New Delhi: Anhad, 2014).

of nearly 8 between 2014 and 2018.³⁰ Attacks on minorities have been tacitly encouraged by the refusal of state officials and the police to hold perpetrators of violence accountable for their actions. In recent years, the courts and government bodies have sometimes overturned convictions or withdrawn cases that accused Hindu militants of involvement in violence against Muslims. As reported by Human Rights Watch, "The BJP government's discriminatory and divisive policies have led to increased violence against minorities, creating a pervasive environment of fear and a chilling effect on government critics. Instead of holding those responsible for abuses to account, the authorities chose to punish the victims, and persecuted anyone who questioned these actions."³¹

The Modi years witnessed several large-scale episodes of majority-on-minority violence. Consider just a few examples. In 2020, violence erupted in New Delhi as Muslims and others protested the CAA. Approximately fifty people were killed in the riot, most of them Muslim, the police doing little to intervene on behalf of the victims and some even participating in the violence.³² Ahead of India's 2024 general election, Prime Minister Modi kicked off his reelection campaign by inaugurating a new Hindu temple in Ayodhya, built over the site of the Babri Masjid mosque that had been demolished by Hindu extremists thirty-one years prior. Following Modi's remarks, BJP supporters and Hindu mobs took to the streets to support the temple's construction, and communal violence and clashes broke out shortly thereafter across India's northeast.³³ Christians, too, have come under increasing attack by militant Hindus. In 2023, violent ethnoreligious clashes erupted in Manipur between the state's majority Hindu Meitei community and the minority Christian Kuki population, following protests over Hindu Meitei privilege with respect to jobs, land rights, and political power. The violence, marked by brutal fighting and sexual assaults, was largely one-sided, majority-on-minority hostility. More than 250 churches of different

---

[30] Deepankar Basu, "Majoritarian Politics and Hate Crimes against Religious Minorities: Evidence from India, 2009–2018," *World Development* 146 (2021): 105540.

[31] Human Rights Watch, "India: Increased Abuses against Minorities, Critics," January 11, 2024, https://www.hrw.org/news/2024/01/11/india-increased-abuses-against-minorities-critics.

[32] Jeffrey Gettleman, Sameer Yasir, Subhashini Raj, Hari Kumar, and Atul Loke, "How Delhi's Police Turned against Muslims," *New York Times*, March 12, 2020, https://www.nytimes.com/2020/03/12/world/asia/india-police-muslims.html; "Delhi Riots: Police Trying to Communalise Case, Accused Tells Court," *Times of India*, February 16, 2022, https://timesofindia.indiatimes.com/city/delhi/2020-delhi-riots-police-trying-to-communalise-case-accused-tells-court/articleshow/89623178.cms.

[33] Human Rights Watch, "India: Violence Marks Ram Temple Inauguration," January 31, 2024, https://www.hrw.org/news/2024/01/31/india-violence-marks-ram-temple-inauguration.

denominations were burned or damaged across the state; hundreds were killed; tens of thousands displaced; entire villages razed. Civil rights advocates accused the central government of protecting the perpetrators and exploiting communal divisions for political gain. Despite the severity of the violence, Modi refused to address the conflict for months. Prior to the outbreak of violence, Manipur had been a largely peaceful state.[34]

The alliance between Hinduism and the state has further given rise to a number of different forms of antiminority violence unique to the Indian context, including cow vigilantism, violence surrounding the so-called love jihad, and religious conversion-related attacks. These acts of violence are frequently carried out by mobs and vigilante groups, stemming from a culture of impunity that emboldens Hindu militants to attack minorities.

The first form of violence pertains to attacks carried out by Hindu vigilantes who condemn the sale, purchase, and consumption of beef. Because cows are considered sacred in Hinduism, Hindu nationalists have long sought bans on the cattle trade through legal prohibitions known as "cow slaughter laws."[35] The export of beef is banned nationally. Violent Hindu vigilantes have used such laws to target beef-consuming minorities, namely Christians, Muslims, and Hindus who eat beef.[36] Cow slaughter laws have also threatened the livelihoods of those involved in the leather and meat production industries, disproportionately affecting the poor. The strictest laws governing the slaughter of cattle exist in Delhi, Gujarat, Haryana, Himachal Pradesh, Jammu and Kashmir, Ladakh, Punjab, Rajasthan, Uttar Pradesh, and Uttarakhand. In these states, the slaughter of cattle, including cows, bulls, and bullocks, is banned altogether; those involved in the cattle trade face stiff fines or even imprisonment. Most other states severely restrict the conditions under which cattle can be slaughtered. Since 2014, several states have amended their existing laws protecting cows to impose harsher penalties for the slaughter, transportation, ownership, or sale of cattle or beef. The National Cow Commission (Rashtriya Kamdhenu Aaoyog) mandated

---

[34] BBC News, "Ethnic Conflict and Murder Grip India's State of Manipur," YouTube, September 20, 2023, https://www.youtube.com/watch?v=kyw_QE9cMh4.

[35] Ian Copeland, "History in Flux: Indira Gandhi and the 'Great All-Party Campaign' for the Protection of the Cow," *Journal of Contemporary History*, 49, no. 2 (2014): 410–439; Rohit De, "The Case of the Invisible Butchers: Economic Rights and Religious Rites," in *A People's Constitution: The Everyday Life of Law in the Indian Republic*," ed. Rohit De (Princeton, NJ: Princeton University Press, 2018), 123–168; Kenneth Russell Valpey, *Cow Care in Hindu Animal Ethics* (London: Palgrave Macmillan, 2019).

[36] Cassie Adcock, "Cow Protection and Minority Rights in India: Reassessing Religious Freedom," *Asian Affairs* 49, no. 2 (2018): 340–354.

to protect cows, came into existence in 2019. The central government has proposed introducing a nationwide bill that would prohibit cow slaughter altogether and the sale, storage, or transportation of beef products. Indeed, a de facto federal ban on cattle slaughter came into effect when the Ministry of Education invoked the 1960 Prevention of Cruelty to Animals Act to regulate the sale of cattle for slaughter at livestock markets. Twenty-four of India's twenty-nine states enforce restrictions on the slaughter of cattle.[37]

The passage of restrictions regulating or banning the practice of cattle slaughter has emboldened various cow protection (*gau raksha*) vigilante groups within society who have attacked traders and consumers of beef with increasing frequency and lethality. Cow protection groups patrol highways and inspect trucks extrajudicially, often with the support of law enforcement, to ensure that cattle are not being transported to slaughterhouses or animal fairs. Those accused of trafficking cattle are frequently beaten and sometimes even killed.[38] Data from the Armed Conflict Location and Event Data Project show that violent incidents pertaining to alleged cow slaughter jumped by 40 percent from 2016 to 2017 and by almost 100 percent from 2017 to 2018.[39] Although cow vigilantism is not a new phenomenon and has in fact been occurring for centuries, the jarring spike in cattle-related attacks in recent years coincides with the political empowerment of Hindu nationalism at the state and national level.

A second form of antiminority violence involves attacks by Hindu men against Muslim men accused of seducing, marrying, and converting Hindu women to Islam in order to turn India into an Islamic republic, a conspiracy theory known colloquially as the "love jihad." It is impossible to deduce precisely how many love jihad–related attacks occur in India. However, in 2020 official government statistics recorded more than three thousand murders related to "honor, love affairs, or illicit relationships."[40] The actual number

---

[37] U.S. Department of State, Bureau of Democracy, Human Rights and Labor, "India," in *2016 International Religious Freedom Report*, www.state.gov/j/drl/rls/irf/religiousfreedom/index.htm#wrapper.

[38] Human Rights Watch, "Violent Cow Protection in India," February 18, 2019, https://www.hrw.org/report/2019/02/18/violent-cow-protection-india/vigilante-groups-attack-minorities.

[39] Armed Conflict Location and Event Data Project, "Cow Protection Legislation and Vigilante Violence in India," May 3, 2021, https://acleddata.com/2021/05/03/cow-protection-legislation-and-vigilante-violence-in-india/.

[40] Lauren Frayer, "In India, Boy Meets Girl, Proposes—and Gets Accused of Jihad," NPR, October 10, 2021, https://www.npr.org/2021/10/10/1041105988/india-muslim-hindu-interfaith-wedding-conversion.

may be magnitudes higher. The situation has turned particularly grim in Hindu nationalist strongholds such as Uttar Pradesh and Madhya Pradesh, where Muslim men who have attempted to marry Hindu women have been violently attacked or forced into hiding. Accusations of love jihad helped prompt deadly riots in Muzaffarnagar District of Uttar Pradesh in 2013 that left sixty-two dead. Rather than crack down on perpetrators of this form of violence, Hindu nationalist state governments have created "love jihad laws" that have empowered law enforcement to take action against Muslim men suspected of courting Hindu women.[41] In the case of love jihad–related violence, we see a reciprocal and cyclical relationship between the actions of the state and violence on the ground. Since the BJP's coming to power in 2014, multiple states have introduced or strengthened laws regulating, and in some cases criminalizing, interfaith marriages. These laws and the mandatory public notice requirements for interfaith marriages stir up communal hostilities and facilitate violence against interfaith couples. Hundreds of people have been arrested under these new laws. None, to date, however, has been prosecuted, indicating that the laws' sole purpose is to intimidate Muslims.

Love jihad–related violence represents just one form of general anti-Muslim violence. Violence directed against Muslims occurs within a wider historical context of Hindu-Muslim polarization, seen in the destruction of the ancient Babri Masjid in Ayodhya during a political rally in 1992, triggering riots all over the Indian subcontinent, the scapegoating of Indian Muslims for violence emanating from Pakistan, and anti-Muslim bigotry at the highest levels of government. For example, at the swearing-in ceremony in the Lok Sabha for members of parliament following the 2019 elections, virtually every Muslim MP was met with shouts of "Jai Shri Ram" (Hail Lord Ram) or similar Hindu nationalist slogans hurled by their BJP counterparts.[42] The same phrase has also been shouted by militant Hindus during attacks on Muslims. During the 2024 general election, Prime Minister Modi was widely accused of anti-Muslim hate speech when he claimed that if the Congress Party were to win the election it would distribute the country's wealth to "infiltrators" who "have more children," an

---

[41] Billy Perrigo, "Why India's Most Populous State Just Passed a Law Inspired by an Anti-Muslim Conspiracy Theory," *Time*, November 25, 2020, https://time.com/5915579/love-jihad-uttar-pradesh/.

[42] Prashant, "When Jai Shri Ram Became a Political Tool to Heckle Muslim MPs, It Lost Something," *The Print*, June 22, 2019, https://theprint.in/opinion/newsmaker-of-the-week/when-jai-shri-ram-became-a-political-tool-to-heckle-muslim-mps-it-lost-something/253159/.

apparent reference to the Muslim community. He alleged that in a Congress government, "Muslims" would have "first right over resources."[43]

Finally, "anticonversion laws," officially known as "freedom of religion" laws, which prohibit conversion of Hindus to minority faiths through coercion or enticement, have been exploited by Hindu nationalists to target alleged proselytizers. These statutes regulating conversion have been rapidly spreading throughout India, as has attendant conversion-related violence directed at those belonging to conversionary faiths. Owing to the extremely serious nature of conversion-related violence, I devote the entire following section to its examination.

Antiminority violence in India has occurred within a broader enabling cultural, legal, and political ecosystem that reflects the country's increasing communal polarization and disdain for religious minorities. This ecosystem exists at all levels of government and society, including at the very top: the prime minister. Although Modi has offered tepid condemnations of violence and assurances of religious tolerance, these statements have usually followed egregious cases of antiminority violence and have been offered only in response to strong international condemnation. Among minority communities, such after-the-fact sentiments are seen as lacking sincerity. In some cases, Modi has responded to Hindu violence with studied silence. Beyond Modi, other identifiable agents of Hindu nationalism—the Bajrang Dal, the Rashtriya Swayamsevak Sangh, the Vishva Hindu Parishad, and extremist BJP politicians—have directly promoted attacks on minorities and downplayed these attacks after the fact.

At the national level, the shield provided by Hindu nationalist government agents and the national media has had the effect of signaling to violent religious actors that they need not fear being held accountable for their actions. On the contrary, Hindu vigilantes have not only enjoyed the protection of Hindu nationalist politicians; in some cases they have even been openly celebrated and valorized. Concurrently, the government, using legal measures such as the Unlawful Activities Prevention Act (UAPA) and the Sedition Law, has targeted for repression critical voices that advocate for the rights of minorities.[44] The invocation of these laws is intended to silence critics of

---

[43] Rhea Mogul, "Modi's Muslim Remarks Spark 'Hate Speech' Accusations as India's Mammoth Election Deepens Divides," CNN, April 22, 2024, https://edition.cnn.com/2024/04/22/asia/india-modi-muslim-hate-speech-allegations-intl-hnk/index.html.

[44] Hannah Ellis-Petersen and Aakash Hassan, "How a Terrorism Law in India Is Being Used to Silence Modi's Critics," *The Guardian*, December 10, 2021, https://www.theguardian.com/world/2021/dec/10/how-terrorism-law-india-used-to-silence-modis-critics.

the government through the creation of an atmosphere of fear and intimidation. For example, in 2020 Stanislaus Lourduswamy, an eighty-four-year-old Catholic priest in ill health who had devoted his life to ministering to the poor and vulnerable, was arrested for allegedly violating the UAPA. He died in custody nine months later, his case never proceeding to trial.[45] The government now routinely investigates, harasses, intimidates, and even arrests journalists, human rights activists, and ordinary citizens who document and expose the reality of religious persecution in India.[46] For example, in 2021 the government filed complaints under the UAPA against individuals who tweeted about mosque attacks in the northeastern state of Tripura. The intent behind these actions is clear: to keep the world from knowing the truth about the plight of minorities in India.

At the state level, too, governments have failed to intervene in the face of Hindutva provocations. The police rarely arrest perpetrators of violence against minorities. If they are arrested, they seldom serve time in prison. To make matters worse, numerous local courts—bodies meant to protect the rights of minorities—have themselves been co-opted by the same Hindu nationalism that has engulfed India's political institutions. In this way, law enforcement and courts have greatly contributed to the erosion of political secularism. A culture of impunity has consequently been created that has emboldened Hindu vigilante violence against minorities, insofar as violent vigilantes understand that they need not fear police retribution and will not be brought to book for their actions. For example, very few of those responsible for cattle-related lynchings have even been prosecuted. In the case of love jihad–related attacks, evidence shows that authorities have encouraged the targeting of interfaith couples. At least eight states controlled by the BJP have passed laws to deal with love jihad by prohibiting "forced conversions" through marriage. Antiminority violence also has the perverse consequence of providing Hindu nationalist leaders with a fresh justification for pursuing further discriminatory laws and polices targeted at minorities, whom they scapegoat as being the source of interreligious hostilities. Thus the cycle of legal restrictions, hardening of religious identities, persecution, and violence continues.

[45] Surinder Kaur, "Father Stan Swamy: Courageous Indian Priest Accused of Terrorism," *Christianity Today*, August 22, 2022, https://www.christianitytoday.com/ct/2022/august-web-only/father-stan-swamy-catholic-priest-tribals-terrorism-died.html.
[46] Billy Perrigo, "They Shared a Video of a Muslim Man Being Attacked in India. Now They're Being Investigated by Police," *Time*, June 18, 2021, https://time.com/6073758/india-investigating-muslim-journalists/.

It is important to briefly mention the role of social media in stoking violent communal hostilities, as both government officials and nonstate actors have used it to spread hate and conspiracy theories about religious minorities at lightning speed. The pervasive spread of misinformation through social media platforms like Facebook and WhatsApp has directly contributed to majoritarian violence.[47] Cow vigilante mobs, for example, have often organized online and used social media to spread allegations and misinformation regarding those purportedly involved in the transportation and slaughter of cattle or the sale and consumption of beef. Facebook has been accused of spreading hate speech and even publishing antiminority "hit lists" that have fueled religious violence in India and other parts of Asia.[48] Social media has armed violent vigilantes with an unprecedented means to propagandize, organize, and mobilize. Young people—those most likely to use social media—have been especially susceptible to radicalization via social media, owing to their technological savvy.

In summary, antiminority violence in India, enabled by Hindu privilege coupled with the demonization and securitization of minority communities, has long been an endemic feature of Indian life. The problem, however, has become even more acute since 2014, owing to the political empowerment of Hindu nationalism. As the federal and local governments have escalated their enforcement of antisecular laws and policies in service to promoting a Hindu nationalist agenda, majoritarian violence against the country's minority communities—Christians, Muslims, Sikhs, and others—has increased correspondingly. In particular, we observe an increase in antiminority violence with respect to issues such as cattle slaughter, interreligious marriage, and proselytizing and conversion. Violent religious persecution from below has been reinforced by approval—sometimes tacit, sometimes explicit—from above. The degrading of political secularism and embrace of Hindutva effectively signals to violent vigilantes in society that their actions have the approval of the state. India's alarmingly high level of religious persecution threatens to further cycles of antiminority violence and domestic and regional instability. The following section takes an in-depth look at

---

[47] Rahul Bedi, "Social Media Rumours Lead to Mob Lynching of Two Men in India," *Irish Times*, June 11, 2018, https://www.irishtimes.com/news/world/asia-pacific/social-media-rumourslead-to-mob-lynching-of-two-men-in-india-1.352706.

[48] Kim Arora, "Facebook Post Lists Inter-Faith Couples," *Times of India*, February 6, 2018, https://timesofindia.indiatimes.com/india/facebook-post-lists-inter-faith-couples-calls-forattacks/articleshow/62796340.cms.

the chilling effect that one particular antisecular measure—anticonversion laws—has had on stoking majoritarian vigilantism in India.

The Problem of Anticonversion Laws

In 2021, the southern Indian state of Karnataka became the latest Indian state to formally enact an anticonversion bill. The law authorized the police to conduct door-to-door inspections of churches for the purpose of finding Hindus who had converted to Christianity. Karnataka followed in the footsteps of nine other states that had previously passed similar pieces of legislation: Arunachal Pradesh, Chhattisgarh, Gujarat, Himachal Pradesh, Jharkhand, Madhya Pradesh, Odisha, Uttar Pradesh, and Uttarakhand. Odisha was the first state to enact such a law, in 1967, followed by Madhya Pradesh in 1968. Other states, such as Manipur and Rajasthan, have considered similar bills, while Tamil Nadu repealed its anticonversion law in 2006. The Indian Supreme Court upheld the constitutionality of state-level anticonversion laws in the landmark case *Rev Stanislaus v. State of Madhya Pradesh* (1977), declaring that attempted conversion inhibits religious freedom and that "there is no fundamental right to convert another person to one's own religion."

Formally known as "Freedom of Religion Acts," anticonversion laws, as they are referred to by their critics, are state-level statutes designed to regulate religious conversions done through "forcible" and "fraudulent" means, including "inducement" and "allurement." Originally introduced by Hindu princely states such as Rajgarh, Patna, Sarguja, and Udaipur before independence as a means of preserving Hindu identity in the face of Christian proselytization emanating from the West, these statutes would eventually be reinstated by several Indian states after independence from Britain.[49] The basic structure and content of these laws vary only minimally between states, as newer laws tend to be modeled on earlier statutes in other states. For example, the first of these laws, the Orissa Freedom of Religion Act of 1967 states that "no person shall convert or attempt to convert either directly or otherwise, any person from one religious faith to another by the use of force or by inducement or by any fraudulent means nor shall any person abet any such conversion." The language found in the Orissa bill is virtually identical

---

[49] James Andrew Huff, "Religious Freedom in India and Analysis of the Constitutionality of Anticonversion Laws," *Rutgers Journal of Law and Religion* 10, no. 2 (2009): 1–36.

to that found in the anticonversion laws of other states. Karnataka's law, for example, prohibits "unlawful conversion from one religion to another by misrepresentation, force, undue influence, coercion, allurement or by any fraudulent means."[50] Similar laws have been proposed three times at the national level, but were rejected each time. Punishments for violating the provisions of the laws include fines ranging from 5,000 to 50,000 rupees and prison sentences of one to three years. These penalties increase in the cases of individuals attempting to convert minors, women, or members of scheduled castes away from their faith. Sometimes anticonversion laws require prospective converts to register with authorities their intent to convert to a non-Hindu religion before they can officially leave Hinduism.

Anticonversion laws represent a codification of Hindutva and reflect a fear of intensifying evangelistic activity by Christian missionaries who offer marginalized Hindus the possibility of escaping the oppressive caste system and becoming dignified and equal members of society.[51] Upper-caste Hindus, however, tend to see conversion as a threat to the Hindu nation.[52] Indeed, none other than Mohandas Gandhi opposed proselytization and conversion for this very reason. Contemporary Hindu nationalists fear that the number of Hindus will decline as the number of non-Hindus rises, altering the dynamics of the vote bank.[53] Through these laws, right-wing Hindu groups like the RSS—the ideological arm of the BJP—seek to perpetuate the identity of India as a predominantly Hindu nation by regulating conversions to non-Hindu religions. For example, the Backward Communities Bill of 1960 sought to combat the conversion of Hindus to "non-Indian" religions, including the proselytizing faiths of Islam and Christianity.[54] More recently, several ministers of the ruling BJP have given their support to the adoption of a national anticonversion law as a means to retain India's Hindu character. This goal was explicitly acknowledged by BJP Member of Parliament Tarun Vijay in 2015 in a statement of remarkable candor: "For the first time, the population of Hindus has been reported to be less than 80 percent. We

---

[50] Karnataka Act No. 25 of 2022, "The Karnataka Protection of Right to Freedom of Religion Act, 2022," 2022, https://dpal.karnataka.gov.in/storage/pdf-files/25%20of%202022%20(E).pdf.

[51] David Mosse, *The Saint in the Banyan Tree: Christianity and Caste Society in India* (Berkeley: University of California Press, 2012).

[52] Nathaniel Roberts, *To Be Cared For: The Power of Conversion and the Foreignness of Belonging in an Indian Slum* (Berkeley: University of California Press, 2016).

[53] Sarbeswar Sahoo, *Pentecostalism and the Politics of Conversion in India* (Cambridge: Cambridge University Press, 2018).

[54] Indian Law Institute, "A Study of Compatibility of Anti-Conversion Laws with Right to Freedom of Religion in India," 2015, https://papers.ssrn.com/sol3/papers.cfm?abstract_id=2359250.

have to take measures to arrest [this trend]... and I think a bill of this nature will... allow Hindus to remain a majority in India." That same year, Union Home Minister Rajnath Singh and future minister of home affairs Amit Shah made similar statements in support of a nationwide anticonversion law.[55]

Despite the seemingly good intent of anticonversion laws, critics point out a number of fundamental problems. First, the laws often do not clearly define "inducement" or "allurement." Accordingly, threats of eternal damnation and promises of eternal rewards can easily fall into these restricted categories. Predictably, then, the definitional ambiguity of anticonversion laws leaves government officials with a great deal of discretion regarding what constitutes their violation.[56] Second, some state laws require converts to register their intent to convert with governmental authorities, thus publicly marking them for societal harassment, discrimination, and even violence. Third, anticonversion statutes typically regulate conversions from Hinduism to other religions but do not restrict conversions or reconversions to Hinduism in the same way, thus creating an unbalanced religious playing field for minority faiths. The U.S. Commission on International Religious Freedom found, for example, that anticonversion laws "generally require government officials to assess the legality of conversions out of Hinduism only."[57] Meanwhile, the Indian government, pressured by Hindutva activists, has sponsored numerous *ghar wapsi* (homecoming) campaigns aimed at reconverting to Hinduism those who previously converted to other religions. The *ghar wapsi* initiatives tend to be specifically targeted at the poor.

Minorities would counter that converts are not seduced through incentives or inducements, as Hindu nationalists claim, but that marginalized Hindus voluntarily accept a non-Hindu religion in the hopes of escaping the oppressive caste system, achieving dignity and equality, and finding spiritual fulfillment. Telesphore Toppo, Archbishop of Ranchi, insists, "Forced conversions do not exist. We are free people with a free will and a free conscience and intelligence. No one can force another to convert."[58] Former United

---

[55] *International Business Times*, "BJP Lawmakers Plan Anti-Conversion Bills in LS, RS," 2015, https://www.ibtimes.co.in/bjp-members-introduce-bill-criminalising-religion-conversion-653925.
[56] Goldi Osuri, *Religious Freedom in India: Sovereignty and (Anti) Conversion* (London: Routledge, 2012); Sahoo, *Pentecostalism and the Politics of Conversion in India*, 79–80.
[57] U.S. Commission on International Religious Freedom, "India," in *2016 Annual Report*, http://www.uscirf.gov/reports-briefs/annual-report/2016-annualreport.
[58] World-Wide Religion News, "India: Another State Expected to Pass 'Anti-Conversion' Law," *World Watch Monitor*, August 3, 2017, https://wwrn.org/articles/47230/.

Nations special rapporteur on freedom of religion or belief Asma Jahangir found very little evidence of attempted forced conversions by religious minorities, as the laws themselves have led to few arrests or convictions: "Even in the Indian states which have adopted laws on religious conversion there seem to be only few—if any—convictions for conversion by the use of force, inducement, or fraudulent means. In Orissa, for example, not a single infringement over the past ten years of the Orissa Freedom of Religion Act 1967 could be cited or adduced by district officials and senior officials in the State Secretariat."[59]

Although anticonversion laws are passed by state governments, these governments themselves do not typically engage in violent persecution of religious minorities. A much more dire threat comes from the extralegal enforcement of conversion-related laws and policies by mobs, vigilantes, and terrorists, often with the tacit support of politicians. Thus, anticonversion laws empower extremists associated with the religious majority— Hindus— to attack religious minorities. In short, charges of religious conversion work to kindle passions against those seeking to convert individuals away from Hinduism, motivate vigilantes, and justify acts of violence.

In states enforcing anticonversion laws, Hindu vigilantes have often attacked with impunity individuals, homes, places of worship, and businesses of those believed to be proselytizing and converting Hindus to other faith traditions, using the very laws passed by the state to justify their violence. These episodes can range from relatively minor, isolated incidents to large-scale communal riots. In turn, the state commonly turns a blind eye to violence carried out by Hindus, on whose behalf it inhibits conversion in order to retain its good standing with that religious group. In some cases, the police and government officials have actively incited conversion-related attacks.[60] Hindu vigilantes thus feel empowered to commit acts of violence with little or no fear of governmental reprisal because anticonversion laws, in effect, lend the authority of the state to extremists and reinforce extreme views. India expert Chad Bauman suggests, "One of the particularly troubling characteristics of violence against India's Muslims and Christians is how infrequently the perpetrators are even charged, let alone convicted, and how regularly witnesses become

---

[59] United Nations General Assembly, "Report of the Special Rapporteur on Freedom of Religion or Belief," 2009, http://daccessods.un.org/TMP/5744267.70210266.html.

[60] M. Sudhir Selvaraj, "Acts of Violence? Anti-Conversion Laws in India," *Social & Legal Studies* 33, no. 5 (2024): 790807.

corrupted, or are intimidated into changing their stories in order to exculpate criminals."[61] My analysis of the relationship between anticonversion laws and violence finds that states that enforce anticonversion laws are statistically much more likely to give rise to violent persecution against minorities, and in particular Christians, than states where such laws do not exist.[62]

Consider the case of Madhya Pradesh, a large, centrally located state where anticonversion laws have their roots. Madhya Pradesh's Freedom of Religion Act was enacted in 1968 and subsequently amended in 2006. This law requires individuals seeking to convert to a different religion to give prior notice to the district magistrate. It also prohibits conversions through force, inducement, or fraudulent means. A number of cases reveal violence against Christians in Madhya Pradesh to be directly related to the issue of conversion. In March 2015, Hindu militants attacked a Bible convention in Jabalpur over allegations that religious conversions were taking place.[63] In 2016, a blind pastor, his wife, and eleven others were accused of proselytizing among some villagers. They were all violently beaten by an angry mob of Hindu extremists and charged under the Madhya Pradesh Freedom of Religion Act. In 2017, a Hindu nationalist group beat Christian parents and a group of children at a railway station in Indore, accusing the parents of kidnaping the children and forcibly converting them.[64] Later that year, right-wing Hindu activists attacked Catholic carol singers in Madhya Pradesh's Satna district and set a priest's car ablaze, accusing them of religious conversion.[65] In January 2018, a group of Hindu extremists broke into a pastor's house in Jhirigamali village and beat his teenage son, accusing them of illegal conversion.[66] In 2021, a mob of around 150

---

[61] Chad Bauman, "Faith and Foreign Policy in India: Legal Ambiguity, Selective Xenophobia, and Anti-Minority Violence," *Review of Faith & International Affairs* 14, no. 2 (2016): 37.

[62] Nilay Saiya and Stuti Manchanda, "Anti-Conversion Laws and Violent Christian Persecution in the States of India: A Quantitative Analysis," *Ethnicities* 20, no. 3 (2020): 587–607.

[63] Siddharth Ranjan Das and Amit Chaturvedi, "Church Attacked in Jabalpur, Christians Threaten to Shut Schools If Attackers Not Caught," NDTV, March 22, 2015, https://www.ndtv.com/india-news/church-attacked-in-jabalpur-christians-threaten-to-shut-down-schools-if-attackers-not-caught-748560.

[64] The Wire Staff, "Madhya Pradesh High Court Hands Over Children to Parents in Alleged 'Forced Conversion' Case," October 31, 2017, *The Wire*, https://thewire.in/communalism/madhya-pradesh-high-court-christian-children-forced-religious-conversion.

[65] Express News Service, "Mob Encircles Christian Priests, One Held for Alleged Conversion in Madhya Pradesh," *New Indian Express*, December 16, 2017, http://www.newindianexpress.com/nation/2017/dec/16/mob-encircles-christian-priests-one-held-for-alleged-conversion-in-madhya-pradesh-1728613.html.

[66] Church in Chains, "Official India: On the Side of Militants," 2018, https://www.churchinchains.ie/wp/wp-content/uploads/2018/03/India-Report-PUBLIC-2018-.pdf.

Hindus barged into a prayer hall and proceeded to beat the worshipers gathered there with sticks and batons. The attackers alleged that the group had been engaging in forced conversions.[67] These and dozens of other cases reveal the severity of violent, antiminority persecution related to the issue of conversion. As demonstrated in many of these cases, the act of charging Christian *victims* of violence under the anticonversion law indicates how it contributes to the persecution of Christians by empowering Hindu vigilante extremists.

In summary, while anticonversion laws are passed for the ostensibly noble purposes of safeguarding the integrity of India's religious communities and traditions, shielding lower-caste groups from exploitation, fighting coerced conversions, and preserving social harmony, they actually serve to coerce religious conformity, silence opposing religious views, and weaken the forces of moderation. Indian anticonversion laws legalize discrimination against minority religious groups and codify the existing reality of religious persecution in society. Such laws enmesh Hinduism and the authority of the state to the detriment of religious minorities. Anticonversion laws produce majority-on-minority violence in much the same way that blasphemy laws do in the Muslim world. Laws inhibiting conversion create and sustain environments of hostility toward religious minorities, thus empowering the voices of extremism and promoting religious conflict between majority Hindus and minorities. Ironically dubbed "freedom of religion" bills, these laws have the twofold effect of obstructing peaceable religious conversion through the threat of arrest and incarceration and encouraging harassment and violence against religious minorities accused of engaging in "forcible conversions" by vigilantes who claim they are simply enforcing the law. Because anticonversion laws are often passed at the behest of Hindu nationalist groups who fear that India's Hindu character is under siege owing to the growth of competing faiths, they disproportionately target religious minorities, especially Muslims and Christians, both groups for whom proselytism is central to the teachings of their faiths. Laws regulating interfaith conversion appear to be growing in popularity. Uttar Pradesh's chief minister, Yogi Adityanath, for example, has threatened to deploy hundreds of government agents under

---

[67] ADF India, "New Anti-Conversion Law in Madhya Pradesh Used to Target Minority Communities," April 2021, https://adfindia.org/stories/passing-of-anti-conversion-bill-in-madhya-pradesh-accelerates-violence-against-christians/.

the National Security Act to forcibly stop conversions from Hinduism.[68] Calls for a nationwide anticonversion bill remain strong among Hindutva activists.

Summary

Owing to its massive population size, largely democratic history, and potential to shape global developments well into the future, India represents perhaps the world's most troubling case of a country that has turned its back on political secularism. The country's early leaders imagined a country where political identity would not be based on or derived from any particular faith tradition. Under the guidance of India's first prime minister, Jawaharlal Nehru, they rejected the religious nationalism of Hindu intellectuals like V. D. Savarkar and M. S. Golwalkar, who envisioned India as a land for Hindus to the exclusion of minorities.[69] Though Nehru was personally no admirer of religion, he and his contemporaries had witnessed firsthand the devasting role played by communalism in dividing India into two separate countries. They understood that effectively managing India's tremendous linguistic, ethnic, and religious diversity required a commitment to political secularism in order to hold the nascent country together. In fact, they recognized that the privileging of one religion over others had the potential to upend India's democratic experiment. In short, whereas Savarkar and his ilk believed that India's religious identity should overlap with its territorial boundaries—hence Savarkar's maxim "Hindu, Hindi, Hindustan"—India's secular leaders following independence championed the principle of "unity in diversity." Nehru, in particular, drawing on India's ancient ideals of interreligious tolerance and harmony, understood that the country's diversity was its greatest strength. His inclusive nationalism not only helped mobilize Indians against British colonialism, but it also inaugurated the world's largest experiment in democratic governance.

Yet these secular ideas met with immediate resistance from those who saw political secularism as a foreign imposition that obscured India's identity as a Hindu country—a sentiment that has contended with political

---

[68] Asim Ali, "India's Hindutva Hardliners Treat Religious Conversion as Security Threat," *The Diplomat*, July 2, 2021, https://thediplomat.com/2021/07/indias-hindutva-hardliners-treat-religious-conversion-as-security-threat/.

[69] V. D. Savarkar, *Hindutva: Who Is a Hindu?* (New Delhi: Hindi Sahitya Sadan, 2003).

secularism for the soul of the country since independence. Nehru's contemporary, Gandhi, was murdered by Hindu nationalist Nathuram Godse in 1948, one year after India declared its independence. Ironically, Nehru's daughter, Indira, and grandson, Rajiv, both paved the way for the rise of Hindu nationalism by appealing to Hindu nationalists in an attempt to secure their vote banks.

Since then, the forces of Hindutva have been on the march. Hindu nationalism has experienced a major renaissance in the twenty-first century. Today India's future as a politically secular country dedicated to safeguarding its unmatched diversity finds itself in jeopardy. Whereas India's postindependence leaders saw the country's religious, ethnic, cultural, and linguistic heterogeneity as a source of strength, a resurgent religious nationalism believes pluralism constitutes a threat to the unity and harmony of Indian society. A Hindu nationalist movement, built around the BJP and its charismatic leader Narendra Modi and drawing on the ideas of Hindutva, has greatly accelerated the destruction of the secular Indian political system in favor of a system based in religious privilege for the majority Hindu population. Hindu nationalists look to the state to defend Hindu civilization against perceived threats stemming from religious conversions, interfaith marriages, and immigration. This goal is best accomplished by placing Hinduism at the center of the country's political and cultural life and coercing minorities into accepting Hindu dominance. Since the 2014 election, the BJP has made impressive political gains, as it has captured political territory long held by its rivals. The BJP's landslide victories in consecutive elections led Sanjaya Baru, an advisor to former prime minister Manmohan Singh, to refer to the era of BJP dominance as the "birth of India's second republic," marking the "end of the 'Nehruvian dynasty.'"[70]

While the coming to power of Modi and the BJP certainly represented a fateful turning point for India's minorities, it would be a mistake to pin the erosion of political secularism solely on a political party. Rather, the attacks on secular political institutions reflect a much deeper and systemic problem that cuts across political parties. True, the BJP attained power at both federal and state levels largely owing to its rejection of political secularism—and the plight of minorities has indeed worsened since 2014—but the other major party in Indian politics, the historically dominant Congress Party

---

[70] TNN, "Birth of 2nd Republic under Modi: Sanjaya Baru," *Times of India*, July 27, 2014, https://timesofindia.indiatimes.com/india/birth-of-2nd-republic-under-modi-sanjaya-baru/articleshow/39078542.cms.

that has governed India for most of its postindependence history, has itself often wavered in its commitment to political secularism. Some of the most problematic legal instruments undermining political secularism—including anticonversion statutes and the Foreign Contribution Regulation Act—were originally formulated and implemented by those affiliated with the Congress Party. Even ostensibly secular politicians associated with the Congress Party who have championed a secular nationalist vision for India have opportunistically manipulated and exploited majoritarianism when they believed they could gain political benefit by doing so. The tenure of Indira Gandhi demonstrates the point most strongly.[71]

Indeed, some of India's most egregious and widespread cases of majority-on-minority religious violence have occurred when the Congress Party has been in control of government. The anti-Sikh massacres in 1984, the violence in Ayodhya surrounding the destruction of a historic mosque in 1992, the 2002 Gujarat pogrom, and the 2008 Odisha riots all occurred under the rule of the Congress Party. Even today it appears that the Congress Party has abandoned its support for political secularism, perceiving it as politically disadvantageous at a moment in time when Hindu nationalism is waxing. By brandishing their Hindu credentials, Congress leaders hope to make electoral inroads among potential Hindu nationalist constituencies. It is therefore too simplistic to claim that the rise of the BJP explains India's deficit of political secularism and its consequent religious violence. It may be more accurate to see the rise of the BJP as a symptom of deeper societal dysfunctions rather than a proximate cause of antiminority discrimination and violence.

Given the systemic nature of antiminority discrimination in India, one might expect minority communities to be prone to violence. While religious violence in India has at times been perpetrated by minority communities, it has occurred with far greater frequency at the hands of the Hindu majority and has been directed against minorities. Hindu extremists have been emboldened by the laws and policies that have tilted the religious playing field in their favor. In the states of India enforcing anticonversion laws, for example, violent vigilantes justify their violence on the grounds

---

[71] Gyan Prakash, *Emergency Chronicles: Indira Gandhi and Democracy's Turning Point* (Princeton, NJ: Princeton University Press, 2021); Christophe Jaffrelot, *The Hindu Nationalist Movement in India* (New York: Columbia University Press, 1998), 272–277; Christophe Jaffrelot and Pratinav Anil, *India's First Dictatorship: The Emergency 1975–77* (New York: Oxford University Press, 2021).

that they are simply upholding the law. As India has become a less politically secular country, it has simultaneously become a more violent and dangerous one, especially for religious minorities. Political secularism thus remains indispensable for the future health of the world's largest democracy, most populous country, and a country that will be one of the world's most important players in the coming decades.

India remains the non-Western world's most important project in political secularism.[72] A country containing one-sixth of humanity and one-quarter of its voters, what happens in India will have enormous ramifications not just for that country but for the Asia-Pacific region and beyond. Should Delhi continue down its current path of embracing Hindutva and dithering in its commitment to political secularism, the consequences for the world may well be disastrous. However, if India's leadership reverses course and recovers its unique and venerable tradition of political secularism, it could well save the country from a bleak future characterized by religious hostilities and violence. A politically secular India could help stabilize the region of South Asia and stem the tide of faith-based violence that has engulfed the subcontinent since the turn of the century. Only if Hindus committed to the principles of political secularism are able to seize the high ground from proponents of Hindutva will India be able to survive as the world's largest secular country.[73] If India does decide to resist the forces of Hindu supremacism and rebuild a culture of religious harmony, it need not look for models beyond its own ancient and impressive traditions of religious pluralism and political secularism.

The following chapter turns to the world's fourth-largest faith tradition and, like Hinduism, one not commonly associated with violence: Buddhism. A religious tradition that was originally birthed in India, Buddhism has become the dominant religion in several Asian countries. Despite the obvious theological differences between nontheistic Buddhism, polytheistic Hinduism, and the monotheistic religions of the West, the conditions under which violence arises in Buddhism strongly parallel the dynamics underpinning violence in every other religion. As the chapter demonstrates, even a religion known for its pacifism and tolerance can become violent in the absence of political secularism.

---

[72] Sumantra Bose, *Transforming India: Challenges to the World's Largest Democracy* (Cambridge, MA: Harvard University Press, 2013).
[73] Shashi Tharoor, *Why I Am a Hindu* (New Delhi: Aleph, 2018).

Chapter 5
Buddhism

Buddhism is the world's fourth-largest religion, claiming about 1 billion global adherents, or 12 percent of the global population. Large concentrations of Buddhists exist in East, Southeast, and South Asia. In fifteen countries, Buddhism is the dominant religion, and sizable populations of Buddhists can be found in India, North and South Korea, and Nepal. Nearly a quarter-billion Buddhists live in China alone.

Like Hinduism, Buddhism finds its roots in India and in a variety of beliefs central to Jainism. Born into a life of luxury, the religion's founder, Prince Siddhartha Gautama, the son of a warrior-king, left his sheltered existence as a young man to experience the world on his own. He witnessed firsthand the suffering of the world. Siddhartha devoted his life to understanding the sources of this suffering. Finding that neither asceticism nor indulgence led to happiness, he came to understand that a life in between the extremes—the "middle way"—was the wisest way to live in a world that abounds in suffering, which he believed stemmed from selfish desires. Siddhartha developed an eightfold plan whereby people could reduce selfish cravings and thus diminish suffering, eventually finding "enlightenment"—a state of compassion, understanding, rootedness, and peace. After finding enlightenment himself, Siddhartha transformed into the Buddha, or "Enlightened One." He traveled throughout India teaching others how they too could reach the same state through right speech, right goals, and love for others. For Buddhists, actions are more important than beliefs.

Buddhism is a religion commonly and widely associated with peace, tolerance, and compassion, pacifism being one of its defining features. The first of the Buddha's five precepts prohibits followers from killing or harming living beings. Buddhist teachings emphasize that violence harms not only the victim but the perpetrator as well, insofar as violence destroys inner peace and that absent inner peace one cannot reach enlightenment. To hurt another living being is to hurt oneself. Buddhist traditions thus emphasize peaceful methods of conflict resolution.

Yet Buddhism, too, like every other one of the world's great religious traditions, has a violent side, belying its stereotype of being "exclusively pacifist" and "irenic."[1] Buddhist soldiers in sixth-century China achieved the noble status of "Bodhisattva" upon killing their enemies. In feudal Japan, warrior Buddhist monks known as the Sōhei used force to defend territory and fight against those associated with rival schools of Buddhism.[2] In sixteenth-century Thailand, Buddhist holy men staged bloody revolts against the government. During the Second World War, Zen Buddhism provided a strong foundation for Japanese militarism, including the imperial Japanese military's use of suicide warfare.[3] Recent history, too, evinces that violence has been justified and carried out by Buddhist actors, especially in the Buddhist-majority states of South and Southeast Asia, where distinctively Buddhist forms of violent nationalism have been observed in countries such as Sri Lanka, Myanmar, Cambodia, and Thailand.[4] One of the most serious acts of terrorism in the modern world involved a deadly chemical weapons attack in Tokyo carried out by a Buddhist-syncretistic doomsday cult called Aum Shinrikyo.[5] In 1995, members of Aum released sarin gas in crowded commuter trains, killing a dozen people and injuring thousands of others. The attack could have been much deadlier had the poisonous gas used been properly weaponized. During the political unrest that gripped Tibet in 2008, hundreds of Buddhist monks participated in deadly riots that resulted in the deaths of dozens of people. Buddhist violence figured prominently in a decades-long civil war in Sri Lanka and plays a crucial role in an ongoing ethnic cleansing campaign in Myanmar and in simmering conflicts in other parts of Asia.[6]

---

[1] Michael Jerryson, "Buddhist Traditions and Violence," in *The Oxford Handbook of Religion and Violence*, ed. Mark Juergensmeyer, Margo Kitts, and Michael Jerryson (New York: Oxford University Press, 2013), 41–66.

[2] Michael Jerryson and Mark Juergensmeyer, eds., *Buddhist Warfare* (New York: Oxford University Press, 2010).

[3] Brian Daizen Victoria, *Zen at War* (New York: Weatherhill, 1997).

[4] Christian Caryl, "Weren't Buddhists Supposed to Be Pacifists?," *Foreign Policy*, April 23, 2013, https://foreignpolicy.com/2013/04/23/werent-buddhists-supposed-to-be-pacifists/; Charles Keyes, "Theravada Buddhism and Buddhist Nationalism: Sri Lanka, Myanmar, Cambodia, and Thailand," *Review of Faith & International Affairs* 14, no. 4 (2016): 41–52; Michael Jerryson, *If You Meet the Buddha on the Road: Buddhism, Politics, and Violence* (Oxford: Oxford University Press, 2018).

[5] Juergensmeyer, *Terror in the Mind of God*, 103–117.

[6] Peter Lehr, *Militant Buddhism: The Rise of Religious Violence in Sri Lanka, Myanmar, and Thailand* (London: Palgrave Macmillan, 2018).

This chapter examines Buddhist violence in light of the global crisis of political secularism, a crisis that also afflicts several of the Buddhist-majority countries of Asia. Because of the social prestige enjoyed by monks in Buddhist-majority countries, governments have sought to co-opt them for political gain. For their part, nationalist monks have looked to the state to promote Buddhist values, maintain social order, and perpetuate the purity and legitimacy of the Buddhist state.[7] As argued here, the mutually reinforcing relationship between temple and state means that Buddhism has become complicit in the violence of the state and the state in the violence carried out by radical Buddhists.

This chapter proceeds in four parts. The first examines the role of Buddhism in Sri Lanka's postindependence violence, including a twenty-six-year-long civil war that engulfed the country from 1983 to 2009. The second considers the close relationship between Buddhism and the state in making possible a genocide against Muslims in Myanmar. The third turns to Buddhist warfare in Thailand. The concluding section highlights the central paradox of this chapter: that the world religion most well-known for its commitment to nonviolence has not been immune from a violent outgrowth when it has found itself in a position of privilege bestowed by the state vis-à-vis its religious competitors.

Sri Lanka

Of the world's Buddhist-majority states, Sri Lanka, the tiny island nation situated at the southern tip of the Indian subcontinent, has the longest history of Buddhism. About 70 percent of the population subscribes to Theravada Buddhism, the official religion of the island, while Tamil Hindus, Tamil Muslims, non-Tamil Muslims, and Christians comprise Sri Lanka's minority religious traditions. Buddhism dominates Sri Lanka's public life, Buddhist monks playing an important role in the island's politics. Ethnic and religious issues are thus deeply embedded in the political sphere, symbolized by presidents and prime ministers bowing down to Buddhist monks during their swearing-in ceremonies, seeking their blessings. The monks, in turn, have exerted pressure on lawmakers to yield to their demands.

---

[7] Mark Juergensmeyer, "The Global Rise of Religious Nationalism," *Australian Journal of International Affairs* 64, no. 3 (2010): 268.

In the earliest years of Sri Lanka's (then Ceylon's) independence from Great Britain, the government pursued policies in which the country's natural diversity was recognized and protected. However, shortly thereafter the Buddhist sangha (order of monks) demanded the protection and privileging of Buddhism and worked to bridge Buddhism and the state. In 1951, the All Ceylon Buddhist Congress presented a resolution to the prime minister informing him that he was "legally and morally bound to protect and maintain Buddhism and Buddhist institutions" and advised him to raise Buddhism to the "paramount position of prestige which rightfully belongs to it."[8] During the 1956 general election, the Sri Lankan Freedom Party, comprised mainly of Sinhala Buddhists, promised the Buddhist majority a privileged status in the country's civic and political life in exchange for its backing. After the party triumphed in the election and its leader, S. W. R. D. Bandaranaike, became prime minister, non-Buddhists soon found themselves relegated to the status of second-class citizens. However, when Bandaranaike failed to sufficiently fulfill his "Sinhala only" campaign pledge, he was assassinated by an extremist Buddhist monk in 1959, a classic example of violent outbidding discussed in chapter 1 From the 1960s onward, religious and ethnic identity became interwoven: to be Buddhist was to be Sinhala, and vice versa.[9] The Sri Lankan Constitution does not declare the country to be a Buddhist state, but it does give Buddhism "the foremost place" and mandates the state to "protect and foster" the Buddhist religion. The alliance between Buddhism and the state sees Sri Lanka as a Sinhala Buddhist country, not one that should be multireligious or multi-ethnic, and threatens to destroy religious pluralism and any shared sense of belonging.

Sri Lanka's first thirty-five years following its independence from Great Britain were relatively peaceful, periodic rioting and a severe persecution of Tamils by the state in 1958 notwithstanding. However, from 1983 to 2009 the country became embroiled in a sanguinary civil war fought between a militant group known as the Tamil Tigers and the Sinhala government, a war which featured the first widespread use of suicide bombings. The Tamil Tigers fought to create an independent state in the northeastern part of the

---

[8] All Ceylon Buddhist Congress, *Buddhism and the State: Resolutions and Memorandum of the All Ceylon Buddhist Congress* (Maradana: Oriental Press), 3.

[9] Mirjam Weiberg-Salzmann, "The Radicalization of Buddhism in the Twentieth and Twenty-First Centuries: The Buddhist *Sangha* in Sri Lanka," *Politics, Religion, & Ideology* 15, no. 2 (2014): 283–307.

country called Eelam. More than 800,000 Tamils fled the country, and over 100,000 civilians perished in the course of the conflict. The war came to an end in 2009 when the Sri Lankan armed forces finally triumphed over the Tamil Tigers. Although the war had numerous causes, among the most prominent was the co-optation of Buddhism and the repression of Tamils by Sinhala political elites, a situation made possible by monks who provided spiritual justification for the violence of the state.[10] Not only did Buddhist nationalists help escalate the conflict; they also repeatedly resisted peace initiatives that could have potentially ameliorated tensions.[11] The elements within Sri Lankan Buddhism desiring peace remained marginalized, as the fighting reinforced Sinhala Buddhist fears of the Tamil minority.

When the civil war ended in 2009, ordinary Sri Lankans and foreign observers alike hoped that the de-escalation of violent communal hostilities would lead to the reestablishment of harmonious religious and ethnic relations among the various communities in the country. Instead, the end of the war gave rise to a widening gulf between the country's ethnic and religious groups and a renewed Sinhala-Buddhist nationalism, supported by an establishment that feared alienating the dominant Buddhist population.[12] Buddhist extremists quickly looked for and found a new enemy: Muslims.

A new facet of resurgent religious nationalism in Sri Lanka involves a shift in the nature of communal conflict from ethnoreligious to more straightforwardly religious. Part and parcel of this shift has been the growing resentment toward and mobilization against the Muslim community by extremist Buddhist organizations.[13] For decades, periodic tensions between

---

[10] K. N. O. Dharmadasa, *Language, Religion, and Ethnic Assertiveness: The Growth of Sinhala Nationalism in Sri Lanka* (Ann Arbor: University of Michigan Press, 1992); Stanley J. Tambiah, *Buddhism Betrayed? Religion, Politics and Violence in Sri Lanka* (Chicago: University of Chicago Press, 1992); David Little, *Sri Lanka: The Invention of Enmity* (Washington, DC: U.S. Institute of Peace Press, 1994); Tessa J. Bartholomeusz, *In Defense of Dharma: Just-War Ideology in Buddhist Sri Lanka* (London: Routledge, 2002); Tessa J. Bartholomeusz and Chandra R. de Silva, eds., *Buddhist Fundamentalism and Minority Identities in Sri Lanka* (Albany: State University of New York Press, 1998); Mahinda Deegalle, ed., *Buddhism, Conflict and Violence in Modern Sri Lanka* (London: Routledge, 2006).

[11] Christopher S. Queen and Sallie B. King, *Engaged Buddhism: Buddhist Liberation Movements in Asia* (Albany: State University of New York Press, 1996).

[12] Sarah Byrne and Bart Klem, "Constructing Legitimacy in Post-War Transition: The Return of 'Normal' Politics in Nepal and Sri Lanka?," *Geoforum* 66 (2015): 224–233; Nira Wickramasinghe, *Sri Lanka in the Modern Age: History of Contested Identities* (Honolulu: Hawaii University of Hawaii Press, 2015).

[13] James John Stewart, "Muslim-Buddhist Conflict in Contemporary Sri Lanka," *South Asia Research* 34, no. 3 (2014): 241–260; John Clifford Holt, ed., *Buddhist Extremists and Muslim Minorities: Religious Conflict in Contemporary Sri Lanka* (New York: Oxford University Press, 2016); Athambawa Sarjoon, Mohammad Agus Yusoff, and Nordin Hussin, "Anti-Muslim Sentiments and

Buddhists and Muslims, who comprise about 10 percent of Sri Lanka's population, had been far eclipsed by the ethnoreligious civil war fought largely between Sinhala Buddhists and Hindu Tamils. Muslims remained largely neutral during the war.[14] The recent and spreading prejudice against Muslims has occurred, in large measure, as a response to Sri Lanka's growing Muslim population and increasing economic competition over resources.[15] Growing animosity toward Muslims also coincides with an increasingly autocratic regime in Colombo.

Buddhist nationalists believe that the shifting religious landscape threatens the Buddhist character of the island. Led by activist monks who promote an extreme form of nationalism, groups like Bodu Bala Sena, Sinhala Ravana, and the Sinhale Jathika Balamuluwa have launched massive campaigns, both online and on the ground, to restrict Sri Lanka's religious pluralism by, among other things, calling for a ban on different forms of the full-faced Islamic veil, the elimination of halal certification and cattle slaughter, the limiting of mosque construction, the boycotting of Muslim businesses, and the regulation of travel to the Middle East. They have spread Islamophobic conspiracy theories—including that Muslim-owned businesses were secretly distributing products to sterilize Sinhala Buddhist women and that Muslims were deliberately spreading COVID-19—among Buddhist communities through protests, rallies, and leaflet campaigns, fostering a climate of paranoia about and fear of Muslims.[16] In short, Muslims have largely replaced Hindu Tamils as the Buddhist nationalist object of wrath in contemporary Sri Lanka.

Militant Buddhist nationalism in Sri Lanka has accompanied a renewed alliance between sangha and state. For example, the Gotabaya Rajapaksa government donated valuable land in Colombo for the construction of a Buddhist cultural center. In 2013, Rajapaksa was a guest of honor at the opening ceremony of a Bodu Bala Sena training center.[17] The government has also tacitly (and in some cases overtly)

Violence: A Major Threat to Ethnic Reconciliation and Ethnic Harmony in Post-War Sri Lanka." *Religions* 7, no. 10 (2016): 1–18.

[14] Dennis B. McGilvray, "Rethinking Muslim Identity in Sri Lanka," in *Buddhist Extremists and Muslim Minorities*, ed. John Clifford Holt (New York: Oxford University Press), 54.

[15] Benjamin Schonthal, "Environments of Law: Islam, Buddhism, and the State in Contemporary Sri Lanka," *Journal of Asian Studies* 75, no. 1 (2016): 137–156.

[16] Syed Abbas Hussain, "Fighting a Pandemic of Misinformation," Asia Foundation, September 28, 2022, https://asiafoundation.org/2022/09/28/fighting-a-pandemic-of-misinformation/.

[17] Benjamin Schonthal and Matthew J. Walton, "The (New) Buddhist Nationalisms? Symmetries and Specificities in Sri Lanka and Myanmar," *Contemporary Buddhism* 17, no. 1 (2016): 95.

supported rallies by militant groups against minorities, frequently turning a blind eye to violence orchestrated by them. As A. R. M. Imtiyaz and Mohamed-Saleem observe, "[T]here is recognized sympathy among the government coalition members . . . for the [Bodu Bala Sena] campaign."[18]

What effect has resurgent Buddhist nationalism and antipathy toward Islam and Muslims had on stability and security in Sri Lanka? Five years after the end of its civil war, Sri Lanka witnessed communal rioting in 2014 between Buddhists and Muslims, resulting in the displacement of about ten thousand people. The riots were precipitated by a speech by the firebrand founder and secretary general of Bodu Bala Sena, Galagoda Aththe Gnanasara Thero, at a rally in Aluthgama. Gnanasara thundered, "This country still has a Sinhala police. A Sinhala army. If a single Sinhala is touched, that will be the end of [all Muslims]."[19] Minutes later, hundreds of his supporters, many of whom had been brought in from other areas of the country, rampaged through a nearby Muslim neighborhood targeting mosques, Muslim-owned businesses, and Muslim homes for arson and destruction.[20] The police were widely accused of standing by and, in some cases, even assisting the rioters. The riot came to an end only after the imposition of a military curfew, but the perpetrators of violence themselves were not brought to justice. The police eventually arrested Gnanasara for his role in instigating a series of anti-Muslim hate crimes, and the courts sentenced him to six years in prison. However, he received a presidential pardon following an intensive lobbying campaign on the extremist monk's behalf by his supporters.

Anti-Muslim violence escalated in the years following the Aluthgama riot. In 2017, Buddhist nationalists, including a large contingent of monks, forced a group of Rohingya refugees from Myanmar to flee to a United Nations shelter in Colombo. In 2018, Sinhala Buddhist mobs attacked Muslims in a series of religious riots in the towns of Kandy and Ampara, following the murder of a Sinhala lorry driver. Calm was restored only when the government took extremely stringent measures, imposing a social media blackout and declaring a state of emergency. Both the 2014 and 2018 riots

---

[18] A. R. M. Imtiyaz and Amjad Mohamed-Saleem, "Muslims in Post-war Sri Lanka: Understanding Sinhala-Buddhist Mobilization against Them," *Asian Ethnicity* 16, no. 2 (2015): 194–195.

[19] *Colombo Telegraph*, "Unedited Full Video: BBS Gnanasara's Pre-Riots Speech," June 19, 2014, https://www.colombotelegraph.com/index.php/unedited-full-video-bbs-gnanasaras-pre-riots-speech/.

[20] Jerryson, *If You Meet the Buddha on the Road*, 35.

demonstrated the inability—or, more scandalously, the unwillingness—of the government to take meaningful and sustained action against Bodu Bala Sena and related groups. Although the government and Sinhala Buddhist groups condemned the attacks, there is widespread acknowledgment that a number of politicians and extremist monks had discretely maintained close relations with leaders of the mobs. Some of the perpetrators of violence were arrested but not convicted, including several prominent Buddhist activists. Although many police and security forces had been deployed on the streets, evidence shows that they took little action to prevent the riots from occurring or stopping them once in motion. The minister for justice Rauf Hakeem accused his own government of failing to protect vulnerable Muslim communities.[21]

Riots are not the only form of antiminority violence to have emerged in recent years. Hate crimes directed against Muslims have also increased since the end of the civil war. Buddhist extremists, exploiting long-simmering resentment among the dominant Sinhala Buddhist majority, have regularly burned to the ground Muslim shops and homes. Much of the anti-Muslim violence that has gripped the island has been abetted by social media, where allegations of Muslim wrongdoing spread like wildfire and vigilante groups cohere in response.[22] My analysis of religious violence in Sri Lanka shows that from 2013 to 2017, Buddhist extremists carried out almost fifty identifiable attacks against Sri Lankan Muslim targets, including shrines and mosques. (Dozens more attacks occurred that were likely committed by extremist Buddhist groups, but the perpetrators of these strikes could not be clearly identified.) During that time, Muslims did not commit a single identifiable act of terrorism.

Nevertheless, the growing discrimination against Muslims by the state and demonization of Muslims by Buddhist nationalists in society have contributed to increasing resentment among the country's Muslim population. On Easter Sunday 2019, a series of coordinated suicide attacks struck crowded churches, bustling luxury hotels, and a housing complex, resulting in the deaths of 259 people, mostly Christian worshipers. The perpetrator of the attack, National Thowheeth Jama'ath, was a local militant Islamist

---

[21] Human Rights Watch, "Sri Lanka: Muslims Face Threats, Attacks," July 3, 2019, https://www.hrw.org/news/2019/07/03/sri-lanka-muslims-face-threats-attacks.

[22] Carolina Holgersson Ivarsson, "Lion's Blood: Social Media, Everyday Nationalism and Anti-Muslim Mobilisation among Sinhala-Buddhist Youth," *Contemporary South Asia* 27, no. 2 (2019): 145–159.

group with ties to ISIS. The bombings represented a watershed moment in Sri Lankan history. Up to this point, Sri Lankan Islam had remained largely neutral and nonviolent.

Although the Easter Sunday bombings targeted Sri Lanka's Christian community, they had the effect of reinforcing the fears of the Sinhala Buddhist majority about the threat posed by Islam. Buddhist nationalist groups stood ready to exploit the opening provided by the bombings. Shortly after the attacks, Buddhist mobs, organized on social media, launched a spate of revenge attacks against Muslim communities, torching hundreds of Muslim businesses, homes, and places of worship, the police doing little to halt the violence. All Muslim cabinet ministers, state ministers, and deputy ministers resigned their positions. The Colombo attacks and their aftermath served as an unfortunate and troubling reminder of the country's long history with communal violence.

The government's response to the attacks was to double down on policies restricting religious pluralism. It quickly imposed a state of emergency, during which it arrested thousands of Muslim men in connection with plotting the attacks under emergency terrorism laws. Though most were eventually released for lack of evidence, hundreds remained detained for extended periods of time, in some cases without formal charges. In the days following the attacks, Colombo took the unusual step of banning face coverings as part of emergency legislation. The law banned any facial garment that "hinders identification." "The ban is to ensure national security. . . . No one should obscure their faces to make identification difficult," then president Maithripala Sirisena said in justifying the decision. The president's office argued that the ban would develop "a peaceful and reconciled society."[23]

A week after the Easter Sunday attacks, Sri Lanka entered its general election season. The election inspired the creation of a group calling itself the Sinha-Le (Lion's Blood) that aimed at capturing the Sinhala Buddhist vote bank for Rajapaksa. Some Buddhist monks attempted to politicize the Easter Sunday attacks, making common cause with the Sinha-Le in order to protect Buddhism from the perceived threat posed by Islam. The election split the country along religious lines. Ultimately, Rajapaksa's People's Front Party, with the support of Buddhist nationalist groups such as Bodu Bala Sena, secured nearly 60 percent of the vote and nearly 65 percent of Parliament

---

[23] Presidential Media Division of Sri Lanka, "Steps to Ban Covering One's Face to Defy Identification," Official Website of the President of the Democratic Socialist Republic of Sri Lanka, April 28, 2019, http://www.president.gov.lk/steps-to-ban-covering-ones-face-to-defy-identification/.

seats. Rajapaksa was elected president, largely owing to the overwhelming support he received from the Sinhala-Buddhist majority. Sri Lanka experts attributed the success of the People's Front partly to its ability to successfully manipulate widespread fears over Islam. Upon his election, Rajapaksa rewarded Buddhist nationalists for their support by appointing Gnanasaro, the militant monk behind the 2014 Aluthgama riot, head of the country's "One Country, One Law" policy intended to protect the Buddhist character of Sri Lanka by, among other things, ending customary Muslim law.[24] Rajapaksa further deployed the draconian Prevention of Terrorism Act of 2021—a law that allows the Ministry of Defense to detain anyone it suspects of undermining social cohesion for up to eighteen months without judicial process—cracking down Sri Lanka's Muslim communities. The law effectively allowed authorities to securitize Islam by circumventing standard due process procedures in conducting counterterrorism operations. Critics alleged that the law targeted Muslims and suspended the civil rights of minorities. For example, Sri Lankan human rights attorney Hejaaz Hizbullah was imprisoned for twenty-two months under the law for his alleged role in the Easter Sunday attacks, despite there being no credible evidence against him.

In 2022, Buddhist violence in Sri Lanka took another unexpected turn. In that year, thousands of people stormed the presidential residence in Colombo, ousting from power President Rajapaksa and forcing him to flee to Thailand. Protests began in April amid surging fuel and food prices, record inflation, and an overwhelmed healthcare system. Sri Lankans blamed the president for the island's worst economic crisis in its postindependence history. As the riot unfolded, Buddhist leaders, who had previously allied with Rajapaksa, could be seen participating in the violent protests and storming the president's residence. At the time of this writing, the country remains ravaged by domestic turmoil and could well collapse altogether. The future of the island will be determined, in part, by the interactions between Buddhism, state, and society.

In summary, hardline Buddhists in Sri Lanka have long promoted fears that the Buddhist character of the island is under threat, first from British colonists, then from Hindu Tamils, and now from Muslims. The triumph of

---

[24] "Lankan President Appoints Task Force Led by Controversial Monk for 'One Country, One Law,'" *Times of India*, October 27, 2021, https://timesofindia.indiatimes.com/world/south-asia/lankan-president-appoints-task-force-led-by-controversial-monk-for-one-country-one-law/articleshow/87307728.cms.

the armed forces in the war against the Tamil Tigers was widely seen as a victory for the Sinhala Buddhist majority, President Rajapaksa once declaring that the war's conclusion had left a country with no religious minorities. However, the island enjoyed a mere five years of relative calm before becoming embroiled in yet another religious conflict, this time involving the country's minority Muslim community. Today extremist Buddhist movements continue to threaten the country's religious minorities. Led by groups like Bodu Bala Sena, they have made common cause with a government supportive of the idea that Sri Lanka should be a Buddhist state. The resurgence of a muscular Buddhist nationalism in Sri Lanka, which preys on the fears of the majority Sinhala Buddhist community, has helped create a less stable and more violent social climate, as demonstrated by increasing riots, mob attacks, and terrorist strikes by majoritarian Buddhist groups. How the government responds to this reality will matter greatly for the future stability of Sri Lanka, as the country continues to grapple with weaponized religions. If it takes a hardline stance and refuses to address systemic issues of bias and discrimination—as seen in the state's response to the Easter Sunday attacks—it will only continue to fertilize a breeding ground for extremism and violence. In this case, Sri Lanka might well stand on the verge of a new age of terror.

Myanmar

Paralleling developments in Sri Lanka have been similar trends in the Southeast Asian country of Myanmar. Like Sri Lanka, Myanmar is an ethnically and religiously diverse country. About two-thirds of the population are ethnically Burmese (Bamar), and the overwhelming majority of them subscribe to Buddhism. A number of ethnic minority groups—the Chin, Karen, Karenni, Mon, Naga, Rakshine, Shan, and Wa—also call Myanmar home. Many of these groups adhere to minority religious traditions, including Islam and Christianity. Overall, about 90 percent of the population is Buddhist, with Muslims and Christians comprising the most important religious minority communities.

After Myanmar (then Burma) gained independence from Great Britain in 1948, successive governments sought to partner with the sangha in order to bolster their legitimacy. Political leaders, hoping to cloak themselves in an aura of spiritual transcendence, have publicly participated in Buddhist rites and affirmed the dominant status of Buddhism. Every regime since the country's independence has either endorsed Buddhism as the state religion or adopted "Buddhist values" to build political legitimacy. The Ministry of Religious Affairs exists to purify, perpetuate, promote, and propagate "the Theravada Buddhist [religion]."[25] In turn, the sangha lends the state spiritual authority to shape the country's policy. In 1961, Prime Minister U Nu, himself a committed Buddhist, enacted a bill enshrining Buddhism as the official religion of the country. Prime Minister Than Shwe promoted a series of laws that defined Myanmar in terms of "one race, one language, one religion."[26] The state's privileging of Buddhism has been coupled with its marginalization, and at times violent persecution, of those communities that are ethnically and religiously distinct from the Burmese Buddhist majority.[27]

The relationship between Buddhism and the state, however, is also more fraught in Myanmar than in Sri Lanka, owing to the military regime's authoritarian control over the country. After General Ne Win took power in a swift, bloodless coup d'état in 1962, all the Burmese governments have been headed by the military, save for a brief experiment in democracy from 2015 to 2021. In 1988, the military brutally cracked down on pro-democracy protests, and as many as five thousand people were killed. Even after the National League for Democracy (NLD) won the election of 1990, the military refused to hand over power, placing the party's leader, Noble Peace Prize winner Aung San Suu Kyi, under house arrest. She would be repeatedly arrested and released over the next decades. From 2015 to 2021 she was detained once again after having served in the role of state counselor for six years. The sangha has regularly participated in antistate protest movements in defiance of the heavy-handed tactics and authoritarianism of the regime. For example, in 2007 the short-lived Saffron Revolution provided a glimmer of hope that democracy and peace could take hold in Myanmar after five decades of military rule.[28] Led by saffron-clad monks, the

---

[25] U.S. Commission on International Religious Freedom, *Burma: Religious Freedom and Related Human Rights Violations Are Hindering Broader Reforms: Findings from a Visit of the U.S. Commission on International Religious Freedom* (Washington, DC: U.S. Commission on International Religious Freedom, 2014), 4.
[26] Mikael Gravers, "Spiritual Politics, Political Religion, and Religious Freedom in Burma," *Review of Faith & International Affairs* 11, no. 2 (2013): 48.
[27] Monique Skidmore, "Darker Than Midnight: Fear, Vulnerability, and Terror Making in Urban Burma (Myanmar)," *American Ethnologist* 30, no. 1 (2003): 5–21.
[28] Benedict Rodgers, "The Saffron Revolution: The Role of Religion in Burma's Movement for Peace and Democracy," *Totalitarian Movements and Political Religions* 9, no. 1 (2008): 115–118.

protests challenged the legitimacy of the military dictatorship. The generals responded swiftly and violently, brutally suppressing the demonstrations and beating, killing, and jailing thousands of monks. The junta's violent crackdown, however, delegitimated the government in the eyes of many.[29] The junta formally stepped down in 2011 but seized power once again in 2021, following a landslide electoral victory by the NLD.

Still, as in Sri Lanka, political secularism finds itself in crisis. Although the Burmese military has demonstrated its willingness to crack down on Buddhism when deemed necessary, it has also worked to co-opt Buddhism when possible. At the same time that the military has cracked down on those elements of the sangha that refuse to support its actions, it has publicly demonstrated strong support for monks who support the junta, its violent crackdown on Burmese society, and its targeting of ethnoreligious communities, lavishing them with gifts and forging a shared ultranationalist narrative. Conversely, monks who protest the junta frequently find themselves jailed or disrobed. In an effort to recover its religious legitimacy following the Saffron Revolution, the junta quickly worked to restore its alliance with Buddhism. For example, Article 361 of the country's 2008 Constitution recognizes the "special position of Buddhism as the faith professed by the great majority of the citizens of the Union."

Majoritarian privilege has been coupled with minority repression. At times, the state has conducted brutal operations against the Muslim minority, for example, a 1977 operation called "Dragon King" under the direction of General Ne Win that forced over 200,000 Muslims living in Rakhine State to flee the country. The operation resulted in "widespread reports of forced labor, torture, rapes, and mass killing."[30] Fifteen years later, the junta once again cracked down on Rakhine Muslims in an operation dubbed "Clean and Beautiful Nation," this time forcing over a quarter-million to flee for their lives. Militant Buddhists applauded these ethnic cleansing campaigns.

Although postindependence Myanmar has exhibited a generally cooperative relationship between the sangha and the state, it is also clear that Buddhist violence has tracked closely with the increasing entanglement of religion and state. In the 1970s and 1980s, Buddhist violence in Myanmar

---

[29] Stephen McCarthy, "Overturning the Alms Bowl: The Price of Survival and the Consequences for Political Legitimacy in Burma," *Australian Journal of International Affairs* 62, no. 3 (2008): 298–314.

[30] Kurt Jonassohn and Karin Solveig Bjornson, *Genocide and Gross Human Rights Violations in Comparative Perspective* (New Brunswick, NJ: Transaction, 1998), 263.

tended to occur only sporadically. Thereafter, however, as the sangha and the government moved closer together and the state began to suppress minorities, Buddhist violence intensified greatly. In 1997, deadly riots broke out in Mandalay when a mob of at least a thousand Buddhist monks waged a campaign of targeted violence against Muslims. The riots featured the burning of religious books, physical assaults, and the vandalizing of Muslim-owned establishments. The military junta turned a blind eye to the ransacking of mosques and attacks on Muslim homes and businesses.

The integration of Buddhism and the state reached new heights in the 2010s, when the president supported the drafting of a new national law prohibiting interfaith marriage, known as "Safeguarding the National Identity," a measure promoted by nationalist monks to prevent Buddhist women from marrying Muslim men as a means to "preserve race and religion." In 2012, thousands of monks participated in marches supportive of President U Thein Sein's proposal to forcibly remove Rohingya Muslims from Myanmar. Monks have seized upon—and often helped create—a widespread belief among Burmese Buddhists that Muslims living in Myanmar seek to undermine the country's Theravada Buddhist identity.

Behind the ubiquitous hatred of Muslims have been militant Buddhist monks who have spread their message of hate and instigated violence on social media.[31] The contemporary militant Buddhist nationalist movement in Myanmar has encompassed two major organizations: the 969 Movement and the Organization for the Protection of Race and Religion, known by its Burmese acronym MaBaTha. Both groups formed in tandem with incremental political liberalization reforms by the state following the 2007 Saffron Revolution.[32] Both have also orchestrated campaigns of discrimination and violence against the Muslim minority.[33]

The 969 Movement, a loose network of monks and lay Buddhists, formed in 2012 and swiftly gained notoriety. The number 969 refers to the nine virtues of the Buddha, the six great qualities of his teachings (dhamma), and

---

[31] Paul Mozur, "A Genocide Incited on Facebook, with Posts from Myanmar's Military," *New York Times*, October 15, 2018, https://www.nytimes.com/2018/10/15/technology/myanmar-facebook-genocide.html.

[32] Ronan Lee, "The Dark Side of Liberalization: How Myanmar's Political and Media Freedoms Are Being Used to Limit Muslim Rights," *Islam and Christian-Muslim Relations* 27, no. 2 (2016): 195–211.

[33] Niklas Foxeus, "The Buddha Was a Devoted Nationalist: Buddhist Nationalism, Ressentiment, and Defending Buddhism in Myanmar," *Religion* 49, no. 4 (2019): 661–690; Niklas Foxeus, "Buddhist Nationalist Sermons in Myanmar: Anti-Muslim Moral Panic, Conspiracy Theories, and Socio-Cultural Legacies," *Journal of Contemporary Asia* 53, no. 3 (2023): 423–449.

the nine virtues of the monastic order (sangha). While these numbers may appear innocuous, they were deliberately chosen to represent the cosmological opposite of "786," the number representing Islam.[34] In the months following its formation, 969 stickers began appearing outside Buddhist businesses and homes throughout the country. The 969 Movement is led by Ashin Wirathu, a militant but charismatic monk who rejects the traditional nonviolent teachings of his faith. Nicknamed "the Buddhist bin Laden," Wirathu teaches that Muslims represent an existential threat to the Buddhist character of Myanmar and compromise the country's religious purity.[35] "They would like to occupy our country, but I won't let them. We must keep Myanmar Buddhist," he declared in 2013.[36] In 2003, Wirathu was sentenced to twenty-five years in prison for his role in inciting mob violence, but he was released only seven years later.

The 969 Movement began as a campaign by monks encouraging Buddhists to boycott Muslim-owned businesses and patronize only businesses owned by Buddhists. In some parts of the country, Buddhists aligned with the 969 Movement have prohibited Muslims from buying or renting land or houses. The group has also promoted anti-Muslim violence; leading figures have openly called for attacks on Muslim communities living in Myanmar. In 2017, Wirathu praised the killers of a prominent Muslim attorney.[37] Buddhist mobs, drawing inspiration from Wirathu, have violently attacked Muslims.

In contrast to the 969 Movement, MaBaTha, until it was outlawed in 2017, was a more formally organized group. Founded in 2013, the organization's name reflects its belief that religion, ethnicity, and race should comprise the three ingredients of Burmese national identity. If the 969 Movement operated primarily at the level of society with the goal of raising awareness regarding the threat posed to Buddhism by the spread of Islam, MaBaTha emerged as the political arm of the Buddhist nationalist movement, courting political parties, staging demonstrations, and promoting legal measures pertaining to the regulation of interfaith marriage, monogamy, religious

---

[34] Alex Bookbinder, "969: The Strange Numerological Basis for Burma's Religious Violence," *The Atlantic*, April 10, 2013, https://www.theatlantic.com/international/archive/2013/04/969-the-strange-numerological-basis-for-burmas-religious-violence/274816/.
[35] Alex Preston, "The Rohingya and Myanmar's 'Buddhist Bin Laden,'" *British GQ*, February 12, 2015, https://www.gq-magazine.co.uk/article/myanmar-rohingya-muslim-burma.
[36] Hannah Beech, "The Face of Buddhist Terror," *Time*, July 1, 2013, http://content.time.com/time/magazine/article/0,9171,214,600,000.html.
[37] U.S. Commission on International Religious Freedom, *2017 Annual Report* (Washington, DC: USCIRF, 2017), 24.

conversion, and population control that would protect Myanmar's identity as a Buddhist country. These bills, collectively known as the "race and religion protection laws," became law in 2015. MaBaTha further oversaw the rapid growth of Buddhist schools for children that offered informal religious education classes to young people.

As in Sri Lanka, Buddhist privilege and religious co-optation have paved the way for antiminority violence by extremist Buddhists. Doubtless, the most significant target of violent religious persecution by militant Buddhists has been a Muslim minority living in the Western part of the country close to the border separating Myanmar and Bangladesh known as the Rohingya, a group that has suffered decades of violent religious persecution and a campaign of ethnic cleansing.[38] The government, along with the country's Buddhist nationalists, have long portrayed the Rohingya as illegal aliens who recently migrated from Bangladesh, despite the fact that a majority of Rohingya have lived in Myanmar for generations. Some trace their roots in Myanmar to the seventeenth century. Nevertheless, the government has long refused to recognize the Rohingya as a distinct ethnic group and has denied them citizenship, making the Rohingya one of the largest stateless populations in the world.[39] They enjoy no property rights, no equal protection under the law, and no access to healthcare and education.[40]

Since the 1990s, the Rohingya have suffered accelerating waves of violence, and Rohingya refugees have been fleeing the country at a staggering rate over this time.[41] The government's targeting of the Rohingya has prompted Buddhist vigilantes to do the same. In May 2012, anti-Rohingya violence engulfed the northern part of Rakhine State, including the state capital Sittwe and surrounding areas, following the alleged rape and murder of a Buddhist woman by a group of Muslim men. Violence against the Rohingya quickly spread to other parts of the country, including Mandalay and Meiktili. The following month, a Buddhist mob lynched

---

[38] Arifa Sarmin, "Ongoing Persecution of the Rohingya: A History of Periodic Ethnic Cleansings and Genocides," *Intellectual Discourse* 28, no. 2 (2020): 675–696.

[39] A. K. M Ahsan Ullah, "Rohingya Refugees to Bangladesh: Historical Exclusions and Contemporary Marginalization," *Journal of Immigrant & Refugee Studies* 9, no. 2 (2011): 139–161; A. K. M Ahsan Ullah, "Rohingya Crisis in Myanmar: Seeking Justice for the Stateless," *Journal of Contemporary Criminal Justice* 32, no. 3 (2016): 285–301.

[40] Mary Kate Long, "Dynamics of State, *Sangha* and Society in Myanmar: A Closer Look at the Rohingya Issue," *Asian Journal of Public Affairs* 6, no. 1 (2013): 79–94.

[41] Greg Constantine, "Exiled to Nowhere: Burma's Rohingya," last modified 2018, www.exiledtonowhere.com/.

ten Muslims in central Myanmar. The violence would continue over the following months, resulting in the deaths of hundreds of Rohingya, the destruction of over a dozen holy sites and thousands of Muslim homes, and the displacement of over 100,000 people.[42] Human Rights Watch documented collusion between state authorities, militant monks, and community leaders.[43] Although the government declared a state of emergency and deployed troops to restore calm, Muslims, particularly in Rakhine State, continued to be killed, injured, or displaced at alarming rates. The overwhelming majority of perpetrators of violence have never been brought to justice.

Inciting much of the violence has been the Burmese military, known as the Tatmadaw. It has institutionalized discrimination against the Rohingya, denying them fundamental human rights. In 2017, the Tatmadaw, led by General Min Aung Hlaing, engaged in mass killings, rapes of Rohingya women, and the forced displacement of hundreds of thousands. The military's violent persecution of the Rohingya has only increased since 2017, reaching a climax following the 2021 coup. The Tatmadaw has closely aligned itself with Buddhist nationalists in an attempt to buttress its legitimacy.

Over 1 million Rohingya have fled Myanmar since the 1990s, many of them settling in the world's largest and most densely populated refugee camps, located in Cox's Bazaar, Bangladesh, the majority of them women and children.[44] The squalid camps have themselves experienced escalating violence between different religious communities. Of the Rohingya still in Myanmar, many remain internally displaced or held in internment camps. The United Nations has described the Rohingya as the most persecuted minority in the world.[45] Scholars and practitioners of human rights have depicted the situation as a genocide.[46] UN Commissioner for Human Rights Zeid Ra'ad al Hussein referred to the plight of the Rohingya as "a textbook

---

[42] Neghinpao Kipgen, "Conflict in Rakhine State in Myanmar: Rohingya Muslims' Conundrum," *Journal of Muslim Minority Affairs* 33, no. 2 (2013): 398–410.

[43] Human Rights Watch, *All You Can Do Is Pray: Crimes against Humanity and Ethnic Cleansing of Rohingya Muslims in Burma's Arakan State* (New York: Human Rights Watch, 2013).

[44] UN Refugee Agency, "Rohingya Refugee Crisis," UNHCR, 2022, https://www.unrefugees.org/emergencies/rohingya/.

[45] Lindsey N. Kingston, "Protecting the World's Most Persecuted: The Responsibility to Protect and Burma's Rohingya Minority," *International Journal of Human Rights* 19, no. 8 (2015): 1163–1175.

[46] Azeem Ibrahim, *The Rohingyas: Inside Myanmar's Genocide* (London: Hurst, 2018); Ronan Lee, *Myanmar's Rohingya Genocide: Identity, History, and Hate Speech* (London: I. B. Tauris, 2021).

example of ethnic cleansing."[47] At the time of this writing, a case regarding violations of the Genocide Convention is pending at the International Court of Justice.

Expectedly, the genocidal campaign against the Rohingya has spawned a violent minority backlash.[48] A group calling itself the Arakan Rohingya Salvation Army (ARSA) has claimed responsibility for sporadic attacks against security forces based in Rakhine State.[49] The group has continued to expand its activities. My analysis of terrorist incidences in Myanmar shows that from 2016 to 2020, ARSA carried out sixty identifiable attacks throughout Myanmar, resulting in about a hundred fatalities. Attacks by ARSA have provided a pretext for large-scale and wildly disproportionate military operations against the general Rohingya population and massive forced migrations. Even accounting for attacks by Rohingya extremists, the violence has been clearly one-sided and genocidal in its intent and scope, marked by extrajudicial killings, forced disappearances, sexual violence, looting, and property destruction.

Militant Buddhists have also targeted other minorities living in Myanmar, especially Christians living in Kayin, Kachin, and Chin states. Like the Rohingya, Christian minorities have reported forced conversions, attacks on sacred sites, forced labor, and displacement.[50] Entire Christian villages have been razed to the ground, their inhabitants forced to flee. In Kachin State, more than 100,000 Christians have been internally displaced as a result of civil conflict. Since 1996, the military has destroyed more than three thousand Christian villages, leaving more than 1 million people displaced. Tatmadaw troops have destroyed dozens of historic churches.[51]

In 2021, the Tatmadaw seized power in a coup, arresting members of the civilian government, including Suu Kyi, but freeing militant monks,

---

[47] United Nations, "UN Human Rights Chief Points to 'Textbook Example of Ethnic Cleansing' in Myanmar," *UN News*, September 11, 2017, https://news.un.org/en/story/2017/09/564622-un-human-rights-chief-points-textbook-example-ethnic-cleansingmyanmar#:~:text=%E2%80%9CT he%20situation%20seems%20a%20textbook, access%20to%20human%20rights%20investigators.

[48] Laura Steckman, "Myanmar at the Crossroads: The Shadow of Jihadist Extremism," *Counter Terrorist Trends and Analyses* 7, no. 4 (2015): 10–16.

[49] Iftekharul Bashar, "Rohingya Crisis and Western Myanmar's Evolving Threat Landscape," *Counter Terrorist Trends and Analyses* 11, no. 6 (2019): 14–18; Ronan Lee, "Myanmar's Arakan Rohingya Salvation Army (ARSA)," *Perspectives on Terrorism* 15, no. 6 (2021): 61–75.

[50] Christian Solidarity International, "East Asia: Burma," *CSW*, January 11, 2018.

[51] Christian Solidarity International, "East Asia."

including Wirathu. The coup not only abruptly ended Myanmar's experiment in democracy; it also facilitated the breakdown of law and order and economic collapse that directly led to the escalation of violence. The military violently suppressed peaceful, pro-democracy protests, killing at least thirteen hundred. Hundreds of thousands of Burmese found themselves internally displaced, and millions in dire need of humanitarian aid. Conspicuously absent from the widespread protests against the regime have been privileged Buddhist leaders. Some monks have even served as militia fighters, marching alongside soldiers against armed pro-democracy groups. The leader of the coup, General Hlaing, has cast himself as the protector of the nation's majority Theravada Buddhist religion, in the style of a long line of warrior-kings.[52]

Many expressed hope that the resounding victory of Suu Kyi's NLD in 2015 would herald a brighter future for the beleaguered Rohingya community. Instead, Suu Kyi refused to condemn the atrocities of the state against the Rohingya, and even declined to call the Rohingya by name, thus perpetuating the claim of Buddhist nationalists that the Rohingya are actually illegal Bengali immigrants who have no place in Myanmar.[53] Indeed, it stands to reason that her stance against the Rohingya has contributed to her popularity. To make matters worse, the international community, including leaders of Muslim-majority countries, has done little to address the plight of the Rohingya.[54] Thus the Rohingya remain the world's largest stateless people and most persecuted religious group.

Auspiciously, though, the promotion of violence has not been the only role played by Buddhism in Myanmar. Many Buddhist monks abhor the militancy of their chauvinist counterparts and reject the idea that Myanmar should be a country only for Buddhists. Monks participated in the 1988 uprising that brought Suu Kyi to prominence. Buddhist monks clad in their saffron robes courageously and nonviolently fought for democracy in 2007.

---

[52] Thu Thu Aung and Poppy Mcpherson, "Monk Militia: The Buddhist Clergy Backing Myanmar's Junta," Reuters, December 8, 2022, https://www.reuters.com/world/asia-pacific/monk-militia-buddhist-clergy-backing-myanmars-junta-2022-12-08/.

[53] Ronan Lee, "A Politician, Not an Icon: Aung San Suu Kyi's Silence on Myanmar's Muslim Rohingya," *Islam and Christian-Muslim Relations* 25, no. 3 (2014): 321–333; Peter A. Coclanis, "Aung San Suu Kyi Is a Politician, Not a Monster," *Foreign Policy*, May 14, 2018, https://foreignpolicy.com/2018/05/14/aung-san-suu-kyi-is-a-politician-not-a-monster/.

[54] Navine Murshid, "Bangladesh Copes with the Rohingya Crisis by Itself," *Current History* 117, no. 798 (2018): 129–134; Gershon Dagba and Israel Nyaburi Nyadera, "Position of Responsibility: International Response to the Rohingya Refugee Crisis—The Case of Western Countries," in *Rohingya Refugee Crisis in Myanmar: Ethnic Conflict and Resolution*, ed. Kudret Bülbül, Md. Nazmul Islam, and Md. Sajid Khan (London: Palgrave Macmillan, 2022), 313–336.

Whether the conventional Buddhist teachings on tolerance and goodwill can eventually win the day has yet to be seen. Much will depend on whether those espousing the peaceful face of Buddhism can effectively dissociate Buddhism from the state.

In summary, although the image of saffron-clad Buddhist monks inciting carnage against innocent civilians, rampaging through neighborhoods, and ransacking homes and businesses contradicts stereotypical perceptions of the religion, Buddhist nationalists in Myanmar have indeed engaged in sectarian violence and oppression. The weaponization of Buddhism in this manner stems from the country's crisis of secularism. A symbiotic relationship between the sangha and the state has propelled a nationalist discourse that aims to protect Buddhist national identity, which Buddhist nationalists believe to be threatened by the presence and growth of religious minorities. The generals have long attempted to portray themselves as devout Buddhists, participating in religious rituals and giving alms. The most important national Buddhist body, the State Sangha Maha Nayaka Committee, has largely failed to publicly condemn the rhetoric and activities of militant movements. Government leaders, too, have been largely supportive of the issues championed by these groups and have frequently defended anti-Muslim monks in public. The most significant target of antiminority vitriol has been the Rohingya. Backed by radical monks, the government has refused to recognize the Rohingya as citizens of Myanmar, paving the way for a genocidal campaign against them.

Thailand

The case of Thailand, a country where 95 percent of the population identifies as Buddhist, differs from Sri Lanka and Myanmar. While Buddhism has long been a basis for Thai national identity, religious freedom and nondiscrimination have also been constitutionally protected. For example, although the 1997 Thai Constitution mandates that "[t]he King is a Buddhist and Upholder of religions," it does not declare Buddhism to be Thailand's national religion and guarantees the full rights of citizenship to minority communities. The promotion of inclusive policies by the state facilitated the integration of religious minorities into Thai society. Some Buddhists, though, believed that the equal treatment of religions made possible by the Constitution threatened the superiority of Buddhism. A fringe group of monks lobbied for the Constitution to declare Buddhism the official religion of the state, but their efforts were rebuffed.[55] The country's Buddhists have historically rejected the militant Buddhism found in Sri Lanka and Myanmar, and monks have comparatively little influence over the state. For its part, the state has historically viewed with suspicion exclusionary Buddhist nationalist movements. Expectedly, Buddhist violence has historically remained low, save for a campaign in the mid-1990s by the Myanmar-based group known as the Democratic Karen Buddhist Army against refugee camps along the Thai-Myanmar border. The spate of attacks, though, appears to have been driven more by events in Myanmar than in Thailand.

Nevertheless, recent developments in Thailand present reasons for concern that it, too, may be retreating from its commitment to political secularism—a development that has coincided with the country's democratic recession. After the end of the Cold War, economic and political liberalization moved Bangkok away from the alliance between the monarchy and Buddhism that characterized the military dictatorship, when the integration of temple and state reached its zenith.[56] However, in 2014 the Royal Thai Armed Forces launched a coup against the democratically elected government and established a junta called the National Council for Peace and Order. Supportive of the military have been Buddhist nationalists who claim that Buddhism is losing its aura in Thailand and that it must remain a key marker of Thai national identity. They have thus demanded protection and privilege from the state and more authority over social and political affairs.[57] Within three years, the military government adopted a new constitution, one that clearly moved the country in the direction of Buddhist establishment.[58] Article 67 of the document declares, "In supporting and protecting Buddhism, which is the religion observed by the majority of Thai people for a long period of time, the State should promote and support education and dissemination of dharmic principles of Theravada Buddhism for

---

[55] Keyes, "Theravada Buddhism and Buddhist Nationalism," 47.

[56] Somboon Suksamran, "Buddhism, Political Authority, and Legitimacy in Thailand and Cambodia," in *Buddhist Trends in Southeast Asia*, ed. Trevor Lind (Singapore: Institute of Southeast Asian Studies, 1993), 101–153; Peter A. Jackson, "Withering Centre, Flourishing Margins: Buddhism's Changing Political Roles," in *Political Change in Thailand: Democracy and Participation*, ed. Kevin Hewison (London: Routledge, 2002), 75–93.

[57] Katewadee Kularbkeaw, *The Politics of Thai Buddhism under the NCPO Junta* (Singapore: ISEAS, 2019).

[58] Eugénie Mérieau, "Buddhist Constitutionalism in Thailand: When Rājadhammā Supersedes the Constitution," *Asian Journal of Comparative Law* 13, no. 2 (2018): 283–305.

the development of mind and wisdom, and shall have measures and mechanisms to prevent Buddhism from being undermined in any form. The State should also encourage Buddhists to participate in implementing such measures or mechanisms."

Of the five recognized religions, Buddhism receives a disproportionate allocation of resources. The relationship between temple and state in Thailand today resembles the historical relationship between Buddhism—a traditional pillar of Thai nationalism—and the monarchy that existed during the colonial era and Siam's transition to modern Thailand.[59] Just as the king served as the patron of the sangha during this time—a symbiotic relationship known as the "Two Wheels of Dhamma"—contemporary Thai Buddhist nationalists look to the state for protection from their perceived religious competitors and intrareligious schisms (especially between mainstream Buddhism and a heterodox sect known as the Dhammakaya Temple).[60]

A recent and growing strain of Buddhist nationalism, coupled with a renewed alliance between Buddhism and the state, has coincided with a deadly and protracted insurgency that has occurred in the overwhelmingly Muslim and ethnically Malay southern part of the country known as the "Deep South," a region that has witnessed periodic fighting between insurgents and the Thai government since the 1940s. The Malay Muslim insurgents are fighting for a separate independent state comprising Thailand's Muslim-majority southern provinces—Pattani, Yala, Narathiwat, and parts of Songkhla—a region that was for centuries an independent Islamic sultanate with its own culture and language. In the 1990s, political and economic reforms by the Thai government led to an amelioration of tensions, many believing that the insurgency had come to an end. However, in 2004 the fighting resurfaced as new insurgent groups formed.[61] In that same year, the state declared martial law in southern Thailand. In 2019, the conflict escalated ahead of elections as the government heightened its military engagement in the southern regions, prompting deadly attacks by

---

[59] Somboon Suksamran, *Political Buddhism in Southeast Asia: The Role of the Sangha in the Modernization of Thailand* (New York: St. Martin's Press, 1977); Stanley J. Tambiah, *World Conqueror and World Renouncer: A Study of Buddhism and Polity in Thailand against a Historical Background* (Cambridge: Cambridge University Press, 1977); Joseph Chinyong Liow, *Religion and Nationalism in Southeast Asia* (Cambridge: Cambridge University Press, 2016), 6–7.

[60] Khemthong Tonsakulrungruang, "The Revival of Buddhist Nationalism in Thailand and Its Adverse Impact on Religious Freedom," *Asian Journal of Law and Society* 8 (2021): 74.

[61] Frank Bures, "Muslim Unrest Flares in Thailand," *Christian Science Monitor*, January 7, 2004, https://www.csmonitor.com/2004/0107/p06s01-wosc.html.

insurgent groups that resulted in civilian casualties and temporary displacement. Since 2004, over seven thousand people, both Buddhists and Muslims, have perished in the conflict.

The Thai government has responded with a heavy hand, giving near blanket immunity to the military for its operations in the restive South. The military's presence in the southern provinces has been guided by special emergency laws that infringe on civil liberties, further alienating an already marginalized population. This has also encouraged Buddhist vigilantism.[62] The bloodshed in the Deep South has led to the emergence of "soldier monks"—members of the military who ordain as monks, some even carrying weapons under their robes and donning saffron-colored bulletproof vests.[63] These soldier monks have formed a loosely connected resistance movement to protect Buddhism from the perceived threat posed by the growing presence of Islam and to reassert Buddhism's preeminent place in society. In 2014, for example, vigilante monks attempted the extrajudicial killing of an imam before murdering his three sons.[64] At the same time, Buddhist spaces, including temples and schools, have become increasingly militarized, and military spaces increasingly religionized. At the order of the queen, the government has armed local Buddhist militias known as Village Defense Volunteers as a means to counter the Muslim insurgency. These organizations remain distinct from the armed forces and law enforcement agencies of the state and train on Buddhist temple compounds. The state's alliance with these groups has deepened the sectarian dimension of the conflict in southern Thailand.[65]

The Deep South conflict has fed a sense of anxiety, particularly fears over Islamist extremism, receding Buddhist dominance, and the erosion of national identity, among Thai Buddhists throughout the rest of Thailand.[66] Rising Islamophobia in society, fed by the insurgency, has become commonplace. Mobs have protested the building of mosques and the standardization

---

[62] Michael K. Jerryson, *Buddhist Fury: Religion and Violence in Southern Thailand* (New York: Oxford University Press, 2011), 119.

[63] Duncan McCargo, "Thai Buddhism, Thai Buddhists and the Southern Conflict," *Journal of Southeast Asian Studies* 40, no. 1 (2009): 1–10; Duncan McCargo, *Tearing Apart the Land: Islam and Legitimacy in Southern Thailand* (Ithaca, NY: Cornell University Press, 2008), 183–187; Jerryson, *Buddhist Fury*, 85.

[64] Zachary Abuza, "Religion in the Southern Thailand Conflict," *The Interpreter*, October 10, 2014, https://www.lowyinstitute.org/the-interpreter/religion-southern-thailand-conflict.

[65] Michael Jerryson, "Appropriating a Space for Violence: State Buddhism in Southern Thailand," *Journal of Southeast Asian Studies* 40, no. 1 (2009): 33–57.

[66] Duncan McCargo, "The Politics of Buddhist Identity in Thailand's Deep South: The Demise of Civil Religion?," *Journal of Southeast Asian Studies* 40, no. 1 (2009): 11–32.

of halal food.[67] Several prominent monks have openly endorsed violence in the name of protecting Thailand's Buddhist identity.[68] In 2019, a prominent monk publicly declared that for each monk killed in Thailand's Deep South, "a mosque should be burned, starting from the northern part of Thailand southwards."[69] (The monk, Phra Maha Apichat, was subsequently expelled from his monastic community.) While Buddhist violence remains relatively low compared to Sri Lanka and Myanmar, it is still present and could well see an explosion in the future should current trends persist.

Islamophobia can also be seen in the realm of politics. The Buddhist nationalist Pandin Dharma Party has parlayed anxiety over Muslim ascendance into an electoral victory at the polls. In a country traditionally tolerant of religious differences, the rise of a pro-Buddhist party marks a new and worrying trend. The emergence of the party reveals how the insurgency has deepened the alliance between Buddhism and the state. In this quid pro quo, the state offers protection to the sangha in exchange for the sangha's support of the state. As a result of this mutually advantageous grand bargain, Thai Buddhism is able to recover its receding hegemony as the state buttresses its legitimacy.

In summary, the case of Thailand presents a cautionary tale regarding the future of Buddhist nationalism in Asia. For much of its history, Thai society was among the most open in all of Asia, and was largely inclusive of minorities. Most Thai Buddhists rejected militant Buddhism. Yet, as in Sri Lanka and Myanmar, certain elements within the sangha and laypeople are now advocating for a closer relationship between temple and state. They perceive Buddhism as embattled and in need of state protection; they fear that Buddhism is at risk of losing its cultural superiority; and they see Buddhism as intrinsically intertwined with the Royal Thai government, which, for its part, has worked to construct Thai identity on the basis of religion. Thai Buddhist extremists have taken particular aim at Islam, as they have in Sri Lanka and Myanmar. Incited by the conflict in the Deep South, they have spread conspiratorial canards about the country's minority Muslim population, accusing them of deliberately subverting the country's Buddhist identity and asserting Muslim cultural dominance. Militant Buddhism in

---

[67] Tonsakulrungruang, "The Revival of Buddhist Nationalism in Thailand and Its Adverse Impact on Religious Freedom," 83.
[68] Jerryson, *Buddhist Fury*, 182–186.
[69] *Pime Asia News*, "Bangkok: Monks Leading a Buddhist Extremist Movement for a Confessional State," April 11, 2015, https://www.asianews.it/news-en/Bangkok:-monks-leading-a-Buddhist-extremist-movement-for-a-confessional-state-35778.html.

Thailand has been abetted by the country's turmoil since the beginning of the twenty-first century: bloody political protests, a coup and governmental instability, unprecedented climate catastrophes, and continuing unrest in the Deep South. Triggered by these crises, Buddhism and the state are reforging their once strong alliance to the detriment of minorities. The Pew Research Center notes that social hostilities involving religion remain at a high level, reflecting, in part, activities of nationalist Buddhist groups such as the Buddhism Protection Organization for Peace.[70] Conspicuously absent have been Buddhist calls for peace and reconciliation or condemnation of abuses by Thai security forces, reflecting the deepening entanglement of Buddhism and the state.

Summary

Most Buddhists steadfastly follow the nonviolent path of the Buddha. They affirm Buddhism's emphasis on love for others, condemn violence in every form, and practice the virtue of ahimsa (non-violence). Even today, Buddhist activists fight extremists by calling for interfaith harmony. They seek to bring healing to societies wounded by incessant violence by increasing knowledge, tolerance, and empathy.

Yet, in line with the argument of this book, Buddhism also has a dark side, belying the irenic stereotype many outsiders have of the world's fourth-largest religion. Although Buddhist teachings emphasize tolerance, harmony, nonviolence, and peace, Buddhist leaders have sanctioned violence and war throughout the religion's history. War and violence can be seen in each of Buddhism's major traditions—Theravada, Mahayana, and Vajrayana—challenging romanticized notions of Buddhism as a faith uniquely devoted to peace and nonviolence. Put in proper context, even among Buddhists one can discern the Janus-faced, multivocal character of religion.

In recent times, the weaponization of Buddhism in certain parts of Asia has shaken the religion's pacifist foundations. As political scientist Janjira Sombatpoonsiri notes, this violence stems from "Buddhist majoritarian movements" whose goal is "to expose the public to what they view as virulent

---

[70] Pew Research Center, *Globally, Government Restrictions on Religion Reached Peak Levels in 2021, While Social Hostilities Went Down*, 39.

threats against the Buddhist majority."[71] Multiple Buddhist-majority countries have witnessed serious religious hostilities between Buddhists and minority religious traditions. In Sri Lanka, militant Buddhist nationalist groups such as the Bodu Bala Sena fight for the country to retain its Buddhist character. The same forces previously helped fuel a twenty-six-year-long civil war against a different minority community, the Tamils. In Myanmar, radical monks have abetted a genocidal campaign against the country's Rohingya Muslim population. In Thailand, Buddhist militarism has coincided with a democratic recession. These cases upend common stereotypes of *two* religions—Buddhism and Islam—for in each case Buddhists have been the perpetrators of violence and Muslims the victims. In all three countries, antiminority violence can be understood as the result of the "religionization of politics."[72] To be sure, the threat to Buddhist identity owing to perceived Muslim demographic growth, cultural and economic ascendancy, and proneness to violence is largely imagined; what matters, however, is that many Buddhists *believe* these things to be true. This fear has proven to be a powerful tool in the mobilization of Buddhist majoritarianism.

Although the most serious cases of violent Buddhist extremism have been confined to the countries surveyed in this chapter, there is growing concern that it could spread to other parts of Asia where Muslims have a small but visible presence.[73] Also concerning is the growing possibility for extremist Buddhist groups to more easily forge alliances across countries as they continue to harness the power of social media. Indeed, insipient cross-country partnerships between hardline Buddhists have already been created, such as the 2014 pact between Sri Lanka's Bodu Bala Sena and Myanmar's Wirathu for the purpose of protecting embattled Buddhists from the growing threat posed by Islam to their respective societies.

In the end, the cases in this chapter complicate the simplistic picture of Buddhism being an inherently pacifist religious tradition, revealing that Buddhism is susceptible to nationalism and violence, as is every other of the world's great religious traditions. Majoritarian violence in these countries has been greatly abetted by deficits in political secularism, as Buddhist nationalists seek to take over their states and governments lend their support

---

[71] Janjira Sombatpoonsiri, "Buddhist Majoritarian Nationalism in Thailand: Ideological Contestation, Narratives, and Activism," *Journal of Contemporary Asia* 53, no. 3 (2022): 398–422.

[72] Sascha Helbardt, Dagmar Hellmann-Rajanayagam, and Rüdiger Korff, "Religionisation of Politics in Sri Lanka, Thailand and Myanmar," *Politics, Religion & Ideology* 14, no. 1 (2013): 36–58.

[73] Elaine Coates, "Interreligious Violence in Myanmar: A Security Threat to Southeast Asia," *RSIS Commentaries* 117 (2013): 1–3.

to destructive sectarian forces. In these settings, Buddhist majoritarian movements see the presence of religious pluralism as a threat and strive to solidify national identity on the basis of their own religion. In response, they seek out alliances with their states so as to respond to the presence and growth of religious minorities. The resulting Buddhist nationalism throughout the region has greatly contributed to social fragility and violence, chiefly carried out by Buddhist vigilantes, supported by the laws and policies of the state, against religious minorities. In the end, the violent manifestations of Buddhism explored in this chapter demonstrate that privilege carries the power to weaponize even what is arguably the world's most peaceful religion.

How, then, can the peaceful face of Buddhism triumph over the forces of division, hatred, and intolerance? To start, the vast majority of Buddhists who uphold the religion's "live and let live" approach to life must unequivocally denounce those who seek to weaponize Buddhism against minority religions and affirm nonviolence as central to Buddhist teachings. While this is an important step, the solution also requires an understanding of the crucial role played by religious privilege in stoking communal hostilities. The peaceful face of Buddhism is likely to prevail only under conditions of political secularism that reject Buddhist privilege. Accordingly, in recognition of this reality, Buddhists who abhor violence must commit themselves to rejecting Buddhist nationalism and upholding the separation of Buddhist identities and institutions from the governing apparatus. Only then can "engaged Buddhism" prevail against the forces of "enraged Buddhism."

Having examined the relationship between the global crisis of secularism and violence in the four largest of the world's religions, the next chapter turns to the final case: Judaism. Whereas the present and previous chapters have examined religions numbering in the billions or hundreds of millions of followers, Judaism is a comparatively tiny religion. Still, it is an important case, owing to Israel's location in the tinderbox of the Middle East and the ongoing Israeli-Palestinian conflict. Here again we see a robust relationship between the degrading of political secularism in the form of Jewish privilege and the empowerment of violent Jewish radicals.

Chapter 6
Judaism

Judaism is by far the smallest of the world's major religions, with only 15 million adherents worldwide. Only one country in the world—Israel—has a Jewish majority. Still, Judaism remains one of the world's most important religions for several reasons. First, Judaism gave birth to the world's two largest religious traditions, Christianity and Islam, both of which trace their roots to Abraham, the Hebrew patriarch of the world's monotheistic religions. Second, the world's only Jewish-majority state, Israel, occupies a land considered sacred not only by Jews but also by Christians and Muslims. As such, it has been the location of many wars and conflicts. Third, Judaism, arguably more than any other religion, brings into sharp relief the ambivalence of religion. On the one hand, the Hebrew scriptures contain some of the most violent passages found in any of the world's holy texts. Some passages in the Hebrew Bible appear to command genocide, infanticide, and slavery.[1] In ancient times, an anti-imperialist Jewish insurrectionist group called the *sicarii* conducted stealth assassinations against the Roman occupiers of Judea. In Mandatory Palestine, militant Jewish groups such as the Irgun, the Lehi, and the Stern Gang committed acts of terror against British soldiers and the Arab population in Palestine. More recently, Jewish groups such as Kach, Gush Emunim, Keshet, Bat Ayin Underground, and Lehava have undertaken violence as a means to thwart proposed peace plans between the Israelis and Palestinians, combat the secularization of Israeli society, and protect the Orthodox Jewish way of life.[2]

Yet the Jewish tradition also contains rich resources for peacebuilding and reconciliation. Most important here is the idea of *shalom*—a state of vertical right relationship between oneself and God, of horizontal right relationship between oneself and one's fellow human beings, and of inward peace within oneself. *Shalom* not only renounces the use of force; it forsakes even

---

[1] Leviticus 20:27; 1 Samuel 15:3; Psalm 137:9.
[2] Ian Lustick, *For the Land and the Lord: Jewish Fundamentalism in Israel* (New York: Council on Foreign Relations, 1988); Ami Pedahzur and Arie Perliger, *Jewish Terrorism in Israel* (New York: Columbia University Press, 2011), 31–37.

thoughts of violence or ill will toward others. In this view, the commitment to nonviolence is a natural expression of *shalom*.

If Judaism, reflecting its scriptures, is sometimes violent and sometimes peaceful, what explains this ambivalence? In line with the major argument of this book, I suggest that Judaism's violent and peaceful tendencies can be explained by politics. Among advanced industrial democracies, Israel is highly unique. Modern Israel has its origins in a nineteenth-century Zionist movement that campaigned for the establishment of a Jewish state as the only way to justly end millennia of Jewish persecution. The location of this Jewish home would be in Ottoman-controlled Palestine, the land inhabited by the ancient Israelites. On Friday, May 14, 1948, in the city of Tel Aviv, Zionist leader David Ben-Gurion officially declared the establishment of an independent, sovereign Jewish state. Today Israel is the world's only Jewish country, with approximately 7 million Jews calling Israel home. About 73 percent of the population is Jewish, the rest belonging to Muslim, Christian, Druze, and nonreligious minorities, the vast majority of whom are of Arab/Palestinian descent. Even though Israel was conceived as a Jewish state from the beginning, the founder of modern political Zionism, Theodor Herzl, was an atheist who envisioned a secular governing apparatus that would not be influenced by religion, modeled on a European-style religion-state arrangement. In Herzl's ideal Israeli state, the rabbis would be confined to their synagogues, and the state would stay out of religious affairs. Ze'ev Jabotinsky, the leader of the Zionist movement during the interwar years, also defined Jewishness in secular nationalist terms. We have seen similar founding secular visions in countries like Egypt, India, Pakistan, and Türkiye in previous chapters.

Israel's political leaders, however, did not share this vision. Ben-Gurion, the founder of the Israeli state, formed a government that included Jewish parties and relaxed the assumption that governmental and religious institutions should be separated. He also made important concessions to influential rabbis, granting the state rabbinate jurisdiction over the personal status of all Jewish citizens, guaranteeing the sanctity of the Sabbath in the public sphere, and promising cultural autonomy to Israel's ultra-Orthodox community. As might be expected in a country that identifies as a "Jewish state," religion and government have been inextricably intertwined in Israel from its founding. That Israel was established as an officially Jewish state has naturally produced religious tensions between different communities. Minorities have lashed out against being treated as second-class citizens. Violent fringes of the Jewish majority have partaken in bloodshed in an effort to keep Israel religiously pure.

This chapter proceeds in three parts. The first surveys the state of political secularism in Israel. It argues that among the world's advanced industrial democracies, Israel features a highly anomalous religion-state arrangement, one that explicitly envisions a country for one particular religious community, namely Jews. That Israel was founded as a Jewish state necessarily means that it has suffered from the lack of political secularism from its establishment. The second section examines the interaction between religious privilege, Jewish nationalism, and attacks by militant Jews against minorities and the state itself. Here we see how the absence of political secularism has helped produce multiple pathways to majoritarian violence. The concluding section situates the discussion in the context of Israel's future as a "Jewish democracy."

Political Secularism in Israel

Zionism holds that Judaism is not just a religion but a nationality, one that deserves a state of its own. Early European Zionists argued that, given millennia of anti-Jewish persecution, the Jewish people had a right to settle in their historic homeland in the Middle East. The Zionist movement gained support in the first decades of the twentieth century, with tens of thousands of European Jews migrating to the Holy Land. Following the Holocaust, many more Jews permanently left Europe for British Palestine. In 1947, amid growing sectarianism between Jews and Arabs, the United Nations devised a plan to divide Palestine into two separate states, one for Jews (Israel) and one for Arabs (Palestine). Jerusalem, a city considered sacred by Jews, Christians, and Muslims, would be internationally administered. The Jews accepted the plan and declared their independent state on May 14, 1948.

Although the founders of Israel decided to omit any reference to God from the country's Declaration of Independence and guaranteed universal religious freedom in this same document, they made no effort to separate synagogue and state. The Declaration of the Establishment of the State of Israel proclaims, "The Land of Israel was the birthplace of the

Jewish people. Here, their spiritual, religious, and political identity was shaped." Consequently, Judaism thoroughly infuses social and political life in Israel. The 1992 Basic Law: Human Dignity and Liberty defines Israel as both a "Jewish and democratic state." The Law of Return allows for any Jew, or any child or grandchild of a Jew, anywhere in the world to immigrate to Israel and gain full citizenship with his or her spouse and children, but this right is not conferred to non-Jews. At the level of society, legally recognized marriages must be performed by a rabbi, divorces by a rabbinical council. The law declares Shabbat and Jewish holidays as national days of rest. Accordingly, many businesses are closed on Saturdays, including many forms of public transportation and the Israeli airline, El Al. Only kosher food is allowed at army bases and in government buildings. The flag of Israel resembles a Jewish prayer shawl (*tallit*) that features the Star of David at its center. The national coat of arms displays a seven-branched menorah flanked on both sides by olive leaves. The national anthem contains well-known lines from Jewish prayers. In practical terms, Israel has the highest level of government intervention in religion of any democratic state, Orthodox Judaism serving as a de facto national religion.[3]

The intertwining of Judaism and Israeli public life in these myriad ways has led some scholars to describe Israel as a "theocratic democracy"[4] or "semi-secular democratic state."[5] To be sure, Israel remains friendlier to minorities than surrounding Muslim-majority states. Minorities living in Israel generally enjoy basic political rights and civil liberties, including freedom of religion, freedom of speech, and freedom of assembly. These rights, though, do not extend to minorities living in the West Bank. Palestinians in the Occupied Territories cannot receive permanent resident status in Israel or East Jerusalem even if they marry Israelis. While Israelis can leave and reenter the country at will, Palestinians generally cannot fly out of Israel's international airport and often find themselves subject to other restrictions on movement. Palestinians are denied the right to vote. This unequal state of affairs has led many, including former American president Jimmy Carter,

---

[3] Jonathan Fox and Jonathan Rynhold, "A Jewish and Democratic State? Comparing Government Involvement in Religion in Israel with Other Democracies," *Totalitarian Movements and Political Religions* 9, no. 4 (2008): 524.
[4] Nachman Ben-Yehuda, *Theocratic Democracy: The Social Construction of Religious and Secular Extremism* (New York: Oxford University Press, 2010).
[5] Almond, Appleby, and Sivan, *Strong Religion*, 131.

to criticize Israel for functioning as an apartheid state.[6] For these reasons, Israel cannot be considered a politically secular country.[7]

Not only does the Israeli state discriminate against non-Jews; it also discriminates against non-Orthodox Jews. Since its founding, the state has favored Orthodox denominations of Judaism over Conservative or Reformed Judaism. Some government policies have been based on an Orthodox understanding of religious law (*Halacha*). For example, only marriages and divorces performed by Orthodox rabbis are recognized by the state. Jews who marry or divorce without the Chief Rabbinate's authorization face prison sentences. The Chief Rabbinate does not always recognize as Jews Israeli citizens who self-identify as Jewish, including converts to Reformed and Conservative Judaism. The Rabbinate also determines which Jews can be buried in Jewish cemeteries, limiting this right to those considered Jewish by Orthodox standards. The government subsidizes Orthodox religious and educational institutions through the Ministry of Religious Services, but does not extend the same support to schools or organizations affiliated with other Jewish traditions.[8] The financial support offered to Orthodox institutions comes with strings attached, however, as beneficiaries are prohibited from rejecting the existence of Israel as a "Jewish and democratic state." Most ultra-Orthodox Jews known as the Haredi (comprising about 13 percent of the population) are exempt from the compulsory military service required of the rest of Israeli citizens, so that they can instead focus on their religious studies.[9] On some public bus lines, riders are segregated by gender, men sitting at the front and women at the back.

Arguably, the commitment of Israel's political leaders to political secularism has never been lower than it is at the time of this writing. The most recent coalition government, comprising several nationalist and religious parties (including one whose leader was once convicted of anti-Arab racism) and led by embattled prime minister Benjamin Netanyahu, might

---

[6] Jimmy Carter, *Palestine: Peace Not Apartheid* (New York: Simon & Schuster, 2006).

[7] Guy Ben-Porat and Bryan S. Turner, "Introduction: Contemporary Dilemmas of Israeli Citizenship," in *The Contradictions of Israeli Citizenship: Land, Religion, and State*, ed. Guy Ben-Porat and Bryan S. Turner (London: Routledge, 2011), 12.

[8] Joshua Mitnick, "Israel Moves to Improve Religious Freedom—for Jews," *Christian Science Monitor*, June 6, 2012, www.csmonitor.com/World/Middle-East/2012/0606/Israel-moves-toimprove-religious-freedom-for-Jews.

[9] Enver Torregroza Lara and Sebastián Cote Pabón, "Secularism and Democracy in Israel: Military Service as Case Study," *Middle East Policy* 26, no. 3 (2019): 134–150.

be the most far-right government in Israel's history.[10] The most important ministerial posts have been assigned to right-leaning or ultra-Orthodox politicians. Upon the formation of the government, twenty-seven Israeli human rights organizations issued a joint statement averring that the governing coalition sought to make "Jewish supremacy" its "official policy."[11] Prime Minister Netanyahu himself declared in a series of tweets, "The Jewish people have an exclusive and unquestionable right to all areas of the Land of Israel" and "[T]he government will promote and develop settlement in all parts of the Land of Israel—in the Galilee, the Negev, the Golan, Judea, and Samaria."[12] The Jerusalem-based human rights organization B'Tselem points out that the dozens of laws that discriminate against indigenous Palestinians and favor Jews are designed to advance and perpetuate the "supremacy of one group—Jews—over another—Palestinians" throughout the "territory between the Jordan River and the Mediterranean Sea."[13] The problem is compounded by the reality of high population growth rates among the ultra-Orthodox. In 2023, massive demonstrations erupted across the country. The protestors rallied against a proposed legal reform plan put forward by Netanyahu that would have virtually eliminated Israel's system of checks and balances. Importantly, throughout the upheaval Netanyahu maintained the support of his ultra-Orthodox constituency.[14]

In 2018, Israel's Parliament passed a controversial new Basic Law, Israel—The Nation State of the Jewish People, colloquially known as the "Nation-State Law." The law defines the country as the "national homeland of the Jewish people." Although the law grants individual rights for all citizens, it bestows *national* rights only on Jewish citizens. The bill affirms Israel's Jewish character, recognizes Jewish law as an inspiration for legislation, promotes Jewish communities that enforce rules that exclude Israeli

---

[10] Raffi Berg, "Israel's Most Right-Wing Government Agreed under Benjamin Netanyahu," *BBC News*, December 22, 2022, https://www.bbc.com/news/world-middle-east-63942616.

[11] Daoud Kuttab, "Is 'Jewish Supremacy' Translating into Anti-Christian Violence in Jerusalem?," Religion News Service, February 3, 2023, https://religionnews.com/2023/02/03/is-jewish-supremacy-translating-into-anti-christian-violence-in-jerusalem/.

[12] Nasim Ahmed, "Jewish Supremacy Is State Policy, Says Netanyahu," *Middle East Monitor*, January 3, 2023, https://www.middleeastmonitor.com/20230103-jewish-supremacy-is-state-policy-says-netanyahu/.

[13] B'Tselem, "English," 2023, https://thisisapartheid.btselem.org/eng/#1.

[14] *The Economist*, "Binyamin Netanyahu Is Exploiting Israel's Divisions," March 16, 2023, https://www.economist.com/middle-east-and-africa/2023/03/16/binyamin-netanyahu-is-exploiting-israels-divisions?utm_medium=social-media.content.np&utm_source=twitter&utm_campaign=editorial-social&utm_content=discovery.content.

Palestinians, defines Israel's national holidays and symbols, acknowledges Jewish settlement as a "national value," and drops Arabic as one of Israel's national languages, leaving Hebrew as the state's only official language. It further recommends that judges use Jewish jurisprudence and heritage as a source of legal principles in cases where no judicial precedent exists. Essentially, the bill made the right to national self-determination "unique to the Jewish people." Supporters of the bill contend that it represents a symbolic affirmation of an existing reality; its purpose is to foster Jewish unity, but it has no bearing on the day-to-day lives of citizens. Critics, including many international Jewish groups, allege that the law threatens Israel's democratic foundation and future insofar as it discriminates against the 20 percent of Israeli citizens belonging to minority communities, relegates them to the status of second-class citizen, denies the history and legitimacy of indigenous Palestinian communities, and bolsters an existing apartheid state. Essentially, they claim that the law makes Palestinians strangers in their own homeland and denies them full equality by failing to grant them the same rights as Jews.[15] In the months that followed the bill's passage, tens of thousands of people took to the streets in protest, including both Jewish and Arab Israelis. As a Basic Law, the legislation has constitutional standing.

It is important to note that Jewish privilege in Israel has been supported by its greatest ally abroad, the United States. Historically, Washington has provided Israel with a remarkable level of economic, military, and diplomatic support.[16] American backing of Israel has been enabled, in large part, by conservative evangelical Christians in the United States who believe that God gave the physical land of Israel to the Jewish people for all eternity.[17] This belief has translated into a political outgrowth known as "Christian Zionism," a form of Zionism that predates its Jewish counterpart. In this view, the United States must stand steadfastly by the state of Israel if it is

---

[15] Yousef Jabareen, "Enshrining Exclusion: The Nation-State Law and the Arab-Palestinian Minority in Israel," in *Defining Israel: The Jewish State, Democracy, and the Law*, ed. Simon Rabinovitch (Cincinnati, OH: Hebrew Union College Press, 2018), 249–263.

[16] John J. Mearsheimer and Stephen M. Walt, *The Israel Lobby and U.S. Foreign Policy* (New York: Farrar, Straus and Giroux, 2008).

[17] Pew Research Center, *Many Americans Uneasy with Mix of Religion and Politics* (Washington, DC: Pew Research Center for the People & the Press, 2006), 20; Michael Lipka, "More White Evangelicals Than American Jews Say God Gave Israel to the Jewish People," Pew Research Center, October 3, 2013, https://www.pewresearch.org/fact-tank/2013/10/03/more-white-evangelicals-than-american-jews-say-god-gave-israel-to-the-jewish-people/; Lifeway Research, "Evangelical Attitudes toward Israel Research Study," December 1, 2017, http://lifewayresearch.com/wp-content/uploads/2017/12/Evangelical-Attitudes-Toward-Israel-Research-Study-Report.pdf.

to fulfill its own calling as a Christian nation.[18] American presidents, too, both Republican and Democratic, have acted on Christian Zionist beliefs in fashioning their policies toward Israel. In 1994, President Bill Clinton, quoting his minister W. O. Vaught, explained Christian support for Israel: "If you abandon Israel, God will never forgive you. . . . It is God's will that Israel, the biblical home of the people of Israel, continue for ever and ever."[19] In 2018, President Donald Trump took the controversial step of moving the American embassy in Israel from Tel Aviv to Jerusalem. The relocation legitimated the claim of Israeli officials that Jerusalem is Israel's undivided capital, despite the fact that Palestinians living in the eastern part of the city also claim it as their capital.

In summary, supporters of Israel tout it as the only democracy in the region. At the same time, Israel inherently rejects political secularism, making its religion-state arrangement highly unique—and problematic—among the world's liberal democratic states. Founded as a Jewish democracy, Israel explicitly favors a certain form of Judaism, while it discriminates against non-Jews and non-Orthodox Jews. A controversial 2018 law codified Israel's status as a Jewish state. Israel's rejection of political secularism has been abetted from abroad by the most powerful country in the world, the United States.

Jewish Nationalism and Violence

Since Israel's founding, violence has been an endemic feature of life there. After Israel declared independence in 1948, forces from surrounding Arab states attacked. The following decade witnessed regular incursions by Arab guerrillas from Syria, Egypt, and Jordan, who carried out attacks against Israeli civilians and soldiers, and reprisal operations by the Israeli Defense

---

[18] Paul Merkley, *The Politics of Christian Zionism, 1891–1948* (London: Routledge, 1998); Alan Mittleman, Byron Johnson, and Lancy Isserman, eds., *Uneasy Allies? Evangelical and Jewish Relations* (Lanham, MD: Rowman and Littlefield, 2007); Stephen Spector, *Evangelicals and Israel: The Story of American Christian Zionism* (Oxford: Oxford University Press, 2008); Donald M. Lewis, *The Origins of Christian Zionism: Lord Shaftesbury and Evangelical Support for a Jewish Homeland* (Cambridge: Cambridge University Press, 2014); Robert O. Smith, *More Desired Than Our Owne Salvation: The Roots of Christian Zionism* (Oxford: Oxford University Press, 2014); Samuel Goldman, *God's Country: Christian Zionism in America* (Philadelphia: University of Pennsylvania Press, 2018).

[19] Bill Clinton, "Address of United States President William Jefferson Clinton to the Knesset," Knesset, October 27, 1994, https://www.knesset.gov.il/description/eng/doc/speech_clinton_1994_eng.htm.

Forces. In 1967, Israel won a war lasting six days against Egypt, Jordan, and Syria, significantly expanding its territory. Six years later, Israel was again attacked by a coalition of countries on the Jewish holiday of Yom Kippur. Throughout the 1970s, Israel fought off a Palestinian insurgency emanating from South Lebanon. From 1985 to 2000, Israel once again became embroiled in a conflict in South Lebanon against forces backed by Iran. Since 2008, Israel has fought periodic wars against the militant Islamist group Hamas in Gaza. The Israeli state has also had to deal with domestic violence, including two bloody Palestinian uprisings known as "intifadas" that took place in 1987–1993 and 2000–2005. In 2021, riots broke out between Jews and Arabs in various cities. In 2023, tensions between the Israelis and Palestinians escalated yet again, with more rockets being fired into Israel than at any point since 2006. On October 7, 2023, Israel suffered the worst terrorist attack in its history when Hamas murdered more than fourteen hundred civilians in an operation called "Al-Aqsa Flood," precipitating an Israeli ground war in Gaza and the most significant military escalation in the region since the 1973 Yom Kippur War. Since its independence, over forty-five hundred Israeli civilians have been killed in Palestinian terrorist attacks, about half the lives claimed since 2000.[20]

With good reason, then, the overwhelming majority of work exploring violence related to Israel focuses on anti-Jewish extremism, especially Palestinian (suicide) terrorism.[21] Not all religious violence in Israel emanates from Arab or Muslim sources, however; militant Jews, too, have taken to the gun. Paradoxically, but also consistent with what we have seen in previous chapters, Israel's integration of religion and state has helped fuel the extremist ideology held by militant Jewish groups that Israel should exist not just as a country where Jews comprise a numerical majority but also as a land that only Jews should be allowed to inhabit. Violent Jewish actors have been emboldened by hardline politicians in the Israeli government. Extremist Jews have targeted both Palestinian civilians, especially those living in the Occupied Territories, and the Israeli state itself.

---

[20] Jewish Virtual Library, "Number of Terrorism Fatalities in Israel," 2021, https://www.jewishvirtuallibrary.org/number-of-terrorism-fatalities-in-israel.

[21] Assaf Moghadam, "Palestinian Suicide Terrorism in the Second Intifada: Motivations and Organizational Aspects," *Studies in Conflict and Terrorism* 26, no. 2 (2003): 65–92; Scott Atran, "Genesis of Suicide Terrorism," *Science* 299, no. 5612 (2003): 1534–1539; Shaul Kimhi and Shemuel Even, "Who Are the Palestinian Suicide Bombers?," *Terrorism and Political Violence* 16, no. 4 (2004): 815–840.

First, extremist Jews have targeted Muslim communities residing in both the Occupied Territories and in Israel proper. Many embrace a theology that teaches that the coming of the Messiah and the subsequent redemption of the Jewish people can occur only once Israel has been cleansed of impure, non-Jewish elements. Such was the theology held by Rabbi Meir Kahane. An American-born Israeli ultranationalist, Kahane called for the expulsion of all Palestinians from Israel, the creation of a religiously pure state comprised solely of Jews, and the adoption of *Halakha* as state law.[22] As he wrote in his 1987 book, *Uncomfortable Questions for Comfortable Jews*, "The pity is—the tragedy is—that most Jews do not believe that Judaism is Divine and therefore do not accept it as the foundation of the state."[23] While serving in the Knesset in the mid-1980s, Kahane proposed numerous laws that would forcibly separate Jews from Arabs in the realms of housing, educational institutions, and civic organizations.[24] The militant rabbi also believed in the necessity of violence to protect the Jewish people and facilitate the purification process. "Jewish violence in defense of Jewish interest is never bad," he explained.[25] Kahane founded the political party Kach that advocated for the expulsion of Arabs from Israel and the Palestinian territories. Kahane's convictions would be taken up by far-right militant groups and individuals. For example, in 1994 an American-born Israeli doctor and supporter of Kahane, Baruch Goldstein, murdered twenty-nine Muslim worshipers and wounded another 125 inside the Ibrahimi Mosque in what became known as the Cave of the Patriarchs Massacre.

After Israel took control of the West Bank—a stretch of land across the eastern border of Israel along the west banks of the Jordan River, where most Palestinians reside—following the Six Day War in 1967, Jewish settlers began to set up homes and villages throughout the area. Although the Israeli government has supported the establishment of these settlements, the international community through the United Nations has long maintained that they are illegal under international law and threaten the

---

[22] Ehud Sprinzak, "Jewish Fundamentalism in Israel," in *Fundamentalism and the State: Remaking Polities, Economies, and Militance*, ed. Martin E. Marty and R. Scott Appleby (Chicago: University of Chicago, 1993), 478.

[23] Meir Kahane, *Uncomfortable Questions for Comfortable Jews* (Secaucus, NJ: L. Stuary, 1987), 265.

[24] Joel Brinkley, "Israel Bans Kahane Party from Election," *New York Times*, October 6, 1988, https://www.nytimes.com/1988/10/06/world/israel-bans-kahane-party-from-election.html.

[25] Sprinzak, "Jewish Fundamentalism in Israel," 480.

possibility of a two-state solution to the Israeli-Palestinian conflict. The rapidly expanding settlements in the West Bank have given rise to numerous episodes of violent conflict between Palestinian communities and Israeli settlers. Many settlers are guided by the belief that God has given the land encompassing the West Bank (biblical Judea and Samaria) permanently to the Jewish people as their covenantal heritage. To Palestinians, though, the settlers are occupying invaders. As settlers with the support of the Israeli state have moved into the West Bank and taken over land belonging to Palestinians, Jewish militants have grown increasingly emboldened.

The Hilltop Youth—a Jewish nationalist organization that sets up settlements in the West Bank—serves as a case in point. Following the teachings of Kahane, the Hilltop Youth adhere to a theology that Palestinians must be expelled from all of biblical Israel, including the West Bank.[26] Members associated with the group have been accused of vandalizing and torching Palestinian schools, mosques, olive groves, and homes.[27] Attacks on Palestinian property are frequently accompanied by anti-Muslim graffiti. Former defense minister Ehud Barak referred to the Hilltop Youth as "homemade terror, Jewish-made terror."[28] Other extremist groups associated with settler violence include Gush Emunim and a group calling itself The Revolt. Instances of settler violence have increased sharply in recent years, hundreds of cases being reported annually.[29]

Beginning around 2010, radical Israeli settlers have carried out violent attacks under the slogan "price tag." A form of revenge violence, price tag attacks are targeted at Palestinians and Israeli security forces in response to the demolition of illegally built Jewish homes. These revenge attacks seek to exact a "price" for actions taken by the government against the attackers'

---

[26] Daniel Byman, *A High Price: The Triumphs and Failures of Israeli Counterterrorism* (New York: Oxford University Press, 2011), 291; Ami Pedahzur, *The Triumph of Israel's Radical Right* (New York: Oxford University Press, 2012), 135–137.

[27] Tovah Lazaroff, Yaakov Lappin, and Yaakov Katz, "Palestinians Blame 'Hilltop Youth' for School Arson," *Jerusalem Post*, October 21, 2010, https://www.jpost.com/Israel/Palestinians-blame-hilltop-youth-for-school-arson; Chaim Levinson, "Israel Police Scrambles to Stop Mosque Arsonists from Striking Again," *Haaretz*, December 14, 2011, https://www.haaretz.com/2011-12-14/ty-article/israel-police-scrambles-to-stop-mosque-arsonists-from-striking-again/0000017f-ecbf-d639-af7f-edffc6290000.

[28] Lourdes Garcia-Navarro, "Israel Cracks Down on Radical 'Hilltop Youth,'" NPR, January 9, 2012, https://www.npr.org/2012/01/09/144918870/israel-cracks-down-on-radical-hilltop-youth.

[29] Amos Harel, "Settler Attacks on Palestinian Spike, Reflecting Israel's Systemic Failure," *Haaretz*, November 19, 2021, https://www.haaretz.com/israel-news/2021-11-19/ty-article/.premium/settler-attacks-on-palestinian-spike-reflecting-israels-systemic-failure/0000017f-e228-d38f-a57f-e67aa5090000.

interests. Most of the time, the victims of price tag violence have no relation to the initial grievance of settlers. In one case, Jewish militants torched a Palestinian home in the village of Duma, killing an eighteen-month-old boy and his parents. The perpetrators spray-painted in Hebrew the words "revenge" and "price tag" and a Star of David on the house.[30] The attack is suspected to have been in response to the Israeli government's demolishing of illegally built houses in Beit El settlement.[31] In the following months, a wave of interreligious violence gripped Jerusalem, the West Bank, and Gaza. Palestinians living in the West Bank have experienced scores of cases of price tag violence.[32]

A commonly overlooked aspect of the ongoing Israeli war in Gaza concerns the impact it has had on Jewish extremism in the West Bank. As the international media turned its attention to Gaza following the 2023 attack by Hamas and the subsequent Israeli siege, religious conflict also surged in the West Bank, where violent Israeli settler attacks against Palestinians skyrocketed. From September to October 2023, the number of settler attacks more than tripled, from approximately 70 to more than 230. The number of attacks increased still more over the following year.[33] Extremist settlers have been emboldened and even aided by the Israeli security forces and the policies of the government. It is noteworthy that Prime Minister Netanyahu's coalition government included several religious Zionist parties that supported further annexation of the West Bank. The United Nation's Office of the High Commissioner for Human Rights referred to the rising tide of settler violence, which was already at a record high level in 2023, as "alarming and urgent." It also noted that the settlers "have been acting with the acquiescence and collaboration of Israeli forces and authorities."[34] Settler violence in the West Bank has forced the displacement of entire communities.

---

[30] Elior Levy, Yoav Zitun, Itay Blumenthal, "Palestinian Baby Dies in 'Price Tag' Arson Attack," *Ynet News*, July 31, 2015, https://www.ynetnews.com/articles/0,7340,L-4686046,00.html.

[31] Mohammed Daraghmeh and Tia Goldenberg, "Jewish Attack on Palestinian Home Kills Toddler," *U.S News and World Report*, July 31, 2015, https://www.usnews.com/news/world/articles/2015/07/31/israeli-military-child-killed-in-west-bank-attack.

[32] Anti-Defamation League, "Price Tag and Extremist Attacks in Israel," May 3, 2022, https://www.adl.org/resources/backgrounder/price-tag-and-extremist-attacks-israel.

[33] Mona Chalabi, "Settler Violence against Palestinians in the West Bank—Visualized," *The Guardian*, April 22, 2024, https://www.theguardian.com/world/2024/apr/22/israel-settlers-violence-against-palestine-west-bank.

[34] UN Office of the High Commissioner for Human Rights, "Alarming, Urgent Situation in the Occupied West Bank, Including East Jerusalem," United Nations, November 3, 2023, https://www.ohchr.org/en/press-briefing-notes/2023/11/alarming-urgent-situation-occupied-west-bank-including-east-jerusalem.

Beyond the Occupied Territories, Jewish militants have also violently clashed with Palestinians within Israel proper. In May 2022, more than seventy thousand people filled Jerusalem's narrow cobblestone streets for the annual Jerusalem Day march. For Jewish nationalists, the day commemorates Israel's capture of East Jerusalem, a predominantly Palestinian city, and the Western Wall, the holiest site in Judaism. For Palestinians, the march represents an act of provocation, as Jewish nationalists carry Israeli flags through Jerusalem's Arab quarter—an area that is usually a bustling gathering place for Palestinians—on their way to their final destination, the Western Wall. As they paraded through the streets carrying Israeli flags, some chanted "Death to Arabs." Among the marchers were representatives of far-right, militant Jewish supremacist groups. Despite the deployment of thousands of police officers ahead of the march to maintain order, tensions between Jews and Palestinian protestors quickly boiled over, and violent clashes ensued. Scores of Palestinians were injured. Violence also broke out at the Al-Aqsa Mosque, one of the holiest sites in Islam, after Israeli security forces escorted more than a thousand Jews to the gates of the mosque, where they sang, danced, and waved flags. Former Israeli foreign minister Shlomo Ben-Ami attributed the violence to "Jewish supremacism."[35] The provocation occurred during the Islamic holy month of Ramadan and came on the heels of weeks of heightened tension between Israelis and Palestinians. Clashes surrounding the previous year's Jerusalem Day march led to an eleven-day war between Israel and Hamas, the conflict resulting in the deaths of hundreds of Palestinians, including scores of children. In 2023, tensions between Jews and Palestinians surged once again following an Israeli police raid on the Al-Aqsa Mosque compound, again during Ramadan.

The violence at the 2022 march appears to have been instigated primarily by two far-right groups: Lehava and La Familia. The former advocates for the segregation of Israeli society; the latter is an ultranationalist group which supports the Israeli Premier League football club Beitar Jerusalem. Despite growing calls for the banning of both groups, including by then defense minister Benny Gantz, the Israeli government has so far not acted on these appeals.[36] The inaction on the part of the state has fed into narratives that it does not take the threat of Jewish extremism seriously.

---

[35] Daniel Estrin, "A Look at Jewish Extremism in Israel," NPR, June 2, 2022, https://www.npr.org/2022/06/02/1102728946/a-look-at-jewish-extremism-in-israel.
[36] *Haaretz*, "La Familia Must Be Outlawed," editorial, October 20, 2021, https://www.haaretz.com/opinion/editorial/2021-10-20/ty-article-opinion/la-familia-must-be-outlawed/0000017f-e6ea-d97e-a37f-f7ef83220000.

In addition to targeting Palestinian civilians in both the Occupied Territories and Israel proper, Jewish militants have waged war against their own state. One of the most important pathways to violence in Israel concerns the dynamic of outbidding discussed in chapter 1. That Israel was founded as a "Jewish democracy" has left it vulnerable to the accusation by extremist groups that the state compromises its Jewish purity whenever it enters into dialogue with Arab countries or affirms rights for Palestinians. Every time the government seemed to be moving in a direction considered accommodating of Palestinians, these groups have feared the loss of their privileged station, some lashing out violently. Militant groups such as the Jewish Underground, Keshet, Yad La'achim, and Kach have grounded their violence in the claim that the Israeli state has compromised its Jewish character and has therefore lost its legitimacy. Put differently, militant Jewish groups, seeing themselves as the vanguards of authentic Jewish values, believe that government favoritism of Judaism does not go *far enough*. These groups aspire to create a purer state through the force of arms in accordance with their interpretation of the Hebrew Bible. Some groups, such as The Revolt, go further, claiming not only that the secular Israeli state has no right to exist but also that they have a divine mandate to establish a Jewish kingdom in Israel. Accordingly, such groups might reasonably be classified as "anti-Zionist."[37]

Consider the assassination of Israel's seventh prime minister, Yitzhak Rabin, in 1995. Rabin was murdered by a twenty-five-year-old Orthodox Jewish radical named Yigal Amir. Shaped by militant rabbis, Amir killed the prime minister in an attempt to derail the Israeli-Palestinian peace process following Rabin's signing of the Oslo Accords two years prior, which, Amir believed, was a traitorous act that would have prevented Israel from establishing sovereignty over "Eretz Yisrael," a Jewish state whose territory matches that of the largest expanse of biblical Israel. Accordingly, any peace agreement that divided the land of Israel and denied Jews their God-given heritage by ceding parts of the Occupied Territories to the Palestinians ran counter to the will of God and had to be opposed at all costs, including murder.[38] Amir was associated with the radical Eyal movement, which, in turn, had been greatly influenced by Kahanism. The assassination of Rabin achieved Amir's objective: dealing a death blow to the Oslo peace process. Importantly, Amir acted not as one

---

[37] Yoav Zitun, "A Revolt and a King: The Ideology behind Jewish Terrorism," *YNet News*, January 3, 2016, https://www.ynetnews.com/articles/0,7340,L-4747848,00.html.
[38] Pedahzur and Perliger, *Jewish Terrorism in Israel*, 107.

who hailed from a marginalized or suppressed minority but as one from a majoritarian community that enjoyed official religious privilege. Similar situations have occurred in Israel since Rabin's assassination. One decade later, when another prime minister, Ariel Sharon, announced that Israel would unilaterally disengage from Gaza and officially hand it over to Palestinian governance, extremist Jews plotted attacks against state targets in the following months.[39]

At other times, Jewish vigilantes monitor their own Jewish communities. Militant Jewish outfits such as Sikrikim, an extremist group of radical Haredi Jews, police Jewish society and target those who deviate from their strict interpretation of Jewish law. In 2005 a Haredi Jew named Yishai Shlisel, claiming to be acting on orders from God, stabbed three marchers in a gay pride parade in Jerusalem. Just three weeks after being released from prison in 2015, Shlisel stabbed and injured six marchers at that year's Jerusalem gay pride parade.[40] The Sikrikim have garnered international attention for violence committed against Orthodox Jewish institutions and individuals who fail to comply with their demands.[41]

Finally, in an alarming trend, violent Jewish extremists have also turned against the Christian minority living in Israel, the birthplace of Christianity and a land where Christians have maintained a continuous presence for over two thousand years. In 2023, the minister general of the Order of Friars Minor—the Franciscan group charged with maintaining Christian holy sites in Jerusalem—issued a statement of concern detailing the rise in anti-Christian violence at the hands of Jewish extremists. The statement reported instances of vandalism of Christian cemeteries and churches, attacks on Christian tourists, and death threats against Christians. The report concluded, "It is no coincidence that the legitimization of discrimination and violence in public opinion and in the current Israeli political environment also translates into acts of hatred and violence against the Christian community."[42] The coming to power of Prime Minister Netanyahu's far-right government in 2022 emboldened acts of anti-Christian hatred

---

[39] Pedahzur and Perliger, *Jewish Terrorism in Israel*, 123–128.

[40] *TOI* Staff, "Six Stabbed at Jerusalem Pride Parade by Same Assailant Who Attacked Parade in 2005," *Times of Israel*, July 30, 2015, https://www.timesofisrael.com/six-stabbed-at-jerusalem-pride-parade-by-same-assailant-who-attacked-parade-in-2005/.

[41] Maayan Lubell, "Religious Zealots Attack 'Immodest' Jerusalem Shops," Reuters, October 18, 2011, https://www.reuters.com/article/cnews-us-israel-ultraorthodox-idCATRE79H1HT20111018/.

[42] Francesco Patton and Alberto Joan Pari, "Acts of Vandalism in the Holy Land: Communiqué from the Custody of the Holy Land and Letter from the Minister General," *Ordo Fratrum Minorum*, February 2, 2023, https://ofm.org/en/statement-of-the-custody-of-the-holy-land-following-the-vandalism-of-thursday-2-february-2023.html.

and violence. The Vatican-appointed Latin patriarch, Pierbattista Pizzaballa, lamented that violent Jewish vigilantes "feel they are protected ... that the cultural and political atmosphere now can justify, or tolerate, actions against Christians."[43] The rising tide of anti-Christian extremism in the Holy Land appears not to be the product of a few rogue elements but rather the consequence of systemic issues of religious privilege and antiminority discrimination, which have fueled an atmosphere of hatred.

Israel's internal security service, Shin Bet, has objected to the government's leniency in dealing with Jewish extremists who seek the ethnic and religious cleansing of the Holy Land. Shin Bet has taken particular issue with the Israeli courts for their failure to use administrative detention against militant Jews who break the law.[44] The security service fears that the state's leniency will only embolden more militants who believe they have little to fear for their violent actions. Furthermore, religious minorities have complained that the police do not investigate attacks on members of their communities.[45] The leniency of the courts coupled with the passivity of the police has contributed to a climate of impunity that has emboldened Jewish vigilantes.

In summary, both the marginalized and the privileged have resorted to violence in Israel. However, although much attention has been paid to violence emanating from Palestinian sources, relatively little consideration has been given to violence carried out by militants associated with the privileged Jewish majority population. Violent Jewish extremists have targeted Muslims, the Israeli government, other Jews, and Christians, resorting to violence and terrorism in order to nudge the country toward a pure, theocratic state. In the West Bank, Jewish vigilantes claim to defend the territory over which they believe Israel has a just claim to national sovereignty. In Israel proper, Jewish fundamentalists regularly clash with minorities, sometimes violently. In an alarming trend, Jewish extremists also appear to be

---

[43] Isabel Debre, "Holy Land Christians Say Attacks Rising in Far-Right Israel," *AP News*, April 14, 2023, https://apnews.com/article/christians-easter-attacks-netanyahu-jerusalem-e287dd6bad32573d1656eaea07223782.

[44] Amos Harel and Chaim Levinson, "Settler Terror Underground Seeks to Overthrow Israeli Government, Say Investigators," *Haaretz*, August 3, 2015, https://www.haaretz.com/2015-08-03/ty-article/.premium/murderers-of-infant-part-of-group-planning-to-ramp-up-jewish-terror/0000017f-f434-d497-a1ff-f6b43b960000.

[45] U.S. Department of State, Office of International Religious Freedom, "2021 Report on International Religious Freedom: Israel, West Bank, and Gaza," June 2, 2022, https://www.state.gov/reports/2021-report-on-international-religious-freedom/israel-west-bank-and-gaza/.

targeting non-Muslim minorities in Israel, namely Christians. Militant Jewish groups have been emboldened by a unique religion-state arrangement in a country that is both a democracy and an officially religious state.

Summary

As we have seen throughout this book, the state's privileging of a majoritarian religious tradition at the expense of minorities frequently produces a violent backlash, not only from beleaguered minorities but also from those associated with the privileged religious majority. In the case of Israel, both the Palestinian minority and the Jewish majority have taken up the gun. While much attention has been paid to the dynamics underpinning Palestinian violence, much less has been said about Jewish violence.

Israel reflects a complicated identity, being both a democratic state for all citizens and a religious state for the Jewish majority. Israel stands out for its commitment to democracy and freedom in a region characterized by authoritarianism and minority repression. At the same time, no other liberal democracy in the world rejects political secularism to such a large extent. In Israel, the deliberate and overt privileging of Judaism in the country's laws and policies has produced a violent backlash by Jewish extremists against both minorities and the state itself. It is indeed difficult to imagine that political secularism could ever prevail in a country founded as an explicitly Jewish state. However, unless efforts are made to address issues of systematic bias and privilege, Israel may not be able to create an atmosphere in which extremism, either Islamic or Jewish, has little room to grow, especially as the prospects for a two-state solution grow increasingly grim. Alarmingly, significant numbers of Israelis now fear the possibility of a civil war.[46]

The case of violent Jewish extremism completes our survey of the relationship between religious privilege and religious violence across the world's major religious traditions. The present and preceding chapters have revealed how the forging of close relationships between dominant religious communities and the state have worked to produce majoritarian forms of violence.

---

[46] *Middle East Monitor*, "Israel: Large Majority Believe Violence between Jewish Citizens Is 'Certain,'" February 8, 2023, https://www.middleeastmonitor.com/20230208-israel-large-majority-believe-violence-between-jewish-citizens-is-certain/.

That this relationship exists primarily in countries displaying religious privilege for majoritarian groups suggests that politics and not religion is the major driving force behind religious violence in the modern world.

The preceding chapters have examined numerous cases of countries marked by a paucity of political secularism. The final chapter, by contrast, takes a brief look at several countries, each dominated by a different major world religion, where a commitment to political secularism has helped keep religious tensions at bay. In the cases of the two repeated countries—India and Israel—it shows how historical commitments to secularism and pro-secular contemporary movements can be leveraged to reaffirm the importance of political secularism.

PART III

Chapter 7
Finding Unity in Diversity

Since the 1970s, the world has experienced a resurgence in political movements animated by religious nationalism that threaten states' commitment to political secularism by redefining national citizenship on the basis of religious identity in a manner that marginalizes religious minorities or excludes them altogether. Religious nationalist movements have arisen largely as a byproduct of two simultaneous dynamics: increasing religious diversity and secularization within a country's majority faith tradition. Confronted with changing religious landscapes, religious nationalists attempt to shore up a sense of national community against perceived religious threats.[1] This trend has only accelerated since the turn of the century. Although all of the great world religions emphasize the sanctity of human life, preach love of neighbor, and strive to limit the use of violence, the eroding of political secularism has also had the effect of hardening religious identities and theologies, contributing to the religious polarization of society and religious tensions and conflict.

This book has argued that violent religious hostilities, and in particular majority-on-minority violence, frequently accompany deficits in political secularism. In some cases, religious privilege provides violent religious actors with a green light to attack minorities extrajudicially. Believing they have the law—and God—on their side and that they will not be brought to book for their actions, these majoritarian vigilantes seek to impose their interpretation of proper religion upon society through the force of arms. The cycle continues as majoritarian groups pressure the state to promote their agenda.

On the other hand, majoritarian violence can be dampened in contexts where the government does not give preferential treatment to particular religious groups. Majoritarian violence has a difficult time being sustained in countries marked by a commitment to political secularism, where the

---

[1] Mark Juergensmeyer, "Religious Nationalism in a Global World," *Religions* 10, no. 2 (2019): 262–273.

political environment is not permissive. Given contemporary realities, is it possible for states to affirm a commitment to political secularism? Would majority faith communities ever renounce the quest for dominance over rival faith traditions? These are the questions explored in this concluding chapter.

This chapter is divided into two parts. The first explores a possible remedy to the global crisis of secularism, namely an approach to religion called "covenantal pluralism." The second part reveals that the basic principles undergirding covenantal pluralism can be found in all of the world's major religious traditions and can be observed around the world, including in countries that are characterized by majoritarian religious privilege and repression of minorities, such as India and Israel. Here I briefly survey five "exemplar" countries, each dominated by one of the world's major religious traditions, where the seed of covenantal pluralism has started to blossom. Representing the Eastern religions of Buddhism and Taoism is the multicultural Southeast Asian island state of Singapore, arguably the world's most religiously diverse country in per capita terms. Representing Hinduism is India, a country, as previously shown, that has taken a strong turn toward Hindu privilege in recent years, but one whose own history of interreligious harmony and peace testifies to the possibility of covenantal pluralism. Representing Christianity is the Republic of Botswana, a landlocked country located in southern Africa. Although a developing country, Botswana is a secular democracy known for its religious harmony and tolerance and has experienced virtually no violent religious hostilities. Importantly, the case of Botswana is representative of the larger region of southern Africa. Representing Islam is the West African country of Senegal, whose commitment to pluralism and secularism sets it apart from most Muslim-majority countries. Finally, representing Judaism is Israel, the world's lone Jewish-majority state. In spite of Israel's implicit rejection of political secularism, pro-secular movements on the ground, animated by concerns over justice and equality, offer hope that Israel may be able to reverse course.

Covenantal Pluralism: An Antidote to the Crisis of Secularism?

How can people of faith and those of none live together peacefully in a highly religious, diverse, and volatile world in spite of their fundamental differences? The preceding pages have argued that much of the world's violent religious conflict stems, in large part, from a global crisis of secularism afflicting many of the world's largest and most important countries. States reject political secularism when their political leaders and most important religious groups enter into a kind of quid pro quo wherein majoritarian faith leaders look to the state for special privileges and protection from religious outsiders in exchange for their moral and spiritual legitimization of certain political leaders, parties, or policies. In these settings, the state extends special legal privileges to a particular religious community, which, in turn, legitimates the authority of the government.

Based on this argument, an important solution to global religious violence may appear obvious: states need to (re)affirm a commitment to the principles of political secularism. Such a recommendation would call on governments to uphold the differentiation of the religious and political spheres, withhold political privileges for particular religious groups, remain equidistant from a country's faith traditions, and protect universal religious freedom for both communities of faith and those of none. In principle, the implementation of these recommendations would seemingly result in more robust secularism and the amelioration of violent religious hostilities.

The crisis of political secularism, however, operates at two different levels: the state *and* society. Not only do political leaders seek to co-opt and exploit religion for political purposes, but majoritarian religious groups, too, seek to manipulate the state to solidify their dominance in a country's religious landscape. The relationship is thus reciprocal. While a commitment to secular principles on the part of the state addresses part of the problem, the problem must also be tackled by religious groups in society.

Still, the question remains *why* dominant religious groups would voluntarily forgo the quest for political privilege. After all, religious co-optation is believed to be a win-win situation for both majoritarian religions and political elites. The state gets religious legitimacy; the majority faith tradition gets a leg up on the religious competition.

In reality, though, the reciprocal relationship, though seemingly mutually advantageous, may actually pan out to be a losing proposition for majoritarian faith communities. The classical liberal and critic of majoritarianism, Alexis de Tocqueville, made precisely this argument in his famous work *Democracy in America*, widely considered to be the greatest analysis of American political culture ever written. He famously noted that the United States, in contrast to its European counterparts, stood out for the pervasive influence of religion in its public life. Tocqueville argued that because Christian ministers in America wisely stayed out of politics, they were able to preserve their more vital role of shaping spiritual formation. Having witnessed the damage done to the Catholic Church during the French Revolution, he reasoned that by remaining independent of the state, Christianity in America would avoid suffering the same "vicissitudes of politics."[2] There is no reason to think that this insight would not apply to every other country in the world.

Recent research has affirmed Tocqueville's prescient analysis, revealing that although political leaders believe that they are increasing their legitimacy by allying with a dominant religion, they actually lose credibility and imperil their own political fortunes.[3] On the other hand, although majoritarian religious groups believe that they are securing their privileged status and hegemony by throwing their support behind illiberal political leaders, in reality they too are hurting their cause by making their fortunes dependent on the whims of political elites rather than on the persuasiveness of their theological arguments. Privilege weakens genuine faith. Religion is most authentic when it maintains a sphere of autonomy from the state, rejects political empowerment, and refuses to closely identify with national identities—in short, when it retains its institutional independence from political authorities.[4] On the other hand, communities of faith attempting to curry the favor of the state become distracted from their sacred callings in order to maintain their privileged temporal stations. Moreover, when religious actors are intertwined with the state, they must necessarily accept and promote the goals of the state, often leading to the further compromising of their holy vocations. Unsurprisingly, then, research has consistently shown that countries with a close relationship between religion and state tend to produce *lower* levels of religiosity.[5] The hope thus lies in the possibility that religious and state actors may, out of their *own self-interest*, reconsider the apparent benefits of an alliance between them.

To this end, the concept of covenantal pluralism developed by Christopher Stewart, Chris Seiple, and Dennis Hoover may prove a worthwhile path

---

[2] Alexis de Tocqueville, *Democracy in America* (1835), trans. Harvey C. Mansfield and Delba Winthrop (Chicago: University of Chicago Press, 2002), 279–280.

[3] Fox and Breslawski, "State Support for Religion and Government Legitimacy in Christian-Majority Countries."

[4] Toft, Philpott, and Shah, *God's Century*, 32–39.

[5] Rodney Stark and Roger Finke, *Acts of Faith: Explaining the Human Side of Religion* (Berkeley: University of California Press, 2000); Roger Finke and Rodney Stark, *The Churching of America, 1776–2005: Winners and Losers in Our Religious Economy* (New Brunswick, NJ: Rutgers University Press, 2005); Nilay Saiya and Stuti Manchanda, "Paradoxes of Pluralism, Privilege, and Persecution: Explaining Christian Growth and Decline Worldwide," *Sociology of Religion* 83, no. 1 (2022): 60–78.

forward.⁶ The idea of "covenant" encompasses both *rules* and *relationships*. On the one hand, covenantal pluralism advocates for state secularism—rules—including the constitutional and legal enshrinement of religious equality and religious freedom for all. It implicitly rejects establishmentarianism and other forms of religious or secular privilege or coercion.

On the other hand, realizing that state secularism in itself is not enough, covenantal pluralism further offers a way for people of different faith traditions and those of none to live together in a spirit of amity in multicultural contexts—relationships. A covenant is best understood as a reciprocal relationship between two partners, either individuals or groups, who make binding promises to each other and work together to reach a common goal. Covenants differ from contracts in that they are relational and personal, while also carrying obligations and commitments, whereas contracts are short-term arrangements between parties that cease to exist once the terms have been met. Because covenant is a central idea in many of the world's faith traditions—particularly the monotheistic Abrahamic religions of Judaism, Christianity, and Islam—covenantal pluralism has a potentially broad appeal among adherents of these religions. Although covenant is less central in Eastern religious traditions, here too we see the public virtues associated with covenantal pluralism at work in the history of these faiths. This is crucial because for covenantal pluralism to work in practice it must be perceived as a legitimate approach to religious diversity by the citizens of a country and consistent with their deeply held ethical and religious convictions.[7]

Going beyond a begrudging tolerance of or indifference to religious diversity, covenantal pluralism works toward the cultivation of a public ethic of pluralist virtues involving humility, empathy, patience, courage, trust, and respect between the diverse religious groups in a society and between religious and nonreligious groups. Importantly, covenantal pluralism does not entail a kind of relativism that denies the truth claims of one's own faith tradition. Instead, it recognizes that because no individual, group, or tradition possesses a monopoly on truth, people of faith must have the willingness to engage with and learn from other perspectives through the development of

---

[6] Christopher W. Stewart, Chris Seiple, and Dennis R. Hoover, "Toward a Global Covenant of Peaceable Neighborhood: Introducing the Philosophy of Covenantal Pluralism," *Review of Faith & International Affairs* 18, no. 4 (2020): 1–17.

[7] Robert W. Hefner, "Islam and Covenantal Pluralism in Indonesia: A Critical Juncture Analysis," *Review of Faith & International Affairs* 18, no. 2 (2020): 1–17.

religious literacy. Covenantal pluralism furthermore encourages empathy in stressing that religious groups that are dominant in one country constitute minorities in others. Just as they would wish their coreligionists who happen to be a minority in another country to be treated with dignity and respect, they treat minorities who live in their own countries in like manner.

In summary, the global crisis of political secularism results from a reciprocal relationship between state and religious actors. Addressing this crisis thus requires attention at the levels of both state (rules) and society (relationships). Covenantal pluralism represents a promising way whereby states and societies can navigate a world of immense religious diversity. It entails both a "top-down" dimension—a framework of equal rights and responsibilities encompassed in political secularism—and "bottom-up" norms and practices necessary for the creation of cultures marked by humility, respectful engagement, and reciprocity even amid stark differences in religious beliefs. In short, covenantal pluralism demands both "legal equality and neighborly solidarity."[8] In contrast to tolerance, which implies the grudging acceptance of the troublesome reality of religious difference, covenantal pluralism considers diversity to be inherently valuable, for it is through a multiplicity of beliefs that progress toward truth, love, and peace—the ostensible hallmarks of religion—is made.

Covenantal Pluralism in Practice

Is covenantal pluralism a possibility in the real world? Or is it simply an ideal that can never be achieved in a world marked by deep diversity and fervent religious beliefs? This section shows that manifestations of covenantal pluralism can, in fact, be witnessed around the world and in every faith tradition. Importantly, even in countries where religious majoritarianism is on the march and political secularism is imperiled, people of faith make religious arguments for the importance of living together peacefully in a spirit of harmony and respect. They reject privilege. This section takes a brief look at the practice of covenantal pluralism in each of the world's major religious traditions, highlighting an "exemplar" country for each religion. It proceeds in the same order as the preceding pages, beginning with the world's largest religion, Christianity, and its exemplar country, Botswana.

---

[8] Stewart, Seiple, and Hoover, "Toward a Global Covenant of Peaceable Neighborhood," 5.

Christianity: The Case of Botswana

As explored in the second chapter, the forces of Christian majoritarianism have been on the ascendant in the Americas, Europe, and Africa. Christian nationalism has elevated illiberal populist leaders and far-right political parties that promise to protect Christianity against the threat posed by increasing religious diversity. One surprising region, though, appears to have been remarkably resistant to the forces of religious nationalism sweeping over Christian-majority countries: southern Africa, including Angola, Botswana, Burundi, Lesotho, Madagascar, Malawi, Mozambique, Namibia, Republic of Congo, Rwanda, South Africa, Swaziland, Tanzania, and Zambia. To be sure, some of these countries (Rwanda, Burundi, and South Africa) have a violent or authoritarian past that has involved the politicization of the Christian faith, yet today the region stands out for its commitment to political secularism and harmonious interfaith relations. The only region of the world with fewer violent religious hostilities is the Americas.[9]

Levels of political secularism in southern Africa are strangely high, especially considering that this is one of the most religious regions in the world and almost all of the countries have developing economies. As the case of southern Africa shows, the unusual commitment to political secularism does not necessarily prevent religious groups from cooperating with the state. For example, during the COVID-19 pandemic in 50 percent of southern African countries—a far higher percentage than any other world region—religious groups collaborated with their governments to promote public health measures.[10]

Although virtually any of the countries in the region could be singled out as being a strong representative of an ethic of covenantal pluralism, I select Botswana for its central location in the heart of southern Africa and it being broadly typical of the region. A small, landlocked country sandwiched by Namibia, South Africa, and Zimbabwe, Botswana is a Christian-majority nation with a sizable minority who practice traditional religions or none at all and smaller communities of Muslims, Hindus, Baha'is, Sikhs, and Jews. It is among Africa's oldest democracies and one of the least corrupt countries on the continent.

---

[9] Pew Research Center, *How COVID-19 Restrictions Affected Religious Groups around the World in 2020* (Washington, DC: Pew Research Center, 2022), 39.
[10] Pew Research Center, *How COVID-19 Restrictions Affected Religious Groups around the World in 2020*, 19.

Botswana has a strongly secular Constitution with robust protections for religious freedom, an implicit separation of religion and state (although the state does officially recognize some Christian holidays), and state neutrality in religious affairs.[11] The state does not prefer one religion over any others in its laws or policies, nor does it interfere in the ability of religious bodies to operate freely. At the same time that it offers broad protections for freedom of conscience, the Constitution also prohibits mandatory religious instruction, participation in religious ceremonies, and the taking of oaths contrary to one's religious beliefs. It forbids discrimination on the basis of religion.

The basic secular framework established by the Constitution has enabled not only the free exercise of religion but also a general societal tolerance for religious diversity conducive to the development of robust interfaith relations. Different religious groups have come together to address issues such as HIV/AIDS and gender-based violence. As of this writing, several religious organizations are in the process of forming an official interfaith council, which is expected to include representatives of Christian, Muslim, Hindu, and Baha'i groups. My analysis of religious violence shows that there has not been any recorded incidents of violent faith-based hostilities in the past fifty years. Yet it is noteworthy that religion nevertheless continues to play a significant role in the lives of most Botswanans.

In summary, in southern Africa religion is not so much a source of conflict as a source of hope. Religious institutions and movements are a major force in civil society and a key provider of public goods, especially in the areas of relief and development. Religion's public role is all the more important given the widespread reality of failed states and collapsing government services. Violent religious hostilities have been virtually absent from the region, a happy outcome that has been made possible by a strong commitment to political secularism. It is also a region where we see a strong possibility for the emergence of widespread covenantal pluralism.

Islam: The Case of Senegal

No religion is associated with violence more than Islam. The stereotype predates the terrorist attacks of 9/11 and has only intensified since then, owing

---

[11] D. D. Nsereko, "Religious Liberty and the Law in Botswana," *Journal of Church and State* 34, no. 4 (1992): 843–862.

to the civil wars in Afghanistan and Iraq, the rise of ISIS, the brutality of Islamist political regimes, and the disproportionate role of Islam in global terrorist attacks. As argued in the third chapter, the prevalence of violence in Islam stems largely from the close relationships that exist between mosque and state throughout the Muslim world.

Not every Muslim-majority country renounces political secularism, however. The Republic of Senegal, a relatively small Muslim-majority West African country sitting on the Atlantic coastline, boasts a high degree of secularism, the first article of its Constitution declaring, "The Republic of Senegal is secular, democratic, and social. It assures the equality before the law of all the citizens, without distinction of origin, of race, of sex [and] of religion. It respects all beliefs." Article 5 furthermore makes "religious discrimination" punishable by law, while Articles 8 and 24 guarantee religious freedoms. With respect to politics, the Constitution does not permit political parties to "identify themselves to one race, to one ethnicity, to one sex, to one religion, to one sect, to one language or to one part of the territory." It explicitly maintains, "The institutions and the religious communities have the right to develop themselves without hindrance. They are disengaged from the protection of the State. They regulate and administer their affairs in an autonomous manner." In Senegal, religion has not been politicized as it has in much of the Muslim world where either Islamists seek to fuse religion and state and, in this way, impose their views on the rest of society, or secularist state leaders seek to co-opt, exploit, and manipulate Islam to further their political ambitions.[12]

The overwhelming majority of the population (about 96 percent) practices Islam, with Christian groups and indigenous traditions comprising the minorities. Senegal is a highly religious country; a 2010 survey revealed that about 98 percent of Senegalese say that religion is "very important" to them.[13] The country is home to the largest mosque in West Africa. Islam plays a significant role in public life. Interestingly, many countries in the Muslim world with a similar religious demography and levels of religious devotion exhibit strong deficits in political secularism and experience high levels of religious

---

[12] Alfred Stepan, "Rituals of Respect: Sufis and Secularists in Senegal in Comparative Perspective," *Comparative Politics* 44, no. 4 (2012): 383–384.
[13] Pew Research Center, "Tolerance and Tension: Islam and Christianity in Sub-Saharan Africa," April 15, 2010, www.pewforum.org/2010/04/15/executive-summary-islam-and-christianity-insub-saharan-africa/.

radicalization. This has not been the case in Senegal, leading some scholars to highlight the country's exceptional character.[14] In Senegal, religious cleavages are virtually nonexistent.[15]

Although religious privilege is strongest in the Muslim world, Senegal stands out for its religious pluralism, equality, and harmony.[16] For example, Senegal's first president, Léopold Sédar Senghor, was a devout Catholic. Because interreligious marriage is quite common in Senegal, many families include both Muslims and Christians. Even Senegal's highest officials have married outside of their own faith, including Presidents Abdou Diouf and Abdoulaye Wade, both of whom took Christian wives. Despite being a predominantly Muslim country, Christmas is popularly observed; even the capital, Dakar, is lined with Christmas trees and decorations during Advent season.[17] All this has resulted in a high level of interreligious tolerance. Few countries, inside or outside of the Muslim world, exhibit a spirit of covenantal pluralism to such an extent.

The environment of secularism has encouraged conditions favorable to the emergence of a mystical and peaceable form of Islam known as Sufism, the most prevalent form of Islam in Senegal. The teachings of Sufi brotherhoods such as the Tijaniyya, Qadiriryya, and the Mouridiyya emphasize the importance of personal, spiritual encounters with the divine but de-emphasize the quest for temporal power. This has naturally produced a Senegalese Sufism conducive to democracy, secularism, and interreligious tolerance, which has played a pivotal role in stemming the rise of violent religious hostilities so prevalent in other Muslim-majority states. Consequently, the country has witnessed virtually no violent religious hostilities.

In summary, Senegal stands out in the Muslim world for its commitment to secularism. To be sure, Senegal is not perfectly secular; the government does play a role in religious affairs, cultivating good relations with religious leaders, encouraging peaceful coexistence between faiths, and providing direct financial and material assistance to religious communities. Still, that this involvement in religion does not take on a discriminatory nature, either in the form of secular co-optation by the state or the Islamization of politics

---

[14] Donal B. Cruise O'Brien, "The Senegalese Exception," *Africa* 66, no. 3 (1996): 458–464.

[15] Villalon, *Islamic Society and State Power in Senegal*, 2.

[16] Mamadou Diouf, ed., *Tolerance, Democracy, and Sufis in Senegal* (New York: Columbia University Press, 2013).

[17] Annika Hammerschlag, "Senegal, a Muslim Country That Can't Get Enough Christmas," *VOA News*, December 24, 2019, https://www.voanews.com/a/africa_senegal-muslim-country-cant-get-enoughchristmas/6181575.html.

and society, has enabled the conditions necessary for peaceful coexistence.[18] The Senegalese approach to religion has given rise to a moderate and tolerant Islam, and the country has seen virtually none of the violent religious conflict that has engulfed similar nations.

Hinduism: The Case of India

The fourth chapter of this book discussed the disquieting trend of increasing violent religious persecution in India. Yet because India is by far the most important of the three Hindu-majority states in the world, and because interreligious peace and harmony have been the norm throughout Indian history and remain so even today, I return once again to the world's largest democratic state to consider how a return to political secularism can help keep communal violence at bay as it has in the past.

Although the dramatic increase in communal violence since the 1990s has without question and rightfully given pause to human rights activists, India scholars, and, of course, the people of India, India's indigenous religions, history, and contemporary movements also present reasons for optimism. All of the so-called Indic religions—Hinduism, Jainism, Sikhism, and Buddhism—share in common belief in respect, tolerance, and harmony. These religions lay a strong indigenous foundation for building interfaith trust and acceptance.[19] Arguably, Hinduism, more than any other religion, accepts and celebrates the idea that truth must be sought in a multitude of sources, suggesting that Hinduism is naturally committed to interreligious harmony.[20]

Indeed, the dominant understanding of Hindu nationalism during the independence movement was rooted in an embrace of India's vast diversity. The preeminent leader of the anticolonial struggle, Mohandas Gandhi, drawing on the foundational Hindu principles of *ahimsa* (noninjury) and *satyagraha* (passive resistance), mobilized a mass movement for independence across ethnic, class, and religious lines. He was both a pacifist and a nationalist. But his nationalism was unlike the nativism we see at work across

---

[18] Stepan, "The Multiple Secularisms of Modern Democratic and Non-Democratic Regimes," 132–135.
[19] Dillip Kumar Maharana, "In Defense of Indian Perspective of Multiculturalism," *Indian Journal of Political Science* 71, no. 1 (2010): 69–83.
[20] Elaine M. Fisher, *Hindu Pluralism: Religion and the Public Sphere in Early Modern South India* (Berkeley: University of California Press, 2017).

the world today. Instead, Gandhi practiced a kind of "pluralist nationalism" that rejected the linguistic, ethnic, and religious boundaries associated with the nationalism found in the West.[21] Gandhi's Hindu-inspired vision of postindependence India would be based in a spirit of harmony governing the interactions of India's various religious communities. "If the Hindus believe that India should be peopled only by Hindus, they are living in dreamland. The Hindus, the Mahomedans, the Parsis, and the Christians who have made India their country are fellow countrymen, and they will have to live in unity, if only for their own interest," he straightforwardly surmised.[22] Gandhi's spirit of pluralism and inclusiveness would be enshrined in the Indian Constitution, a governing document that codifies a number of pillars of political secularism, including religious equality, freedom of religion, and minority rights. The secular state apparatus guaranteed that religious minorities would be secure in the newly independent state.[23] Thus the pluralistic and inclusive nature of the Hindu nationalism present during India's independence movement and early years as an independent state bears no resemblance to the exclusivist and illiberal version of Hindu nationalism that characterizes the country today.

Moreover, even today communal tension is not the norm in India, despite its receiving the lion's share of media and scholarly attention. Far more prevalent is what has come to be known as "multiple religious belongings." Many Indians have a deep appreciation and respect for and curiosity about religious traditions outside of their own. They commonly cross religious lines and partake in each other's religious traditions; they celebrate each other's festivals, visit each other's shrines, participate in each other's religious services, and seek healing from each other's deities.[24] A 2021 Pew Research Center survey found that 84 percent of Indians believed that respect for all

---

[21] Diana L. Eck, "Gandhian Guidelines for a World of Religious Difference," in *Gandhi on Christianity*, ed. Robert Ellsberg (Maryknoll, NY: Orbis Books, 1991), 86–88; B. Sreenivasulu Naik, *Unity of All Religions: The Gandhian Way: Sarva Dharma Samabhava* (New Delhi: Mittal, 2018).

[22] Mahatma Gandhi, *The Collected Works of Mahatma Gandhi*, vol. 10 (New Delhi: Government of India, Ministry of Information and Broadcasting, 1963), 29.

[23] Sheila Seshia, "Divide and Rule in Indian Party Politics: The Rise of the Bharatiya Janata Party," *Asian Survey* 38, no. 11 (1998): 1036–1050.

[24] Peter Gottschalk, *Beyond Hindu and Muslim: Multiple Identity in Narratives from Village India* (New York: Oxford University Press, 1999); Anna Bigelow, *Sharing the Sacred: Practicing Pluralism in Muslim North India* (New York: Oxford University Press, 2010); Carla Bellamy, *The Powerful Ephemeral: Everyday Healing in an Ambiguously Islamic Place* (Berkeley: University of California Press, 2011); Carl Ernst, *Refractions of Islam in India* (New Delhi: Sage, 2016); Kerry P. C. San Chirico, *Between Hindu and Christian: Khrist Bhaktas, Catholics, and the Negotiation of Devotion in Banaras* (Oxford: Oxford University Press, 2023).

religions was a hallmark of being "truly Indian." The report notes that "Indians are united in the view that respecting other religions is a very important part of what it means to be a member of their own religious community."[25]

A number of important social movements and grassroots programs dedicate themselves to fostering interreligious engagement, appreciation for pluralism, and respect for diversity, including the Center for Study of Society and Secularism, the Gandhi Peace Foundation, Interfaith Foundation India, the Indian Community Activist Network, and National Campaign on Dalit Human Rights. Perhaps the most important voice for peace that has emerged in recent years is the Caravan of Love (*Karwan e Mohabbat*). Led by human rights activist Harsh Mander, the Caravan of Love describes itself as "a people's campaign devoted to the universal values of the constitution, of solidarity, equality, freedom, justice and compassion ... [that supports] survivors of hate crimes and injustice with legal, social and livelihood help."[26] The Caravan travels to different locations in India, meeting with victims of violence and hate. All of these important endeavors build bridges and help accrue social capital between religious communities by bringing them together for the purpose of promoting interreligious harmony, trust, and empathy. Unfortunately, though, this aspect of interreligious relations in India has not been given the consideration it is due. Disproportionate attention to religious conflict has perhaps skewed perceptions of the nature of public religion in India, reinforcing the stereotype of the country as hopelessly mired in a permanent state of hostility between religious communities.

In summary, India is a country of breathtaking paradoxes. On the one hand, it is a country whose people largely embrace its immense, natural religious diversity. On the other hand, it is a country that witnesses routine outbreaks of violent hostilities between religious groups. Although the problems associated with India's crisis of secularism and attendant and increasing religious violence are cause for great concern, it is important to remember that peaceful coexistence and not interreligious conflict remains the norm for most Indians even today. In the end, if India can recover its splendid tradition of "unity in diversity," it just might be able to beat back the ascendant forces of communalism.

---

[25] Pew Research Center, *Religion in India: Tolerance and Segregation* (Washington, DC: Pew Research Center, 2021), 6.
[26] Harsh Mander, "Karwan e Mohabbat," December 7, 2022, http://harshmander.in/?page_id=26.

Buddhism: The Case of Singapore

In Singapore, the tiny city-state situated at the southernmost point of continental Asia, the Eastern religions of Buddhism and Taoism command the largest following, with about 40 percent of the population subscribing to these traditions. However, the country is also, according to the Pew Research Center, the world's most religiously diverse country, with sizable portions of the population following various other religious traditions: Christianity, Islam, Hinduism, Sikhism, and various folk religions. About one in five Singaporeans has no religious identity.[27]

Some might understandably reason that such a religious constellation would be a recipe for sectarian strife and violence, especially considering that the country is about one-quarter the size of the smallest American state, Rhode Island. The scarcity of land coupled with a highly fragmented religious demography means that people of different religious traditions intermingle on a daily basis, resulting in innumerable potential points of conflict. Astonishingly, though, Singapore has not descended into religious conflict; it has in fact flourished amid its stunning religious diversity. On virtually every metric of human development, Singapore ranks among the top countries in the world. In terms of per capita GDP—the best available indicator of a country's standard of living—Singapore ranks second.[28] Its education system has been consistently ranked one of the highest in the world by the Organization for Economic Cooperation and Development.[29] It is widely considered to be among the world's safest countries, one study finding it has the "lowest levels of fear of violence in the world."[30] The same can be seen in the realm of religion. The Pew Research Center has documented in a succession of annual reports that Singapore consistently witnesses a low level of social hostilities involving religion.[31] Remarkably, Singapore's religious peace has endured even as religious hostilities have escalated in surrounding countries.

---

[27] Pew Research Center, *Global Religious Diversity: Half of the Most Religiously Diverse Countries Are in the Asia-Pacific Region* (Washington, DC: Pew Research Center, 2014), 4.
[28] World Bank, "GDP per Capita, PPP," 2024, https://data.worldbank.org/indicator/NY.GDP.PCAP.PP.CD?most_recent_value_desc=true.
[29] *The Economist*, "What Other Countries Can Learn from Singapore's Schools," August 30, 2018, https://www.economist.com/leaders/2018/08/30/what-other-countries-can-learn-from-singapores-schools.
[30] Institute for Economics and Peace, *Global Peace Index 2021: Measuring Peace in a Complex World* (Sydney: IEP, 2021), 5.
[31] Majumdar and Villa, *Globally, Social Hostilities Related to Religion Decline in 2019*, 65.

What explains Singapore's interreligious harmony in the face of inauspicious conditions that have led to religious tension and conflict elsewhere? The country's remarkable level of interreligious amity has not been the product of good fortune; rather, it has been the result of carefully selected religion-related policies by the state, which have been supported by the country's various faith communities. When Singapore gained independence in 1965, its early leaders quickly recognized the potential for societal strife along religious lines in their highly multicultural country. They understood the wisdom of an approach to religion grounded in political secularism, especially the separation of religion and state, equality among the different religious groups, and freedom of religion, which could ameliorate the centrifugal forces of religious identity. Article 12 of the Constitution, for example, prohibits "discrimination against citizens of Singapore on the ground only of religion." Article 15 grants to every person "the right to profess and practise his religion and to propagate it" and to every religious group "the right to manage its own religious affairs." In practice, the state does not favor any particular religious tradition, nor does it base national identity on any religion. Instead, it has cultivated a strong national identity that overlays Singapore's myriad ethnic and religious identities. By drawing a clear line between religion and politics, the state has guarded against the potential weaponization of religion. Religion-related violence is absent in Singapore.

At the same time, the government, recognizing that social harmony among its many religious groups could not be taken for granted, enabled strong laws that prevent religion from being used as a source of division. The Singapore Ministry of Home Affairs concludes, "Singapore is a multi-racial and multi-religious society. Therefore, racial and religious harmony is vital for Singapore's social cohesion. This harmony does not come naturally—we need to take the effort to build trust and acceptance between different races and religions, and protect the common space that we have."[32] Striving to make religion a source of unity rather than division, the state plays a major role in regulating interreligious relations and managing the peaceful coexistence of religious groups through bodies such as the Religious Harmony Council, the Presidential Council for Minority Rights, and the

---

[32] Singapore Ministry of Home Affairs, "Maintaining Racial and Religious Harmony," 2019, https://www.mha.gov.sg/what-we-do/managing-security-threats/maintaining-racial-and-religious-harmony#:~:text=The%20Ministry%20of%20Home%20Affairs,maintain%20religious%20harmony%20in%20Singapore.

Community Remedial Initiative and through laws such as the Maintenance of Religious Harmony Act. Where the public expression of religious convictions threatens societal harmony, especially in cases of religiously based bigotry or insensitivity, the state acts quickly, decisively, and unapologetically to ensure peaceful coexistence. For example, those found to be making inflammatory remarks directed at particular religious traditions have been charged under the Sedition Act, resulting in fines or jail sentences. Such incidents also appear to have had a strong deterrent effect on like-minded individuals.

In summary, Singapore's proactive version of political secularism—shaped by its unique context of multiculturalism, early episodes of religious tensions, and land scarcity—differs markedly from the laissez-faire form of secularism found in the West. At times it has limited religious freedom when the practice of religious rights infringes on the rights of others, takes the form of insensitive or inflammatory speech, or threatens public order. Yet it has also proven to be highly effective in defusing the same religious tensions that have plagued other religiously heterogeneous countries.[33]

As a consequence of these secular policies, Buddhism in Singapore has not taken on the violent form that it has in Sri Lanka, Myanmar, or Thailand. The same can be said of the other faith traditions present in the country. While isolated cases of communal tensions have occurred throughout Singapore's short history as an independent nation, they have not spilled over into large-scale hostilities between religious communities that could threaten the harmony of Singapore's multicultural society.

Judaism: The Case of Israel

As noted in the sixth chapter, Jewish violence against minorities in the Occupied Territories and in Israel proper has been abetted by a structural context marked by Jewish privilege. The Israeli military and government have at times acted in a manner that has encouraged violent Jewish extremism rooted in Jewish supremacy, racism, and radical anti-Arab ideologies. In other cases, Jewish vigilantes operate independently of the state—and indeed

---

[33] Chan Heng Chee and Sharon Siddique, *Singapore's Multiculturalism: Evolving Diversity* (London: Routledge, 2019); Joseph Chinyong Liow, "Managing Religious Diversity and Multiculturalism in Singapore," in *Navigating Differences: Integration in Singapore*, ed. Terence Chong (Singapore: Institute of Southeast Asian Studies, 2020), 19–35.

may even clash with Israeli security forces—yet remain emboldened in their activities by structural privilege.

Nearly eighty years after the establishment of the modern State of Israel, the global Jewish population remains united behind the idea that Israel is a homeland for the Jewish people. Beyond this conviction, though, there exists a great deal of diversity among Israeli Jews on questions of public policy. Perhaps the most important division surrounds the question of how Judaism and the state should interact. Overwhelmingly, Orthodox Jews (including Haredi and Dati Jews) believe that Israel was given to the Jewish people by God, that Israel's government should promote Jewish beliefs and identity, and that Jews should receive preferential treatment from the state. Secular Jews, on the other hand, strongly favor separation of religion from government policy. Israeli Jews are also divided on how the state should deal with the country's Arab minority. Orthodox Jews are much more likely to believe that non-Jewish Arabs should be expelled from Israel.[34]

There is hope, however. Whereas fundamentalists represent one side of Jewish activism, it is not the only one. In fact, covenantal pluralism may be possible in Israel to an extent it may not be elsewhere. Covenant is central to the Jewish tradition.[35] These covenants run both vertically between God and humanity and horizontally between people. At a time when peace between the Israelis and Palestinians has never seemed so elusive, we nevertheless can see pockets of covenantal pluralism blossoming.

A number of Israeli human rights organizations have emerged that work toward harmonious coexistence between Jews and non-Jews living in Israel and in the Occupied Territories. Such groups include B'Tselem, Bat Shalom, Jewish Voice for Peace, Rabbis for Human Rights, and René Cassin. All of these Jewish groups seek a peaceful resolution to the Israeli-Palestinian conflict and dignity and equal rights for Israel's minority communities. For example, according to its website, B'Tselem "strives for a future in which human rights, liberty, and equality are guaranteed to all people, Palestinian and Jewish alike, living between the Jordan River and the Mediterranean Sea." B'Tselem grounds its advocacy in its interpretation of Genesis 1:27, "And God created humankind in His image. In the image of God did He create them," a passage of scripture it believes represents a "moral edict to

---

[34] Pew Research Center, *Israel's Religiously Divided Society* (Washington, DC: Pew Research Center, 2016), 5.
[35] Genesis 15; Exodus 19–24.

respect and uphold the human rights of all people."[36] Increasingly, ordinary Jewish Israelis are speaking out against abuses of minorities at the hands of the state and societal actors. Particularly among young people, interreligious friendships have become commonplace. In everyday life—schools, businesses, hospitals—Jews and Arabs are working together to forge a better future.[37] A variety of initiatives aimed at promoting coexistence and dialogue between Israelis and Palestinians—among them the Palestinian-Israeli Initiative for Understanding, Nonviolence, and Reconciliation; Ta'ayush Arab-Jewish Partnership; Coalition of Women for Peace; and the Parents Circle–Families Forum—have revealed the possibility of peaceful coexistence on the ground.

In summary, the task of cultivating covenantal pluralism in Israel and the Occupied Territories has never been more important. Decades of conflict, failed diplomacy, and bouts of violence have entrenched deep divisions and mistrust in Israeli society. Nevertheless, Jews and Palestinians lack the luxury of depending on politicians to deliver peace to the beleaguered nation. They must take the lead through grassroots initiatives to secure a brighter future for themselves and their children. Even if a territorial solution to the Israeli-Palestinian conflict is someday achieved, Jews and non-Jews will still have to find ways of living together in spite of their deepest differences and the wounds of the past. Covenantal pluralism can provide a way for ordinary people to prevent cycles of violence, while building trust and relationships conducive to harmonious coexistence and reconciliation that can improve daily life for all.

Concluding Thoughts

Religious diversity is a reality. In a world characterized by accelerating levels of international migration, the extraordinary spread of religious beliefs, unprecedented access to information, exposure to different cultures, and rapidly changing cultural mores and shifting demographics, political leaders have struggled to design policies for effectively dealing with these developments. The default position of many governments has been to partner

---

[36] B'Tselem, "About B'Tselem," 2023, https://www.btselem.org/about_btselem.
[37] Kate Shuttleworth, "The Israelis and Palestinians Who Work Together in Peace," *The Guardian*, July 11, 2016, https://www.theguardian.com/world/2016/jul/11/israel-jews-arabs-palestinians-work-together-peace.

with and privilege dominant faith traditions and to restrict the activities of religious minorities, ostensibly for the sake of maintaining their countries' national cohesion in the face of this increasing diversity, insofar as political leaders often see their states as inextricably intertwined with historically dominant religious traditions. This approach, rooted in the fear of minorities, has largely contributed to the world's current crisis of secularism, a predicament that afflicts every one of the world's major religious traditions.

This book has argued that politics, specifically a dearth of political secularism, and not religion lies at the root of the world's religious violence. In the absence of political secularism, dominant religious groups in society are able to claim the state as their own, "sacralizing" the government in the process. In such situations, they are much more likely to adhere to a theology that emphasizes the fusion of spiritual and temporal power and, once obtained, wield the power of the state against their religious opponents. The price of weaponized faith, though, is being paid in blood.

By contrast, when political secularism thrives, religious communities are more likely to contribute to social harmony, interreligious understanding, and healthy polities. The brief cases in this chapter, in sharp contrast to the cases found in the preceding ones, reveal the possibility of political secularism in each of the world's major religious traditions. In each of these cases, it is clear that majoritarian religious communities do not generally consider the presence of religious out-groups to be threatening; it is often the case that they even welcome religious diversity. Majority religions are much more likely to be accepting of political secularism when they do not isolate themselves in echo chambers, where they interact only with those who hold the same worldviews. When those of different faith traditions interrelate with each other regularly, participate in shared civic organizations, and make efforts to learn from each other, they are much more likely to stand up for each other's rights.

In an approach rooted in covenantal pluralism, the flourishing of society is tied not to the imposition of a dominant religion but rather to a country's commitment to multiculturalism, ideological diversity, and openness. The cases in this chapter show the possibility of harmony in countries comprised of people of diverse backgrounds holding conflicting beliefs and values. When people of faith are able to work together with those of different faith traditions and those of none, they can escape the pitfalls of religious nationalism and strive collectively toward more just social and political orders.

Appendix

This book has argued that contemporary religious violence arises from a global crisis of political secularism afflicting the world today. Whereas much of the literature on the causes of religious violence emphasizes the importance of grievances in encouraging violent tendencies among minority religious communities, I argue instead that religious violence stems centrally from empowered religious majorities, not from embattled religious minorities. When states privilege dominant religious groups, they encourage extremists from those favored groups to undertake violence.

The purpose of this appendix is twofold. First, it provides statistical models supportive of the argument laid out in the first chapter. Second, it provides more detail on the case studies, including case selection, method of analysis, and alternative explanations. Combined, both analyses give robust and triangulated support for the theory delineated in this book.

Statistical Analysis

To establish the relationship between religious privilege and majoritarian religious violence, a statistical analysis of a unique time-series, cross-sectional data set was conducted. The panel data set contains political, economic, geographic, and religious information for 157 countries from 2008 to 2018, the period of time for which relatively complete data are available. The country-year is the unit of analysis. The operationalization of the dependent variable, theoretically central independent variable, and control variables are as follows:

> *Dependent Variable.* The dependent variable is an event count of the number of identifiable cases of physical violence carried out by those identifying with a country's religious majority community (*Majoritarian_Attacks*). Data for the dependent variable are derived and coded from the Global Terrorism Database, an open-source database hosted by the University of Maryland that includes information on terrorist events around the world.[1] A majoritarian attack is defined as any attack carried out by an individual or group associated with a country's dominant religious tradition. These groups were coded at the level of the denomination—Sunni, Shia, Protestant, Catholic—to account for intrareligious violence as well as interreligious violence. *Majoritarian_Attacks* were coded on an annual basis for all of the years in the time series.
>
> *Independent Variable.* The theoretically central independent variable is a measure of religious privilege taken from the Pew Research Center's annual reports on global

---

[1] National Consortium for the Study of Terrorism and Responses to Terrorism, "Global Terrorism Database," START, 2024, https://www.start.umd.edu/gtd.

religious freedom (*Religious_Privilege*).² This variable is a sum of eight different components of favoritism measured on an annual basis:

- *The country's constitution recognizes a favored religion.*
- *One religious group has privileges or government access unavailable to other religious groups.*
- *The government provides funds or other resources to religious groups with obvious favoritism.*
- *The government provides funds or other resources for religious education programs and/or religious schools with obvious favoritism.*
- *The government provides funds or other resources for religious property with obvious favoritism.*
- *The government provides funds or other resources for religious activities other than education or property with obvious favoritism.*
- *Religious education is required in public schools.*
- *The national government defers in some way to religious authorities, texts, or doctrines on legal issues.*

Control Variables. Four sets of control variables were also included in the models that could theoretically be related to the onset of violent religious hostilities. The first set includes three general country variables: the log of a country's geographical area (*Log_Area*), the log of a country's population size (*Log_Population*), and the log of a country's GDP per capita (*Log_GDP_Cap*). These variables are sourced from the World Bank's Development Indicators.³ The second set includes variables related to a country's regime characteristics: political rights (*Political_Rights*), civil liberties (*Civil_Liberties*), institutional democracy score (*Polity*), and regime durability (*Durability*). *Political_Rights* and *Civil_Liberties* are measures of two different aspects of freedom, both of which are sourced from Freedom House, a democracy watchdog best known for advocacy surrounding issues of democracy, political freedom, and human rights.⁴ *Polity* is a measure of the authority characteristics of states that ranges from −10 (strongly autocratic) to +10 (strongly democratic). *Durability* is a measure of political stability that gauges the number of years since a country's last change in regime. *Polity* and *Durability*

---

[2] Pew Research Center, *Global Restrictions on Religion* (Washington, DC: Pew Research Center, 2009); Pew Research Center, *Rising Restrictions on Religion—One Third of the World's Population Experiences an Increase* (Washington, DC: Pew Research Center, 2011); Pew Research Center, *Rising Tide of Restrictions on Religion* (Washington, DC: Pew Research Center, 2011); Pew Research Center, *Religious Hostilities Reach Six-Year High* (Washington, DC: Pew Research Center, 2014); Pew Research Center, *Latest Trends in Religious Restrictions and Hostilities* (Washington, DC: Pew Research Center, 2015); Pew Research Center, *Trends in Global Restrictions on Religion* (Washington, DC: Pew Research Center, 2016); Pew Research Center, *Global Restrictions on Religion Rise Modestly in 2015, Reversing Downward Trend* (Washington, DC: Pew Research Center, 2017); Pew Research Center, *A Closer Look at How Religious Restrictions Have Risen around the World* (Washington, DC: Pew Research Center, 2019); Pew Research Center, *In 2018, Government Restrictions on Religion Reach Highest Level Globally in More Than a Decade* (Washington, DC: Pew Research Center, 2020).

[3] World Bank, "World Development Indicators," 2023, https://databank.worldbank.org/source/world-development-indicators.

[4] Freedom House, "Freedom in the World, 2023," https://freedomhouse.org/report/freedom-world.

are sourced from the Polity V data set hosted at the Center for Systemic Peace.[5] The third set of control variables accounts for countries' predominant religious tradition: Christian (*Christian*), Muslim (*Muslim*), and Eastern religions (*Eastern*). A fourth classification, *Other*, serves as the reference category. A fourth set of control variables accounts for a country's religious demography. This category of variables controls for religious diversity by accounting for the number of groups that comprise at least 5, 10, and 30 percent of a country's population.

Summary statistics for all the variables are presented in Table A.1.

Given the nonnegative count nature of the outcome variable, the dependent nature of values of other observations, and the uneven distribution across observations, the data were modeled using fixed-effects negative binomial regressions. The main results are presented in Table A.2, with Models 2, 3, and 4 progressively adding additional control variables. Model 1 controls for general characteristics of states that might be related to the onset of religion-related violence. The second model additionally controls for the political characteristics of individual states, including regime type and democracy levels. The third model includes the controls for dominant religious tradition. The fourth includes the religious demography variables in addition to all the others.

The results show that religious privilege is positively, consistently, and significantly associated with majoritarian violence. As a country's religious privilege score increases, so too does its level of majoritarian violence, regardless of which control variables are included in the analysis. Across all the models, religious privilege rises to the highest level of statistical significance, meaning that the results are not explainable by chance alone.

Table A.1 Summary Statistics

Variable	Obs	Mean	Std. Dev.	Min	Max
Majoritarian Attacks	1868	13.666	79.917	0	1153
Religious Privilege	1903	3.843	2.618	0	8
Logged Area	1892	11.849	2.142	5.075	16.612
Logged GDP Capita	1833	8.565	1.492	5.351	11.858
Logged Population	1897	15.977	1.854	6.133	21.055
Political Rights	1905	3.587	2.18	1	7
Civil Liberties	1905	3.48	1.881	1	7
Polity	1762	3.943	6.239	−10	10
Durability	1782	29.16	32.017	0	209
Eastern	1914	.092	.289	0	1
Muslim	1914	.31	.463	0	1
Christian	1914	.58	.494	0	1
Groups 5 Percent	1859	2.544	1.24	1	6
Groups 10 Percent	1859	1.982	1.012	1	5
Groups 30 Percent	1859	1.089	.485	0	3

[5] Center for Systemic Peace, "Polity5 Annual Time-Series, 1946–2018," Integrated Network for Social Conflict Research, 2023, https://www.systemicpeace.org/inscrdata.html.

Table A.2 Negative Binomial Regressions of Religious Privilege and Majoritarian Violence

	(1) Majoritarian_Attacks	(2) Majoritarian_Attacks	(3) Majoritarian_Attacks	(4) Majoritarian_Attacks
Religious_Privilege	.503*** (.089)	.325*** (.082)	.215*** (.076)	.214*** (.078)
Logged_Area	.244 (.168)	.114 (.139)	.119 (.136)	.136 (.163)
Logged_GDP_Capita	−.522*** (.142)	.261 (.191)	.245 (.182)	.209 (.193)
Logged_Population	.817*** (.216)	1.037*** (.171)	1.136*** (.191)	1.167*** (.189)
Political_Rights		−.132 (.287)	−.027 (.203)	.01 (.205)
Civil_Liberties		1.257*** (.306)	1.202*** (.244)	1.146*** (.236)
Polity		.188*** (.056)	.221*** (.049)	.221*** (.051)
Durability		−.009 (.007)	−.004 (.006)	−.003 (.006)
Eastern			−2.477** (1.143)	−2.379** (1.194)
Muslim			−.244 (1.109)	−.052 (1.122)
Christian			−1.907** (.954)	−1.672 (1.048)
Groups_5_Percent				.172 (.365)
Groups_10_Percent				−.449 (.385)
Groups_30_Percent				.307 (.391)
_cons	−13.054*** (2.985)	−25.985*** (3.575)	−26.718*** (3.921)	−27.282*** (3.98)
/lnalpha	2.547*** (.132)	2.355*** (.135)	2.134*** (.127)	2.125*** (.128)
Observations	1793	1669	1669	1654

Notes: Standard errors are in parentheses. *** $p<.001$, ** $p<.01$, * $p<.05$.

Of the different religious traditions tested in the models, countries dominated by Eastern religions experience significantly less majoritarian violence than countries dominated by non-Eastern religions.

The results are also robust to a number of alternative model specifications. The results continued to hold if changing the models in the following ways: (1) using the number of victims of majoritarian attacks as the dependent variable; (2) clustering standard errors on countries instead of using fixed effects; (3) using random effects instead of fixed effects; (4) including the previous year's level of majoritarian violence; (5) using bootstrap regressions; (6) including only observations after 2001; and (7) controlling for geographic region. Importantly, substituting minority attacks for majority attacks as the dependent variable does not rise to the level of significance, thus adding further weight to the book's thesis. In short, the statistical analysis is strongly supportive of the argument put forth in this book: where political secularism is in short supply, the likelihood of majoritarian religious violence increases.

To help understand the results, the incidence rate ratios—the rates at which events are expected to change given a 1-unit increase in the independent variable—are presented in Table A.3. The incidence rate ratios show that countries can expect to see an increase in the number of majoritarian attacks by between 23 and 65 percent per 1-unit increase in the favoritism scale, depending on the particular covariates used in the models. In short, both the negative binomial models and the subsequent incidence rate ratios derived from those models provide robust support for the theory outlined in this book.

Case Studies

While the quantitative analysis helps establish broad patterns of the interplay between religion, political secularism, and majoritarian violence, the qualitative analysis enables us to explore the causal mechanisms at work within each of the selected cases.

While the quantitative analysis above showed that increases in religious privilege correspond to higher levels of religion-related violence, the country cases aim to show *how* privilege has emboldened majoritarian vigilantes across cases. The method conforms to John Stuart Mill's "method of agreement," in which cases contain differing background conditions—economics, politics, histories—but similar values on the theoretically central independent variable.[6] If the theory holds water, we should observe that the values of the independent and dependent variables covary over time. The method of agreement helps isolate the cause of the outcome variable in that the dependent variable would be highly unlikely to arise in its absence. The qualitative methodology employed here illustrates the central argument of this book, namely that favoritism of historically and culturally dominant religious traditions has encouraged extremists associated from these very traditions to carry out attacks. In all the cases, we observe that religious privilege has become weaponized against religious outsiders from whom majoritarian vigilantes see threats to the political and cultural hegemony of their own religion.

The qualitative analysis contains two parts: within-case analysis and case comparisons. The first involves demonstrating the causal process mechanisms at work that link secularism deficits to majoritarian violence. Process tracing is used to test the theory within the cases. The case chapters examine majoritarian violence in Christianity, Islam, Hinduism, Buddhism, and Judaism. These religious traditions are widely considered to be the world's most significant in that they either boast the most followers (Christianity, Islam,

---

[6] John Stuart Mill, *A System of Logic*, ed. J. M. Robson (Toronto: University of Toronto Press, 1973), 388–406.

Table A.3 Incident Rate Ratios

	(1) Majoritarian_Attacks	(2) Majoritarian_Attacks	(3) Majoritarian_Attacks	(4) Majoritarian_Attacks
Religious_Privilege	1.650*** (.146)	1.383*** (.113)	1.233*** (.093)	1.238*** (.096)
Logged_Area	1.272 (.214)	1.12 (.115)	1.12 (.093)	1.14 (.186)
Logged_GDP_Capita	.593*** (.084)	1.30 (.250)	1.277 (.232)	1.232 (.238)
Logged_Population	2.264*** (.489)	2.82*** (.481)	3.115*** (.594)	3.211*** (.607)
Political_Rights		.576 (.251)	.974 (.198)	1.010 (.207)
Civil_Liberties		3.52*** (1.076)	3.327*** (.813)	3.145*** (.742)
Polity		1.208*** (.0673)	1.247*** (.061)	1.248*** (.063)
Durability		.991 (.007)	.996 (.006)	.997 (.006)
Other			5.176** (3.820)	9.245*** (7.147)
Eastern			.084** (.096)	.0925** (.110)
Muslim			.784 (.869)	.949 (1.066)
Christian			.149** (.124)	.188 (.197)
Groups_5_Percent				1.189 (.433)
Groups_10_Percent				.638 (.246)
Groups_30_Percent				1.360 (.532)
_cons	2.145*** (2.985)	5.192*** (1.857)	2.491*** (9.771)	1.421*** (5.641)
/lnalpha	2.547*** (.132)	2.355*** (.135)	2.134*** (.127)	2.125*** (.128)
Observations	1793	1669	1669	1654

Notes: Standard errors are in parentheses. *** $p<.001$, ** $p<.01$, * $p<.05$.

Hinduism, and Buddhism) or they represent the parent religion of offshoot traditions (Judaism and Hinduism). Each religion also comprises the majority faith tradition in at least one country in the world, allowing for meaningful tests of the theory. These cases reinforce the validity of the results for two reasons. First, they are considered "crucial" cases of intrinsic importance. If there is truly a global crisis of secularism that produces majoritarian violence, this dynamic should be evident in some of the world's largest and most important countries. Second, the selected cases vary on many factors that could influence the outcome: predominant religious tradition, geographic location, economic development, regime type, and so forth. The heterogeneity within cases allows for the isolation of causal variables across different contexts. Corroborative evidence for my theory across intrinsically important and diverse cases reinforces the theory and the statistical analysis. The cases show (1) how the global crisis of secularism has affected each of the world's major religious traditions and (2) how the increasing entanglement of religion and state has precipitated majoritarian violence.

The second component of the case analysis involves the comparison of positive and negative cases. The former are instances where the outcome of interest has occurred or where the phenomenon being studied is present. The latter are instances where the outcome of interest has not occurred or where the phenomenon being studied is absent. Comparative case studies involve the comparative analysis of multiple cases to identify patterns, similarities, and differences. Chapters 2–6 examine the effect of religious privilege on majoritarian violence in Christianity, Islam, Hinduism, Buddhism, and Judaism, respectively. The concluding chapter shows how "covenantal pluralism" rooted in political secularism has held majoritarian violence at bay in countries dominated by these same religious traditions, including in the histories of two countries surveyed in previous chapters, India and Israel. Taken together, the positive and negative cases provide robust evidence in support of the book's theory.

Finally, like the quantitative analysis, the case studies also help rule out common assumptions about the roots of religious violence in the modern world. This book has surveyed several cases of secular retreats and subsequent majoritarian violence: the United States, Europe, Central African Republic, Uganda, Brazil, India, Sri Lanka, Myanmar, Thailand, and Israel. The diversity of these cases implicitly allows for comparison between the argument put forward in these pages with popular alternative explanations related to politics, economics, predominant religious tradition, or geographical location.

Index

Tables are indicated by an italic t following the para ID.

For the benefit of digital users, indexed terms that span two pages (e.g., 52–53) may, on occasion, appear on only one of those pages.

Adams, John, 67
Adityanath, Yogi, 141–142, 157–158
Afghanistan
　and religious violence, 108–109
　US withdrawal from, 1–2, 108–109
Africa
　Christian nationalism in, 90–92
　covenantal pluralism in, 215–216
ahimsa, 219–220
Ahmadi Muslims, 114, 128–129
Akbaba, Yasemin, 18–19
Akbar, 125
al-Aqsa Mosque, 201
Algeria, 101–102, 114
al-Hussein, Zeid Ra'ad, 2, 178–179
al-Zawahiri, Ayman, 109–110, 126–127
ambivalence of sacred, 14–24
　Judaism and, 189–190
Amir, Yigal, 202–203
Amnesty International, 93
Arakan Rohingya Salvation Army, 179
Assad, Bashar, 101–102
assassinations, 135
　impunity and, 55
　outbidding and, 54, 165, 202–203
Atatürk, Mustafa Kemal, 100
atheism, state and, 36, 47
Aum Shinrikyo, 163

Babri Masjid, 145–146, 148–149
Baha'i faith
　in Botswana, 215
　in Egypt, 115–116
　in Iran, 107–108
Bahati, David, 90–91
Bajrang Dal, 149
Bandaranaike, S. W. R. D., 54, 165
Bangladesh, 112

Baptist Joint Committee for Religious Liberty, 81
Barak, Ehud, 199
Baru, Sanjaya, 159
Basuki Tjahaha Purnama "Ahok," 45
Bauman, Chad, 155–156
Belgium, 48
Ben-Ami, Shlomo, 201
Benedict XVI, pope, 39
Ben-Gurion, David, 190–191
Berger, Peter, 5–7
Berlinerblau, Jacques, 33–34
Bharatiya Janata Party (BJP), 53–54, 135–136, 139–141, 142–143, 145–146, 153–154, 159–160
Bhatti, Shahbaz, 121
Bhutto, Benazir, 54
Bibi, Aasia, 117, 121
Biden, Joe, 1–2, 108–109
Bindi, Federiga, 85–86
bin Laden, Osama, 108–109, 126–127
blasphemy laws, 117–122
　colonial America and, 66
　and impunity, 55
　Iran and, 106–107
　Islam and, 97
　Pakistan and, 111–112
Bodu Bala Sena, 167–169
Boebert, Lauren, 44–45
Boko Haram, 113
Bolsonaro, Jair, 44–45, 93–94
Botswana, 215–216
Bozizé, Francois, 92
Brazil, 44–45, 93–94
Breivik, Anders Behring, 88
Breslawski, Jori, 54
Brubaker, Rogers, 82–83
B'Tselem, 193–194, 225–226
Buddha, 162

Buddhism, 162, 219
   and covenantal pluralism, 222–224
   and religious violence, 2, 163–181
Bush, George W., 69

Calvin, John, 42
Candomblé, 93–94
Caravan of Love, 221
Carter, Jimmy, 192–193
Casanova, José, 33
caste system, 153–155
Catholic Church
   in India, 141–142, 149–150, 156–157
   in Mexico, 94
   Tocqueville on, 212
Cavanaugh, William, 13
Central African Republic, 90–91, 92–93
Ceylon. *See* Sri Lanka
Chansley, Jacob Angeli, 1, 79
Charlottesville riot, 76–78
Christian civilizationalism, 81–90
Christianity, 63
   and covenantal pluralism, 215–216
   decline in Europe, 81–82
   Judaism and, 189
   and religious violence, 1, 63, 88
Christian nationalism, 1
   American, 44–45, 51–52, 64–81
   opposition to, 80–81
   and religious violence, 55–56, 71–74
Christians
   in Algeria, 114
   in Central African Republic, 92
   in India, 135–136, 141–142, 145–146, 153–154, 156–157
   in Israel, 203–204
   in Myanmar, 172, 179
   pseudo-secularism and, 101–102
   in Sri Lanka, 169–170
Christians against Christian Nationalism, 80–81
Christian Solidarity Worldwide, 94
church-state relationship. *See* religion-state relationship
circumcision, Europe and, 86–87
civilizationalism
   Christian, 81–90
   term, 82–83
civil religion, 36–37
civil society, and political secularism, 211
clash of civilizations thesis, 8–11
Clinton, Bill, 195–196

colonialism
   in India, 136–138
   in Sri Lanka, 165
Compassion International, 141–142
Congress Party, India, 140, 148–149, 159–160
Conservative Judaism, 193
conspiratorial thinking
   Buddhism and, 167
   Christian nationalism and, 72–73
Constitution(s)
   Afghanistan, 108
   Algeria, 114
   Botswana, 216
   India, 137
   Iran, 99, 106–107
   Pakistan, 110–111
   Saudi Arabia, 105
   Senegal, 128–129, 217
   Singapore, 223
   Sri Lanka, 165
   Thailand, 181–183
   US, 66–67, 71–72
contract, *versus* covenant, 213
Convening for Equality, 91–92
conversion laws
   India and, 142, 146, 149–150, 152–158
   Iran and, 108–109
co-optation of religion, 47–48
   Buddhism and, 164, 174
   India and, 135
   Muslim world and, 102–104
Coptic Christians, in Egypt, 115–116
cosmic war framing, 13–14
   Christian nationalism and, 72–73, 79
covenantal pluralism, 210–226, 227
   in Botswana, 215–216
   in India, 219–221
   in Israel, 224–226
   in Senegal, 216–219
   in Singapore, 222–224
COVID-19 pandemic, 72–73, 79–80, 142, 167, 215
cow vigilantes, 2–3, 146–147, 150–151
crisis of secularism, 21–23, 31
   antidote to, 210–214
   causes of, 44–49
   and religious violence, 49–59
Crusades, 63

Dati Jews, 225
Dawkins, Richard, 7–8
death penalty

for blasphemy, 117
Iran and, 107, 109
decolonization, 104
Democratic Karen Buddhist Army, 182–183
demonization, 49, 51–52
denialism, and religious violence, 7, 13–14
Dennett, Daniel, 7–8
DeSantis, Ron, 51–52
developing world, Christian nationalism in, 90–94
dharma, 134–135
Diouf, Abdou, 218
discriminatory secularism, Europe and, 83–88
disestablishment
    Botswana and, 216
    US and, 66–67
diversity
    in India, 219–221
    management of, 46
    recommendations for, 209
    in US, 69–70
Dobson, James, 73
duty, religious violence as, 55–56
    US and, 71

Easter Sunday attacks, Sri Lanka, 169–170
Egypt, 101–102
    blasphemy laws in, 122
    religious violence in, 114–116
Enlightenment, 34, 100
equality
    and political secularism, 35–36, 37–38
    victimization and, 50–51, 202
Erdoğan, Recep Tayyip, 101
Ershad, Hussain Muhammad, 112
essentialism, and religious violence, 7–11
establishment, 35–36, 42
    Europe and, 83
ethnic cleansing
    Central African Republic and, 93
    Myanmar and, 2, 178–179
Europe
    and Christian civilizationalism, 81–90
    and political secularism, 34–35, 48
    violent religious hostilities in, 4–5
European Court of Justice, 86
evangelicals, American
    and Israel, 195–196
    See also Christian nationalism
exclusion
    Christian nationalism and, 73
    India and, 3

Eyal movement, 202–203

Facebook, 151
La Familia, 201
favoritism
    and impunity, 55
    and religious violence, 22, 56–57
Feucht, Sean, 79–80
Fields, James Alex, Jr., 76
Finke, Roger, 53–54
Finnbogason, Daniel, 128
FIS. *See* Islamic Salvation Front
Flynn, Michael, 79–80
Foda, Farag, 122
Fox, Jonathan, 11, 40–41, 44, 54, 57–58, 84, 102–103
France
    and Muslims, 83–84, 87–88
    and political secularism, 48
    and securitization, 52–53
freedom, and political secularism, 35–36, 38–39
Freedom from Religion Foundation, 81
freedom of religion
    versus conversion laws, 152–154
    limits on, 39
    US and, 66–67
French Revolution, 48, 100, 212
friendships, interfaith, in Israel, 225–226
Fuentes, Nick, 73

Gandhi, Indira, 135, 159
Gandhi, Mohandas, 153–154, 159, 219–220
Gandhi, Rajiv, 159
Gantz, Benny, 201
Gaza, 196–197, 200
Gnanasara Thero, Galagoda Aththe, 168, 170–171
Godse, Nathuram, 159
Goldstein, Baruch, 198–199
Golwalkar, M. S., 158
Great Replacement theory, 88–89
Guatemala, 47
Gujarat riot, 144
Gurr, Ted, 16–17, 21
Gush Emunim, 199–200

Hakeem, Rauf, 169
Hamas, 196–197
Haredi Jews, 193, 203, 225
Harris, Jaime D., 53–54
Harris, Sam, 7–8

hate crimes, 87–88, 89–90
  in Europe, 87–88
  in Sri Lanka, 169
Hazaras, 109–110
Herzl, Theodor, 190
Hilltop Youth, 199
Hinduism, 134
  in Afghanistan, 109–110
  Akbar and, 125
  in Botswana, 215
  and covenantal pluralism, 219–221
  and religious violence, 2–3, 143–152
Hindutva, 3, 45, 139, 142–143, 153–154
Hitchens, Christopher, 7–8
Hizbullah, Hejaaz, 170–171
Hlaing, Min Aung, 178, 180
Hoover, Dennis, 212–213
Human Rights Awareness, 91–92
human rights organizations
  on blasphemy laws, 118
  on Christian religious violence, 91–92, 94
  on international standards, 43–44
  on Israel, 193–194
Human Rights Watch, 145–146, 177–178
Hungary, 45
Huntington, Samuel, 8–11
Hussein, Saddam, 101–102

Iceland, 82
identity-based explanations of religious violence, 11
ideological extremism, and religious violence, 7, 12–13
immigrants/immigration
  Breivik and, 88
  Christian nationalism and, 73
  Europe and, 82, 84
  India and, 141–142
  US and, 70
impunity, climate of, 55
  in Afghanistan, 109–110
  blasphemy laws and, 120
  conversion laws and, 155–156
  in Egypt, 116
  in India, 145–146, 149–150
  in Iran, 107–108
  in Israel, 203–204
  in Mexico, 94
  in Myanmar, 174–175
  in Nigeria, 113
  in Pakistan, 112
  recommendations for, 132–133

  in Sri Lanka, 168–170
Imtiyaz, A. R. M., 167–168
inclusion, Baha'i and, 107–108
India, 2–3
  and Buddhism, 162
  and covenantal pluralism, 219–221
  crisis of secularism and, 45, 47
  Hinduism in, 134
  minority religious violence in, 20
  and political secularism, 136–143
  and radicalization, 53–54
  and securitization, 52–53
  violent religious hostilities in, 4–5
Indic religions, 219
Indonesia
  crisis of secularism and, 45
  political secularism in, 127–128
  violent religious hostilities in, 4–5
Inglehart, Ronald, 69
instrumentalism, and religious violence, 7, 11–12
insult laws. See blasphemy laws
International Humanist and Ethical Union, 127
Iran, 31, 104, 196–197
  as Islamist, 99
  and political secularism, 46–47
  and religious privilege, 41–43
  and religious violence, 106–109
Iranian Revolution, 46–47, 96–97, 104, 106
Iraq, 101–102
Irish Republican Army, 20
Islam, 96
  and covenantal pluralism, 216–219
  essentialist explanations and, 9–11
  and establishment, 42
  Judaism and, 189
  and religious violence, 1–2, 96–97, 104–116
  variations across time, 124–127
  See also Muslims
Islamic Salvation Front (FIS), 101, 114
Islamic State of Iraq and Syria—Khorasan Province (ISIS-K), 1–2, 109–110
Islamism, 97–99
  and blasphemy laws, 120–121
  and pseudo-secularism, 103–104
  in Sri Lanka, 169–170
Israel, 189
  covenantal pluralism in, 224–226
  and crisis of secularism, 47
  religious violence in, 3

Jabotinsky, Ze'ev, 190

Jahangir, Asma, 154–155
jahiliya, 98
Jainism, 162, 219
Jamaat-e-Islami, 111, 125–126
Jammu and Kashmir, 141–142
January 6, 2021 insurgency, 1, 73, 77–80
Jefferson, Thomas, 67, 71–72
Jericho March, 80
Jerusalem, 3, 11–12, 191, 196
Jerusalem Day march, 201
Jesus Christ, 34, 63
Jinnah, Mohammed, 110–111
journalists, India and, 149–150
Judaism, 189
    Afghanistan and, 109–110
    Botswana and, 215
    and covenantal pluralism, 224–226
    Europe and, 85–86, 87–89
    and religious violence, 3, 196–205
Juergensmeyer, Mark, 12, 13–14, 47–48, 57–58

Kahane, Meir, 198–199, 202–203
karma, 134–135
Karnataka, 152–153
Kelaidis, Katherine, 76–77
Khan, Amjad Mahmood, 119–120
Khan, Pehlu, 2–3
Khomeini, Ruhollah, 31, 46–47, 117
Kimball, Charles, 7–8
Kuru, Ahmet, 125, 130–131
Kurz, Sebastian, 89–90

laïcité, 48, 83–84, 114
Latin America, Christian nationalism in, 93–94
law enforcement
    in India, 145–146, 147–148
    in Iran, 109
    in Israel, 204
    in Saudi Arabia, 105
    in Sri Lanka, 168, 170
Law of Return, 191–192
Lebanon, 196–197
Lehava, 3, 201
le Pen, Marine, 52–53
LGBTQ individuals
    Iran and, 107
    Israel and, 203
    Uganda and, 90–92
Libya, 101–102
Locke, John, 34, 37–38
Lourduswamy, Stanislaus, 149–150
love jihad, 147–150

Lula da Silva, Luiz Inácio, 94

MaBaTha, 175–177
Macron, Emmanuel, 83–84, 89–90
Madeley, John, 36–37
Madhya Pradesh, 156–157
Maha Apichat, 184–185
majoritarian violence, 21–23
    crisis of secularism and, 49–59
    lethality of, 23
    reduction of, recommendations for, 209
    statistical analysis of, 228–232, 230*t*–233*t*
Malay Muslims, 183–184
Mander, Harsh, 221
marriage, interfaith, bans on
    India and, 147–150
    Myanmar and, 175
    versus Senegal acceptance, 218
Marshall, Paul, 118
Maududi, Sayed Abul A'la, 125–126
melting pot, US as, 69–70
Mexico, 93–94
military government
    in Myanmar, 173–174, 178–180
    in Thailand, 182–184
Mill, John Stuart, 37–38, 232
minorities
    Afghanistan and, 109–110
    Egypt and, 115–116
    equality and, 37–38
    Europe and, 84–88, 89–90
    India and, 144–146
    Iran and, 107
    Islamist regimes and, 99
    Israel and, 190–191, 192–193
    Pakistan and, 112
    and privilege, 42
    and religious violence, 16–21, 179
Misionaries of Charity, 141–142
Modi, Narendra, 135, 139–140, 144, 146, 148–149
Mohamed-Saleem, Amjad, 167–168
monks, Buddhist, 164
    in Myanmar, 173–175
    as nonviolent activists, 180–181
    in Sri Lanka, 164–167, 168–171
    in Thailand, 181–182, 184
Montesquieu, Charles de, 123–124
Morocco, 102
Mubarak, Hosni, 101–102
Muhammad, 96–97, 107–108, 122–123
Muhammadiyah, 128

multiculturalism
　Breivik and, 88
　Europe and, 82–83
　India and, 137
Museveni, Yoweri, 90–91
Muslim Brotherhood, 115–116, 125–126
Muslims
　in Botswana, 215
　in Central African Republic, 92
　in Europe, 82–84, 85–86, 87–88, 89–90
　in India, 135–136, 138, 140, 145–146, 148–149
　in Iran, 46–47
　in Israel, 198–199
　in Myanmar, 172, 174–179
　securitization and, 52–53
　in Senegal, 216–219
　in Sri Lanka, 166–167, 168–171
　in Thailand, 183–185
　in US, 52–53, 75–76
　See also Islam
Muslim world
　definition of, 98
　and political secularism, 98–104, 122–131
Myanmar, 2, 51–52, 163, 172–181
　and crisis of secularism, 47
　violent religious hostilities in, 4–5

Nahdlatul Ulama, 127–128
Nasser, Gamal Abdel, 114–115
nationalism
　Hindu, 135–136, 139, 143–152
　Jewish, 196–205
　See also Christian nationalism
National League for Democracy, 173–174
National Thowheeth Jama'ath, 169–170
negative secularism, 39
Nehru, Jawaharlal, 39, 158
Nepal, 45–46
Netanyahu, Benjamin, 193–194, 200, 203–204
neutrality, and political secularism, 35–37
new atheist movement, 7–8, 9–11
New Delhi riot, 145–146
Ne Win, 173–174
Nigeria, 113
　and blasphemy laws, 121
　violent religious hostilities in, 4–5
Nilsson, Desirée, 5
969 Movement, 175–176
nonviolence
　Christianity and, 63
　Judaism and, 189–190

　See also pacifism
Northern Ireland, 20
North Korea, 36, 42–43, 47
Norway, 45–46, 82, 88

Orbán, Viktor, 45, 89–90
Order of Friars Minor, 203–204
Organization for the Protection of Race and Religion (MaBaTha), 175–177
Orthodox Judaism, 189, 192–193, 203, 225
Ottoman Empire, 100
outbidding
　Buddhist regimes and, 165
　Hindu nationalism and, 160
　Islamist regimes and, 113–114
　Jewish militants and, 202–203
　term, 54

pacificism
　Buddhism and, 162
　Gandhi and, 219–220
　See also nonviolence
Pahlavi, Mohammed Reza, 31
Pakistan, 55, 110–112, 138
　and blasphemy laws, 120–121
　as Islamist, 99
Palestine/Palestinians, 190–191, 192–194, 198–201
Pancasila, 127
Pandin Dharma Party, 185
paradox of privilege, 23–24
patronage, 42, 49–50, 54, 102
peace
　Hinduism and, 134–135, 219
　Judaism and, 189–190
Pentecostal groups, 93–94
Perkins, Tony, 74–75
Perry, Samuel, 64–66
persecution. *See* repression/persecution
philosophical secularism, 33–34
Philpott, Daniel, 15, 18–19, 98, 100
Pizzaballa, Pierbattista, 203–204
police. *See* law enforcement
political engagement, faith groups and, 15–16
political secularism, 33–41
　components of, 35–36
　India and, 135, 136–143, 158
　Islam and, 97
　Israel and, 191–196
　issues in, 57–58
　models of, 209
　Muslim world and, 98–104, 122–131

resistance to, 46–47, 64–66
US and, 66–67
variations across space, 124–125, 127–129
political theologies
Christian nationalism and, 64–66, 71–72
and religious violence, 15, 23–24
politicization, 22, 49–50
Judaism and, 190
price tag attacks, 199–200
privilege, religious, 41–42
in Bangladesh, 112
in Europe, 82–83, 88–89
in India, 134
in Israel, 193–196
in Muslim world, 104–116
in Myanmar, 172–173
negative effects of, 132, 212
rejection of, 214
and religious violence, 22, 23–24, 228–232, 230t–233t
versus repression, 42–43
in US, 69, 74–75
prophetic movement, 78
Proud Boys, 75–76, 78
pseudo-secularism
and blasphemy laws, 120, 122
Egypt and, 114–116
Europe and, 83
Muslim world and, 97, 99–104
purity concerns, 54
Israel and, 198, 202

Qaddafi, Muammar, 101–102
QAnon conspiracy, 72–73
Qur'an, 96–97, 117–118
and political secularism, 124–125, 130–131
Qutb, Sayyid, 115–116, 125–126

Rabin, Yitzhak, 54, 202–203
radicalization, 49, 53–56
in India, 151
Rajapaksa, Gotabaya, 167–168, 170–171
Rakhine State, 174, 177–179
Rashtriya Swayamsevak Sangh, 139, 149
ReAwaken America Tour, 79–80
Reformed Judaism, 193
relative deprivation, 16–17
relativism, 37–38
versus covenantal pluralism, 213–214
religion-state relationship
Boebert on, 44–45
Christianity and, 63–64

colonial America and, 66
current changes in, 41
India and, 137, 139–140, 143–152
Islam and, changes in, 125
Israel and, 190–192, 225
Jesus on, 34
Muhammad on, 122–123
Myanmar and, 174–175
negative effects of, 212
and peace, 56
and religious violence, 15
Saudi Arabia and, 105–106
Senegal and, 218–219
Singapore and, 223–224
Sri Lanka and, 167–168
Thailand and, 183
types of, 35–36
US and, 68
religiosity
in Senegal, 217–218
in US, 69
religious identity, politicization of, 22, 49–50
religious literacy, 214
religious resurgence, 6–7, 31
religious violence, 31
blasphemy laws and, 118–120
Buddhism and, 2, 163–181
Christian civilizationalism and, 81–90
Christian nationalism and, 55–56, 71–74, 90–94
crisis of secularism and, 49–59
definition of, 3–4
examples of, 1
explanations for, 7–14
factors affecting, 15
Hindu nationalism and, 2–3, 143–152
increase in, 5
Islam and, 1–2, 96–97, 104–116
Judaism and, 3, 196–205
versus other types, 9–11
persistence of, 3–7
statistical analysis of, 228–232, 230t–233t
repression/persecution
Iran and, 107
Islamist regimes and, 99
versus privilege, 42–43
The Revolt, 199–200, 202–203
ritual animal slaughter bans, Europe and, 86
Rohingya Muslims, 2, 175, 177–180
in Sri Lanka, 168–169
Rouhani, Hassan, 106
Rushdie, Salman, 117

sacred
    ambivalence of, 14–24, 189–190
    politicization of, 49–50
Sadat, Anwar, 54
Saffron Revolution, 173–174
Samoa, 47
samsara, 134–135
Sangh Parivar, 138, 142–143
Sarkozy, Nicolas, 85–86
satyagraha, 219–220
Saudi Arabia, 51–52
    and religious privilege, 42–43
    and religious violence, 105–106
Savarkar, Vinayak Damodar, 139, 158
secularism
    definition of, 32–44, 57–58
    Europe and, 81–82
    optimism on, 5–6
    and peace, 56
    and religious violence, 57–58
    resistance to, 31
    See also crisis of secularism; political secularism
secularization thesis, 5–6
secular nationalism, 99
securitization, 49, 52–53
    US and, 75–76
Seiple, Chris, 212–213
Senegal, 128–129, 216–219
Senghor, Léopold Sédar, 218
separation, and political secularism, 35–36
    elements of, 35–36
September 11, 2001, 96
Shah, Amit, 141–142, 154
Shah, Timothy, 18–19, 137
shalom, term, 189–190
sharia, 98–99, 105, 109
    Egypt and, 114–115
    Pakistan and, 111
Sharon, Ariel, 202–203
Shea, Nina, 118
Shia Muslims
    in Afghanistan, 109–110
    in Iran, 106
    in Saudi Arabia, 105–106
Shin Bet, 204
Shlisel, Yishai, 203
Sierra Leone, 129
Sikhs, 219
    in Afghanistan, 109–110
    in Botswana, 215
    in India, 135–136

Sikrikim, 203
Simentov, Zebulon, 109–110
Singapore, 222–224
Singh, Rajeshwar, 139–140
Singh, Rajnath, 154
Sinhala Jathika Balamulawa, 167
Sinhala Ravana, 167
Sinha-Le, 170–171
Sirisena, Maithripala, 170
Six Days War, 196–197, 198–199
social media
    and conspiratorial thinking, 72–73
    and extremist organizing, 187
    and religious violence, 151
    in Sri Lanka, 169–170
Soldiers of Jesus, 93–94
Sombatpoonsiri, Janjira, 186–187
Soviet Union, 36, 47
Sri Lanka, 163–172
    crisis of secularism and, 47
    minority religious violence in, 20
state
    and use of force, 40
    See also religion-state relationship
Stepan, Alfred, 35–36
Stewart, Christopher, 212–213
Stewart, Katherine, 64–66
Sudan, 20
Sufis
    in Egypt, 115–116
    in Senegal, 218
    in West Africa, 128–129
Suu Kyi, Aung San, 173–174, 179–180
Svensson, Isak, 5, 128
Switzerland, 82
symbolic threat, 50–51
    See also threat perceptions
Syria, 4–5, 101–102

Taliban, 1–2, 108–109
Tamils, 164–166
Taseer, Salman, 121
Tatmadaw, 178–180
Taydas, Zeynep, 18–19
Taylor, Kandiss, 50–51
terrorism
    Buddhism and, 163
    impunity and, 55
    See also religious violence
Thailand, 181–186
Than Shwe, 172–173
theocracies, 42, 98–99

threat perceptions, 50–51
　Hinduism and, 140–141
　India and, 154
　Israel and, 193–194
　Sri Lanka and, 167
　Thailand and, 184–185
Tocqueville, Alexis de, 211–212
Toft, Monica, 5, 18–19
tolerance
　Botswana and, 216
　Hinduism and, 134–135
　US and, 67
Toppo, Telesphore, 154–155
Trigg, Roger, 36–38
Trump, Donald, 1, 52–54
　and Christian nationalism, 72–73, 74–78, 80
　and Israel, 195–196
Türkiye, 100–101, 126–127
twin tolerations, 35–36

Uddin, Asma, 119
Uganda, 90–91
ul-Haq, Zia, 111, 117–118
ultra-Orthodox Judaism, 190–191, 193–194
United Nations High Commissioner for Human Rights, 2, 200
United States
　and Christian nationalism, 1, 51–52, 64–81
　and crisis of secularism, 44–45, 47
　founders, and secularism, 34
　and Israel, 195–196
　and religious violence, 64–81
　violent religious hostilities in, 4–5
U Nu, 172–173
use of force
　Islamism and, 98
　state and, 40
U Thein Sein, 175
Uttar Pradesh, 147–148

Vajpayee, Atal, 52–53
value expectations/capabilities, 21
van Gogh, Theo, 96, 117
Vaught, W. O., 195–196

veil/face coverings, 82–84
　Europe and, 85–86
　Sri Lanka and, 170
victimization, 49–51
　Christian nationalism and, 70, 74
　Hinduism and, 140–142
Vietnam, 4–5
vigilantes
　blasphemy laws and, 118–120
　conversion laws and, 155–157
　and cow protection, 2–3, 146–147, 150–151
　favoritism and, 22
　in Nigeria, 113
　radicalization and, 53–54
　in Thailand, 184
　in Uganda, 91–92
Vijay, Tarun, 154
violent religious hostilities
　definition of, 4–5
　forms of, 4–5
Vishva Hindu Parishad, 149

Wade, Abdoulaye, 218
Wahhabism, 105
Washington, George, 67
West Bank, 192–193, 198–200
Western world
　Islamism and, 98
　and political secularism, 34–35, 123–124
　and pseudo-secularism, 100
White-Cain, Paula, 80
Whitehead, Andrew, 64–66
white supremacy
　and Charlottesville riot, 76–77
　Christian nationalism and, 73–74
　in Europe, 88–89
Wilders, Geert, 51–52, 89–90
Wirathu, Ashin, 2, 51–52, 179–180

Yom Kippur War, 196–197

Zambia, 47
Zen Buddhism, 163
Zionism, 190–191
　Christian, 195–196